A Guide to Early Celtic Remains in Britain

Other Constable titles by Peter Berresford Ellis

A Dictionary of Irish Mythology
The Celtic Empire

A Guide to
Early Celtic Remains
in Britain

Peter Berresford Ellis

Constable · London

First published in Great Britain 1991
by Constable and Company Limited
3 The Lanchesters
162 Fulham Palace Road
London W6 9ER
Copyright © Peter Berresford Ellis 1991
The right of Peter Berresford Ellis to be
identified as the author of this work
has been asserted by him in association
with the Copyright, Designs and Patents Act 1988
ISBN 0 09 471110 0 (PVC)
ISBN 0 09 469200 9 (Hardback)
Set in Linotron 9pt Times by
CentraCet, Cambridge
Printed in Great Britain by
The Bath Press, Avon

A CIP catalogue record for this book
is available from the British Library

Contents

Illustrations

Line drawings

All line drawings by John Mitchell

Introduction

As with the previous titles in this series of Constable Guides, this book is intended to be a guide to visible remains; in this case, remains of the Early Celtic period in Britain. This is frequently referred to as the Iron Age (from the eighth century BC to the coming of the Romans in the first century AD). As our knowledge of the period has expanded, and we recognize more details about the early Celtic civilization, it has become fashionable, and more accurate, to stop referring to 'Iron Age folk' and call the people that inhabited Britain at this time by the more precise term 'Celtic'. This means they were a people who spoke a Celtic language and shared a Celtic culture.

Some will wonder why I have excluded the Bronze Age and will point out that Celticists and many archaeologists now regard the Celtic settlement in Britain as dating to the Urnfield civilization of the Bronze Age (c. 1200–750 BC) which is now called 'Proto-Celtic'. But, as there is still much speculation and argument, I have felt it best to concentrate on the period when we are sure that a Celtic culture held sway all over the island of Britain.

It has been postulated that the Iron Age in Britain came about with an invasion of Celtic-speaking peoples who brought the use of iron into the country. The evidence for a hostile invasion is non-existent. Most Celticists would argue that iron was an innovation adopted peacefully by an already Celtic-speaking people as a result of trading and other links with their fellow Celts on the European mainland.

When Britain became known to the Mediterranean world in the fifth century BC, through the writings of intrepid Greek explorers, it was as a Celtic country. Celtic scholars have suggested that the Goidelic form of Celtic (the ancestor language from which Irish, Manx and Scottish Gaelic developed) was spoken throughout Britain until around the sixth century BC when a language shift took place with the development of what is known now as Brythonic Celtic (the ancestor language from which Welsh, Cornish and Breton derived and which was closely related to

The Tribes of
Celtic Britain

Continental Celtic or Gaulish). While this is a matter of linguistic speculation, we can say with absolute certainty that there is no noticeable trace in place-names or elsewhere of a language earlier than Celtic being used in Britain. All the names mentioned by the early writers on Britain are Celtic.

Britain was referred to as the Pretanic Islands by Polybius, Strabo and Avienus, the name implying that the inhabitants were called Pretani. The name is of uncertain origin. It is thought to be the name by which the Gauls spoke of Britain and which the Romans then copied. Another suggestion lies in the fact that the word *pretan* as a meaning for 'tin' is found in an Egyptian demotic papyrus. Significantly, the Greeks had earlier called Britain Cassiterides – the Tin Islands. The name is also supposed to have been related to the Latin Picti. During the Roman period, the names Britonnes and Britannia came into general use, being, presumably, simply a corruption of Pretani and Pretan. It is also suggested that Albion was an early Celtic name for Britain, soon ousted by Britannia. Certainly, in Old Irish, Albain was used as the name for the whole island before being confined to northern Britain (Scotland). In modern Gaelic, Alba is the name for Scotland and Albannaich the name for a Scotsman.

There is evidence of the movement of some Celtic tribes into Britain from the Continent in the second and first centuries BC. These were the Belgae, (whose name survives in the word Belgium) living in France and the Low Countries, who were forced to move into Britain during the expansion of the Germanic tribes and later the Romans. Commios and his Atrebates from Arras fled to Britain during the Roman conquest of Gaul (*c.* 50 BC) to join a branch of their tribe already established in what is today Hampshire. This appears to have been a relatively peaceful process.

One word of explanation for the linguistically minded about the spelling of Celtic names in this volume: in recording Celtic personal names, Latin writers usually used the -*us* ending. I have reasserted the Celtic -*os* ending, following the argument of Henri Hubert, Kenneth Jackson and other leading Celtic scholars that this is the more correct form. Whereas it is popular to use the

Latin form, for example, of Cunobelin*us*, Professor Jackson has pointed out that in British (ancestor language of the Brythonic group – Welsh, Breton and Cornish – and relative of Gaulish) the name would have been recorded as Cunobelin*os*. A form of declension, similar to Latin, is found in Celtic. Thus when used as the subject of the verb the name would appear as Cunobelin*os*; when the object, Cunobelin*on*; when 'of Cunobelinos' it became Cunobelin*i*; and when 'to Cunobelinos' it became Cunobelin*us*.

To view Early Celtic Britain, we must get rid of the image that has been generally implanted in our minds by some of the propaganda writings of the Romans, particularly those of Julius Caesar, who would have us believe that the natives were almost barbaric, painting themselves, dressing in skins and knowing little, if anything, about weaving, stock-breeding, boat-building, metalwork, art or commerce. That the reverse was true is now accepted through proofs offered by modern archaeological excavation and finds. Celtic Britain, before the coming of the Romans, was a prosperous and fairly sophisticated country. It was run on a tribal system with some tribal rulers such as Cassivellaunos and his successors able to exert their influence on neighbouring tribes. These southern British tribes had begun to issue their own coinage by the second century BC while in other areas iron bars were regarded as currency and, still farther afield, barter was the normal method of exchanging goods. In the centuries before the Romans came, the British Celts traded extensively, not only with their Celtic cousins in Gaul, but with Greek merchants from the Mediterranean.

In Rome, in Julius Caesar's day, it was the height of fashion to own a British woollen cloak (*sagum*) which demonstrates the extent of his propaganda, for he would have us believe that most Britons did not even know how to weave. It was an assertion he must have known to be untrue when he made it. Even Strabo (b. 64 BC, d. after AD 24), Caesar's contemporary, mentions the export in woollen garments to Rome, as well as linen and leatherwork. Archaeology has shown what nonsense Caesar wrote when he claimed: 'Many Britons do not grow corn. They live on milk and flesh and are clothed in skins. All Britons stain their persons with a dye that produces a blue colour. This gives them a more terrible aspect in battle.' Rotary stone querns and other agricultural implements found all over Britain demonstrate just how advanced British Celtic farming was. Even in the more inhospitable climatic regions of the country there is evidence of a wide variety of cereal crops being grown.

The people of Celtic Britain enjoyed an excellent standard of common material culture based mainly on agriculture, including both grain production and stock-breeding, on their crafts, (they were among the foremost metal-workers of the day) and on their architecture. The planning and building of hill-forts, such as Maiden Castle, may be likened in scale to the construction of a cathedral. Their brochs, duns and crannogs, with which we will deal shortly, demonstrate the degree of their building sophistication. At a time when Celtic art was in decline on the Continent, in the years following the Roman conquest of Gaul, it was flourishing in Britain. British Celtic artists were producing magnificent decorated mirrors (the Birdlipp mirror in Gloucester Museum is such an example), not to mention enamelwork and other artefacts whose craftsmanlike precision is simply breathtaking. In the area of Dumfries, Scotland, among the Novantae, there was a flourishing school of Celtic art reaching its highest development in the years immediately after the birth of Christ.

The British Celts were well advanced in the production of iron, tin and copper, and even gold from Wales, and their working into sophisticated items. Bronze-smelting was also an advanced art and had been so for over ten centuries before the Romans arrived.

The war of independence in Gaul, which started in earnest in 53 BC, saved Britain from immediate further invasion and attempted conquest by the Romans. Caesar and his legions were too busy occupied with reducing the Gaulish insurgents, and then came Caesar's assassination in Rome. But the Romans never lost the ambition to add Britain to their empire. With Britain's trade to Europe ever-developing, especially during the rule of Cunobelinos (Shakespeare's Cymbeline), who seems to have exerted his authority over most of the tribes of southern Britain, Rome looked with increasingly envious eyes at the island. Strabo enumerates the tremendous exports from Britain at this time – wheat, cattle, gold, silver, iron, leather goods, hide, woollen garments and hunting dogs. In return, the British Celts imported amber, glassware, jewellery and wine. Amphorae, in which wine was imported from the Continent, are found in large numbers in the country. Britain had, in fact, become a leading commercial centre outside the Roman Empire. Herein lies the reason as to why Rome sought to conquer and incorporate the country into her empire. Although Strabo argued that trade with Britain produced more revenue for Rome than would accrue if the island were to become a Roman province and the Roman treasury had to pay for a standing army and civil service to run the country, the rulers of Rome were not swayed by the economic argument.

The end of a fully independent Celtic Britain occurred in AD 43 when Claudius ordered his armies into Britain to bring it into the Roman Empire. This was the beginning of Roman Britain, with which this volume is not concerned. However, it should be emphasized that the Roman conquest of southern Britain did not put an end to the British Celtic language and culture any more than the incorporation of India into the British Empire ended the Indian languages and cultures. When the Roman Empire collapsed and its troops withdrew from Britain, with the Emperor Honorius telling Britain to look to its own defence in AD 410, Celtic Britain re-emerged as India re-emerged in 1948. Some of the 'upper classes' and civil service spoke Latin as well as Celtic but the language and culture of the people were still Celtic. True, as can be seen by a linguistic examination of Welsh (for example), there were several Latin words which found themselves borrowed into British Celtic, and styles of law, administration and architecture had influenced or displaced the original Celtic forms. Christianity had replaced, in most places in Britain, the old druidic religion. Most importantly, the druidic prohibition on writing no longer existed and the Celts were now free to write not only in Latin (as a *lingua franca*) but in their own languages (as a *lingua materna*). By the sixth century AD, British Celtic (what we now call Early Welsh) was a flourishing literary language.

The real end of Celtic Britain was not, therefore, with the Roman occupation, but began in the middle of the fifth century AD when the ancestors of the English arrived in Britain and commenced to carve the country which became England out of Celtic Britain; the Celts who lived in the conquered territories were annihilated, assimilated or pushed back, west and north, into those areas of Britain where they still survive today.

How to use this book
The book, as I have said, is intended to be a guide to the visible remains of Early Celtic Britain. It does not pretend to give a balanced or complete picture of Britain in this period; for that the reader must turn to the volumes listed in the bibliography. It is, like the other volumes in the series, designed primarily for the ordinary individual who has an interest in the Celtic past of Britain and no prior specialized knowledge.

The book does not contain an all-embracing or complete list of every site in Britain. Patently, there are far too many sites to be listed in such a guide as this. What I have attempted is a review of the more scenic and important sites of the period.

In the listing of visible remains, hill-forts are predominant. This does not mean that the ancient Britons lived under constant threat of attack in a warlike society. It simply means that the main visible remnants of their civilization rest in these vast architectural structures. Traces of settlements and other remains are not as visually exciting as the forts but, nevertheless, they are just as historically important.

It will become obvious to the seeker of Celtic remains that the best preserved of these are in Scotland. The reason for this is simple. Scotland, while invaded by the Romans on several occasions, was never under the *pax Romana* and its defensive structures escaped the destruction visited on the forts and settlements in southern Britain. Here we see the extent of the Celtic ability as architects and engineers. Take, for example, the broch of Mousa from the fourth century BC which still survives to a height of 14m. The intricacies of the artificial islands and crannog dwellings, such as Milton Loch crannog, Kirkcudbrightshire, or the fortified dwellings of duns such as Castlehill Wood in Stirlingshire, make one deeply aware of Celtic building ability.

I have organized the book into areas which are made clear as the reader proceeds. Within the districts, I have dealt with the sites county by county and endeavoured to keep to an alphabetical listing within the county. However, where some sites are close together, I have deviated from this rule. The guide is not meant to be an itinerary. This would be impractical, as not everyone starts from the same point. With regard to remains in Scotland, distance also creates problems and so I have listed the remains by areas as one proceeds rather than strictly alphabetically. The idea is to make things as simple as possible to follow.

The best scheme, when one is searching for Celtic sites, is to turn to the beginning of each chapter, where a listing of the area and counties covered can be found. Then examine the sites discussed in the section and work out your own itinerary. As a matter of even greater convenience, there is an Index of Sites given at the end of the guide.

Against each site listed there occurs the National Grid reference number for the Ordnance Survey maps. Incidentally, Ordnance Survey have published a map of *Southern Britain in the Iron Age* which many might find of use. Sadly, no similar publication relating to Northern Britain has been issued.

Hill-forts
Hill-forts are the most common of Early Celtic remains. There are few major heights in England, Scotland or Wales that do not have the remains of such constructions on them. Built of earth, timber and stone, the vast majority of hill-forts were constructed during the first millenium BC to offer protection to their inhabitants. They can range in scale from between 1 and 12 hectares to some greater constructions measuring over 80 hectares.

We can group hill-forts into five types. There is the *contour fort* whose defences may follow the contours of a hill around its crown. Some scholars argue that the builders were thus unsophisticated and incapable of constructing straight lines. Yet this would have defeated the aim of the contour fort. Indeed, it requires a greater degree of accuracy to construct such a defence work. Hambledon Hill, Dorset is an excellent example of this type.

The *promontory fort* relies on natural defences, usually cliffs on three sides, with the landward side heavily defended by ramparts and ditches. These are fairly numerous and are not always found in coastal areas but also where natural elevations or the confluence of rivers make such a defence work possible. Rame Head in Cornwall or Crickley Hill in Gloucester are examples of such types.

A *plateau fort* is situated on flat ground depending entirely on man-made defences with no natural advantages (such as being on top of a hill). Arbury Bank in Hertfordshire is an example of this type of fort. Then there is the rare *valley fort*, related to the plateau fort, which is low-lying but usually has considerable man-made fortifications – an example is Cherbury in Berkshire.

Finally, we have the multiple enclosure, or *hillslope fort*, which was built on the slope of a hill overlooked by higher ground. Obviously such sites are not in a good military position and I am inclined to believe that these earthworks were not fortifications at all but stock enclosures of a specialized type. It has been noticed that such earthworks are not found outside south-west England and western Wales.

Settlements (towns and villages)
Many Early Celtic settlements have been identified and excavated and this guide has indicated some of the most interesting. But the study of such townships and villages is really a neglected area. In fact, until the 1930s, some scholars argued that before the coming of the Romans the British lived in 'pit dwellings' because numbers of 'pits' had been found in various areas from which artefacts had been recovered. Of course, this was a nonsense for these pits were merely 'storage dumps'. It was not until the excavations of the German archaeologist G. Bersu in 1938 that the 'pit dwellings' concept was dismissed and it was accepted that Early Celts mainly

lived in timbered houses in southern Britain and in more substantial stone and timber constructions in the north. The argument, of course, can be taken further for, in Cornwall, sophisticated stone housing can be found, among other places, at Chysauster. However, the typical lowland British house was a circular timber building, usually with a conical thatched roof.

As well as isolated farmsteads, or more substantial towns, usually enclosed by complicated defence works, a number of small villages or settlements have now been identified. About 140 such villages have been identified in the area of Avon, Somerset and Gloucester alone by the archaeologist Robin Hanley. Hanley argues: 'It is clear that the vast bulk of the population of all Romano-British villages was derived from the native Iron Age communities. There was no influx of new people, just a change in the form of the villages themselves. The population remained largely static.' (*Villages in Roman Britain*.)

Houses in villages and in the larger towns were set alongside a street, and roadways linked the various centres of population.

Herein lies a controversy, for we have always been taught that it was the Romans who made the roads in Britain. In recent years, however, archaeologists have begun to change their minds. There was already a system of Celtic roadways throughout the country before the coming of the Romans and this system was utilized by the Romans and improved on. But the Celts had their own roadway and transport system. That this was so is obvious, firstly from the writings of Diodorus Siculus, Strabo and even Caesar himself. The ease with which the heavy British war-chariots attacked and countered Caesar's troops is evidence in itself, for such heavy vehicles could only move the distances involved and with the speed recorded if there was a particularly good system of roadways available.

Secondly, in recent years there have come to light the fossilized remains of roads, not only in Britain but in Ireland and on the Continent, which demonstrate the sophistication of Celtic road-builders. However, the Celts built their roads and causeways in wood, the most easily accessible local material. The Romans overlaid these roads with stone. Therefore, only where the natural acids of bogs and marshes have preserved the original Celtic roadways can we see how the Celts constructed their highways. The intricacies of Celtic roads are demonstrated by the remains found in 1985, during operations in a Co. Longford bog, Ireland, by Bord na Mona, and taken over by the Department of Archaeology at University College, Dublin. A 1km stretch of roadway was discovered and radio-carbon dated to approximately 200–150 BC. The road was built on a foundation of oak beams placed side by side on thin rails of oak, ash and alder.

Recent archaeological fieldwork in the Severn estuary has brought to light many dramatic finds, not the least of which have been a number of these early Celtic wooden hurdle roadways. The first to be found, known as the Upton Track, in Gwent, has been radio-carbon dated to around the early fifth century BC.

There is a third section of evidence for the advancement of Celtic roadways and transport which lies in linguistics. It has frequently been pointed out that many words connected with transport in early Latin were, in fact, borrowed from Celtic. Words such as *carruca*, a four-wheeled chariot; *carrus*, a baggage wagon; *carpentum*, a two-wheeled chariot (from which, eventually the word for carpenter entered the language); *essedum*, a British war-chariot later adopted by the Romans; *reda* or *rheda*, a travelling carriage, were simply taken over by Latin, demonstrating that the Celts had a highly advanced transportation system.

Duns
The dun, as distinct from a fort, is a fortified dwelling place which has survived only, it seems, in Scotland. These vary from the 'plain' dun, circular, oval or oblong in shape, with walls 3–7m thick, mainly constructed in the first century AD, to more substantial 'galleried' circular duns with walls 5m thick, containing passageways, chambers and steps. These can vary in size up to 22m in diameter. There are numerous insular duns on the islands of Scotland but many of these are from the medieval period.

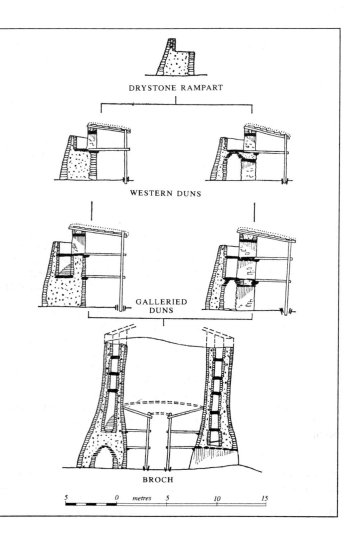

DRYSTONE RAMPART

WESTERN DUNS

GALLERIED DUNS

BROCH

5   0   metres   5   10   15

Brochs

The broch is visually one of the most exciting remains in Early Celtic architecture. Over 500 have been recorded with only a dozen of these outside northern Scotland and the western and northern islands. They are, therefore, considered to be an innovation of the Celtic tribes who later emerged as the Picts. The typical broch is a dry-stone structure, circular, with walls usually about 5m thick and with an internal diameter of 10–13m. There is a single entrance, a door, chambers, and one or more staircases leading to galleries. The most famous example of the broch is that of Mousa (Shetland) where the walls still remain about 15m high. The broch may be considered to be a defended homestead.

Crannogs

A crannog is a circular timber-framed thatched house built on an island in a lake or estuary or marsh. The island was often man-made with a man-made causeway leading from the shore to the house. The majority of crannogs have been found in Scotland (there are also several in Ireland) but excavation shows that such buildings were also constructed in the fens of East Anglia. Crannogs were occupied from 1000 BC until the first century AD.

The crannog is another sign of the ingenuity of Celtic architecture. Once a site was selected, great boulders were rafted out to the spot and sunk so that eventually a low, flat-topped island broke the surface. Great numbers of wooden piles, beams and stakes were cut and incorporated into the boulders and a platform built just above water level. Then a house emerged, sometimes as large as 15m in diameter. A quayside was added and a planked walkway to the shore. The water thus provided the occupants with protection.

Hill carvings

Hill carvings are the rarest of Celtic remains, and are confined to

The evolution of duns (forts) to brochs, according to J. R. C. Hamilton

England. There are only eighteen hill figures to be found, the earliest and perhaps the most famous being the Uffington White Horse in Oxfordshire. Although most hill carvings are of a late date, others of our period are to be found at Cerne Abbas, West Dorset; Stapleford, South Cambridgeshire; and Wilmington, East Sussex. No one has sufficiently explained the purpose of these carvings unless they be tribal symbol (as with the Uffington horse whose stylization bears a distinct resemblance to motifs on Celtic coins of the period) or religious in concept as in the case of the Cerne Abbas Giant which looks like the figure of Dis-Pater or The Dagda, a Celtic 'father of the gods', as described in mythological tales recorded in medieval manuscripts.

Place-names
It perhaps goes without saying that the place-names of Cornwall, Wales and Scotland are obviously Celtic. But the seeker after Early Celtic remains should also be aware that many place-names in England are Anglicizations of Celtic names which date back before the arrival of the ancestors of the English and, indeed, before the arrival of the Romans.

The names of rivers and streams are, to a very large extent, the names given them by the British Celts. Names such as the Aire, Avon, Dee, Derwent (Darwent and Dart), Don, Esk (Axe, Exe), Ouse, Severn, Stour, Tees, Thames, Trent, and Wye are all Celtic, with particular meanings. We have the famous tautology of the River Avon, Avon being the Celtic word for 'river'. Celtic stream names are particularly common in Dorset.

Several hills still carry their Celtic names such as Barr, Brent, Cannock, Chevin, Chiltern, Creech, Crich, Crick, Lydeard, Malvern, Mellor, Penn, Pennard. Some names have the English word for 'hill' added to the Celtic: more tautology.

Some forests in England also cling to their original Celtic names, Chute, Kinver, Morfe, Penge, Savernake, Cheetwood, Chetwode,

Ardanaiseig Crannog, Loch Awe is a good example of a crannog – an Iron Age artificial island built to support a defended homestead

the two last having the old English *wudu* (wood) added to the Celtic name *ceto* (in Welsh, *coed*), a wood.

Some old territorial names, such as Kent, Thanet, Wight, Craven, Elmet and Leeds, are Celtic in origin. The ancient Celtic form is often preserved in the names of English cities and towns, for example London, Carlisle, Dover, Dunwich, Lympne, Penkridge, Reculver, and York, while the English have added *ceaster* or *burg* on to other Celtic place-names to arrive at Dorchester, Gloucester, Manchester, Rochester, Winchester, Countisbury and Salisbury. It is rare to find Celtic village names in England except in those areas where a Celtic language existed until comparatively recent times, as in Cumberland, Hereford, Shropshire, Wiltshire, Devon or Dorset.

There are several Celtic words with a topographical meaning retained in English place-names. For example, the word *cumb, coombe* for 'valley', the words *tor* and *down* for 'hill', the word *carr* for 'rock', *luh* for 'lake', *brocc* for 'badger' and *ecles* for 'church' (as in Eccles).

When in search for the original Celtic population in England it is fascinating to take note of place-names as well as physical remains. A worthwhile companion in such a study is *The Concise Oxford Dictionary of English Place-Names* by Eilert Ekwall. This volume has been reprinted regularly since its first appearance.

Museums
In order to 'put flesh' on the people who lived and worked in Early Celtic Britain, no tour of the remains of hill-forts, brochs, crannogs or other sites would be complete without a visit to a museum. Many of the local museums have artefacts from the period (usually listed as Iron Age) and it is always well worth while calling into those in the vicinity of the sites you are visiting. Readers of the guide will find that special museums are listed within the individual areas, including the British Museum, which has one of the most important Celtic collections in the country, the National Museum of Wales and the National Museums of Scotland. Also listed are some 'living history' museums where

Celtic ('Iron Age') buildings and artefacts have been faithfully recreated, such as the Museum of the Iron Age at Andover, the Butser Farm Project, the Chiltern Open Air Museum and the Cockley Cley Iceni Village Museum.

There are no fewer than 2600 museums in Britain and therefore it is impossible to ensure that every museum which has artefacts from the period in question is given adequate coverage in this volume. Only those of major interest have been mentioned, so the enthusiast in search of the Early Celts is advised to check the local museums in the area in case they include 'Iron Age' artefacts.

Once more, it is emphasized that this is not an exhaustive guide to every hill-fort, settlement, dun, broch and crannog in Britain. But it is a guide to the most visually rewarding of the remains left us by the Early Celtic occupants of this island.

Chapter 1

London and South-east England

Kent, Surrey and Sussex

That London existed in some form before the coming of the Romans is obvious. From the first reference by the historian Tacitus (b. AD 56/7, d. after AD 117), it bears a Celtic name, albeit Latinized. Originally it was probably a small trading settlement of the Trinovantes, an upriver port of this people who traded with Gaul. According to the Greek geographer, Claudius Ptolemaeus (Ptolemy), c. AD 100–178, the Trinovantes' capital was at Camulodunum (Colchester) and covered the northern side of the Thames estuary. We will examine this people in detail in Chapter 5. While some scholars have thought to see the Celtic god Lug in the place-name, as in Lugdunum (fort of Lug) which occurs in many other towns in Celtic Europe such as Lyons (Lugdunum), Léon, Loudan and Laon in France, Leiden in Holand, Liegnitz in Silesia and Carlisle (Luguvalum in Roman times) in England, other scholars believe that the name is derived from the Celtic *londo* meaning 'wild place' – still seen in the Old Irish word *lond* (wild).

The fact that the vast urban conglomeration makes it difficult to reach pre-Roman levels in archaeological terms has caused some to state categorically that there is no evidence to suggest a pre-Roman occupation. However, it was not a usual Roman custom to site a town or city in an area where there was not an existing settlement. Most of the towns and cities in Britain were certainly founded on Celtic settlements. The Romans began to build at 'the wild place' fairly early, around AD 43, which seems to support the theory that they saw a thriving little settlement and port here which could be adapted for their own needs. Even though Camulodunum was the administrative capital for the Romans, London became an important centre and was later appointed the capital of the province soon after AD 80, when Tacitus, who gives us the first literary reference to London, writes that the city was full of traders having arisen from the ashes of the Boudiccan uprising.

London was set by the side of the Thames, the dark or sluggish river – Tamesis. In a recent (1990) BBC television documentary, Professor Richard Bradley of Reading University argued a strong case for the Thames being a sacred river for the Celts, occupying the same role as the Ganges does for the Hindus in India. It is certainly intriguing that Celtic law has its closest parallel in Hindu law, and that firm Indo-European connections are seen in this as well as in Celtic mythology. A fascinating study of such connections was made by Professor Myles Dillon in *Celt and Hindu* (University College, Dublin, 1973). Substantiation for Professor Bradley's argument also comes from the numerous finds made in the river from the Early Celtic period. These, argues Professor Bradley, are votive offerings along the lines of offerings made by Hindus to 'Mother Ganges'. Some of the best examples of exquisite British Celtic craftsmanship, such as the Battersea shield or the Waterloo helmet, numerous swords and other items, have been found in London together with countless skulls from both the Thames and the Walbrook.

In recent years archaeologists have found sites of importance along the Thames. In both Southwark and the City finds have been made which confirm that there were important riverside settlements here which date back to the Late Bronze Age and through the Celtic period.

In the last decade the exact position of a bridge built across the Thames was pin-pointed by excavation. Two Roman roads converging at the same point on the south bank were opposite a structure on the north bank which was identified as a bridge-pier support. The bridge was dated to AD 50 but as Dr Roger Wilson has pointed out it would be 'inconceivable' if there were not an earlier construction at this point and it could well be that the Roman structure obliterated the earlier one.

During the last decade, Dr Stewart Needham of the British Museum has been conducting excavations at Runnymede, beside the Thames, 3km north-west of Egham and famous as the place

where King John signed the Magna Charta. Right on the edge of
the river stood a Celtic township at a spot where many votive
offerings were apparently thrown into the Thames. Dr Needham
argues that the fact that the river was liable to flood here indicates
that the Celts held the Thames so sacred that they even ignored
their own safety in the siting of this particular settlement. When
the English put their own name to the area they called it the
'island of assemblies' which might indicate that there was a
tradition of Celts gathering for religious worship there. Nearby, at
Chertsey (TQ 026676), are the remains of a fortress of the Early
Celtic period.

Three of the rivers which flow into the Thames in and around
London have retained their Celtic names: from the north, the
River Lea which, in its original form, was named after the Celtic
god of light, Lug, and the River Brent, cognate with names such as
Brigantia and the goddess Brigit, meaning high or holy river. From
the south flows the Derwent, meaning the river where oaks are
common. The River Dart in Kent derives from the same root
word.

That the Celts certainly had a hand in naming parts of London is
obvious from the fact that one of the great gates of the city, which
opened on to the river, has come down to us as Billingsgate.
Originally it was called Bile's Gate, Bile being a Celtic god of
death whose task was to transport souls to the Celtic Otherworld.
The Celtic dead of London would be taken out of the city through
Bile's Gate to commence their last journey by river, or perhaps be
disposed of in the river. The Celts revered the head, for in the
head reposed the soul of a person, and they often decapitated their
slain enemies and either kept the heads as a mark of respect or
deposited them in sacred rivers. A larger number of skulls found
in Battersea from the pre-Roman period would support the idea
that the Thames was a sacred place of the dead.

Another gate has retained its Celtic name – Ludgate, the gate of
the Celtic god Lud or Lug, the name also found in the River Lea.
In spite of the replacement of the Celtic population by the Anglo-
Saxons, a folk memory of Lud still hangs across the city where
'King Lud' is often referred to in traditional tales and his name

even adorned a public house at Ludgate Circus. Lud features as the brother of Cassivellaunos in Geoffrey of Monmouth's *History of the Kings of Britain* (c. 1136).

But although Citisights of London introduced a 'Walk through Celtic London' in 1989, in connection with the Museum of London, there is little to be seen of pre-Roman Celtic London outside the museums. Only echoes of the Celts are found here and there. One such echo is the now English tradition concerning the ravens who grace the Tower of London. Legend has it that the Tower will fall if the ravens fly away, so their wings are clipped. The raven is the symbol of the triune goddess of death and battles and the idea is a particularly Celtic one. Whether this idea was picked up by the English from a Celtic tradition which survived in London or whether it was imported from contact with the Celts elsewhere is a matter of speculation.

It is rather like the English tradition which has arisen around the Lia Fáil (Stone of Destiny) which lies underneath the Coronation chair in Westminster Abbey. The Lia Fáil, while not exactly part of the period under question, is worthy of a visit. After it had been brought from Ireland to the Dál Riada kingdom of Argyll (Airer Ghàidheal – seaboard of the Gael), the famous St Colmcille crowned Aidan as king on it, in Celtic tradition. It was kept at Dunstaffnage until AD 848 when Kenneth Mac Alpin took it to Sgàin (Scone) where all Scottish kings (including the famous Macbeth) were crowned on it until it was seized as booty by Edward I (1272–1307) during his invasion and sack of Scotland. Since that time every English monarch has been crowned on it and a legend has arisen that should the stone be taken from Westminster it would mark the end of the English monarchy.

The stone, and others like it, had deep religious significance in Celtic life and the importance of swearing an oath on a sacred stone is frequently stressed in Celtic myth as well as supported by historical event: for example, in the region of James VI two Scottish clans, who had spent centuries in a blood feud, met on Iona and solemnly pledged themselves to peace and friendship on the sacred stones (now vanished).

Citisights of London's 'London Heritage Walks' are worthy of

attendance and are held in connection with the Museum of London. Programmes of the walks can be obtained from Citisights, 213 Brooke Road, London E5 8AB (tel. 071–806 4325). In 1991 Citisights also inaugurated the first 'Day Out in Prehistoric and Celtic London' at the Museum of London Lecture Theatre, which consisted of a series of lectures on the subject, ending with 'Walk through Celtic London'.

No tour in search of Early Celtic Britain within London would, of course, be complete without time spent at the **British Museum** (Great Russell Street, WC1) and the **Museum of London** (London Wall, EC2). Their collections of Celtic artefacts are among the finest in the world.

In the Museum of London, Early Celtic remains (Iron Age) are displayed in the prehistoric gallery. There are four main cases of exhibits: the most outstanding pieces in the collection are a bronze tankard from Brentford, iron daggers in sheaths, bronze and iron horse-bits, bronze 'horn caps' and a bronze terret. Among the many other items are farm implements, pottery, coins of the Cassivellauni and the Trinovantes, including one each of Cunobelinos, Addedormaros and Tincommios, brooches, iron currency bars and replicas of the Battersea shield and the Waterloo helmet.

In the British Museum, Room 39 is dedicated to Celtic artefacts. Next to it, Room 40 deals with the Roman occupation of Britain. There are many fascinating items to be seen here and the Celtic collection includes artefacts not only from Britain but from other areas of Celtic settlement. For example, the bronze flagons from Basse-Yutz in France are outstanding. Those on the trail of the Celts in Britain should note in particular two chariot burials excavated by the British Museum at Garton-on-the-Wolds and Kirkburn. In both, the chariot was dismantled and placed with the skeleton. Chain mail was found in one of these burials (*c.* 400 BC), the earliest occurrence of chain mail found in Britain.

Battersea shield, found in the Thames, is dated to the 1st century BC; an example of total symmetry in design. It is made of bronze with enamel inlay

Also on display are the finds from Aylesford, Kent, including a bucket with bronze fittings from the first century BC, and items from 471 Celtic burials excavated from outside the walls of Verulamium. Breathtaking finds were made in 1965 at Welwyn Garden City, when a Celtic burial was excavated: the corpse was wrapped in fur, showing bear-claws, and no fewer than thirty pots were ranged on the floor of the grave including five Roman amphorae, which would have held 100 litres of wine. The most spectacular find here was the unique set of glass gaming pieces, divided by colour into four sets of six pieces. The grave showed that the British Celts imported Italian wine and tableware, and even silver cups.

Finds from the Thames, supporting the idea of the sacredness of the river, are also on display. Perhaps the most famous is the first century BC Battersea shield, with bronze facing and flowing palmette, the scroll ornament enhanced with red enamel. There are two shield bosses from Wandsworth and a magnificent horned helmet from Waterloo, all dating to the same period. There is also the 1985 find of a bronze shield from Chertsey (Surrey).

The museum has impressive collections of metalwork, especially harness and vehicle fittings from Stanwick (North Yorkshire), Polden Hills (Somerset) and Westhall (Suffolk). These date from the first centuries BC and AD. The gold 'hero' torque from Snettisham (Norfolk) is on display, found in 1948 at the same time as fragments of sixty-one other torques and 158 coins. In 1968 five complete gold torques were found on a building site in Ipswich and another discovered nearby.

The magnificent bronze mirror from Desborough (Northamptonshire) is one of the finest surviving Celtic mirrors and is dated to the first century BC.

One other item of particular interest is the remains of the now famous Lindow Man. This is the upper half of a human body whose skin had been perfectly preserved by the acids of a peat-bog. Found in 1984 at Lindow Moss (Cheshire), this Celt met his death 2000 years ago. He was first knocked unconscious by a couple of blows to the top of the head, then he was garrotted with a piece of animal sinew, which strangled him and broke his neck;

A bronze helmet, dated to the first century BC, found in the Thames by Waterloo Bridge. It is one of the very few Celtic war helmets to have survived anywhere in Europe

finally his killers cut his throat and dropped him face down in the bog. Anne Ross and Don Robins' book *The Life and Death of a Druid Prince: the story of an archaeological sensation* dramatically and imaginatively reconstructs what they see as the events leading to the man's death which was, they claim, a ritual killing with religious significance.

A visit to the Celtic Room of the British Museum is a must for any tour of Celtic Britain for it throws light on the technology used by the Early Celts to manufacture these impressive objects. Jewellery, swords, shields and other weapons, pottery, gaming pieces, utensils and implements from many walks of life all add up to a fascinating collection of items from the Early Celtic period.

The expansion of the city from its original borders into Greater London has destroyed much of the Celtic remains in the area,

which can only offer two hill-forts which are worthy of inspection.
Caesar's Camp, in Holwood Park, Keston, Bromley (TQ 421640)
dates from the second century BC. The small enclosure across the
A233 roadway, in Keston Common, is an annexe to the main fort.
The original fort enclosed 17 hectares and was oval in shape.
However the eastern ramparts were destroyed when Prime
Minister William Pitt, living in Holwood House, ordered some
landscaping to be done. On the west a double bank and ditch still
exist with their counterscarp. The entrance was at the northern
end with a passage some 26m long, composed of flint-faced walling
between timber uprights. A massive fire destroyed the gateway to
the fort at the time of the Roman invasion of AD 43: this is
probably one of the Celtic fortresses reduced by the Roman
commander-in-chief Aulus Plautius during his march to the
Thames.

Another **Caesar's Camp**, Wimbledon (TQ 224711), is situated
on Wimbledon Common. It was originally constructed in the third
century BC and is circular, enclosing 4.3 hectares. The original
entrance was probably on the western side. Although an attempt
was made to level its defences early this century, fortunately little
damage was done and an attempt to cut a water-pipe trench in
1937 showed a bank of 9m wide revetted with posts. The ditch was
10m wide and 3m deep. A storage pit was found with pottery
dating to the third century BC.

Traces of a hill-fort have been discovered at **Enfield** (TQ
321956), where some coins of the Roman period were found. The
site is currently being excavated. Another fort was found at
Redbridge (TQ 436585), whose site revealed Early Celtic and
Roman pottery. But these sites are not visually appealing.

Leaving London, I would begin the search for the trail of the Celts
in Kent, the land of the Cantii or Cantiaci.

'Of all the Britons,' wrote Julius Caesar, 'those that inhabit the
lands of the Cantii are the most civilized and it is a wholly
maritime region. These Cantii differ but little from the Gauls in
habits of life.' Although in this case there is evidence to support

The Aylesford bucket was discovered in 1886 in a burial ground identified
with the Cantii of Kent. It is dated to approximately 50 BC

the words of the Roman general, Caesar's descriptions of Britain and its inhabitants are generally most unreliable. He was simply a military man who wished to depict his enemies as savage barbarians, and thereby give justification for his military campaigns in Britain.

Caesar noted that the Cantii used gold and bronze coinage and weighed iron bars as a means of currency. It is accepted that the Cantii were a Belgic Celtic tribe. Belgic Celtic tribes had settled in south-eastern Britain, among the earlier Celtic inhabitants, in about 180 BC. Some of these tribes, such as the Atrebates of Berkshire and Hampshire, kept close links with their kinfolk who remained in Gaul. Indeed, Commios, the chieftain of the Gaulish Atrebates, had authority over both branches of the tribe. The first Celtic coinage appeared in the land of the Cantii (Kent) in the second century BC. It was imported from Belgic Gaul before chieftains of the Cantii began to strike their own coinage.

When Caesar sent the Atrebate, Commios, to negotiate with the Cantii before his first attempted invasion, he reported that there were four main septs whose chieftains were Cinegetorix, Carnilios, Taximagulos and Segonax. We find a ruler of the Cantii named Dubnovellaunos (c. 15–1 BC) issuing coinage, followed by Vosenios. The coins have typically Celtic complicated animal designs. Then Eppilos (c. AD 10–25), a son of Commios, having been expelled from the Atrebate capital of Calleva (Silchester), seems to have been accepted as chieftain of the Cantii and to have issued his own gold and silver coinage here.

Eppilos, being a son of Commios, must have been quite elderly at this time; we find Cunobelinos (the famous Cymbeline of Shakespeare) exercising authority among the Cantii and using his son Amminos to administer it until a dispute arose and Amminos sought refuge among the Romans.

The capital of the Cantii was at modern **Canterbury** (TR 1457). Nothing is to be seen of the Celtic fort which must have stood here and little of the Roman town which was built in its place. The Cantii called it Durobernia, the fort by the alders or swamp. The Romans called it Durovernum Cantiacorum, recognizing it as the capital of the Cantii. When the Saxons, the ancestors of the

English, arrived they also recognized it as the burgh of the people of Kent – hence Canterbury. The **Royal Museum** (High Street) is especially noted for its collection of Celtic coinage from the area as well as exhibits from the period of Roman occupation.

In July 54 BC, during Julius Caesar's second attempted invasion of Britain, the Roman general ordered an advance from his coastal base-camp near Walmer (the mere of the Welsh – a later Saxon name) into the interior of Britain. The Romans commenced a night march on the evening of 7 July and by morning came upon the Celts who had established a position by the Great Stour River, near Thanington. The Stour (the Celtic name means the strong and powerful river, and is cognate with the Stura in Cisalpine Gaul) was fordable but the Celts contested the crossing. After a fierce engagement, Caesar pushed the Celts back and crossed the river. The Cantii retired into a nearby hill-fort which they had prepared for siege. The approaches had been blocked by the felling of trees. This hill-fort which Caesar now studied, was almost certainly **Bigbury**, Harbledown (TR 116576). It is a large rectangular contour fort enclosing some 10 hectares, protected on all sides by a single bank and ditch. The approaches are from the south-west, although the main entrance is on the eastern side. On the northern side there is a semicircular area which is a cattle enclosure of 2.5 hectares. The main rampart is now only 2.5m high, with a ditch 5m wide and 1.8m deep.

The fort was taken with only small losses to the Romans after Caesar ordered the VII Legion to storm it. Excavations have produced Celtic pottery, a variety of metalwork, including chariot fittings, a chain 5.5m in length with a barrel padlock and iron firedogs. Bigbury is now covered by woods and has been damaged by gravel digging and roadworks.

At Ightham lies **Oldbury Hill Fort** (TQ 582562), one of the largest Cantii fortresses, enclosing some 50 hectares. It is protected on the east by steep, natural cliffs. The first fortification was built around 100 BC and alterations were made about fifty years later. The final construction is a single rampart and ditch protecting the north, west and south, doubled where necessary. At the north-east entrance was a stone revetment and a possible wooden breastwork with a wooden gate. This gate was destroyed by burning, and a large quantity of sling-shots have been found nearby. It is likely that the gate was burnt during the Claudian invasion of Britain in AD 43. Another gate at the south was damaged, although a modern road has destroyed any remains. A great deal of pottery was uncovered during excavations but no clear evidence of dwellings within the fortifications.

Rochester (TQ 7468) is worth a brief visit. Although no Celtic remains can be seen and there are only a few Romano-British sections of the town and fort – especially in the Eagle Court public garden and in the Deanery Garden and cathedral precinct – it is interesting to remember that a major Celtic fortification stood here guarding an important crossing of the River Medway, whose Celtic name means 'Mead-coloured river'. Rochester was called Durobrivae, the stronghold by the bridge. It was here that the Roman invasion of AD 43 under Aulus Plautius met strong resistance from the Celts. The Romans sent their mercenary Batavi cavalry to swim the river while Titus Flavius Sabinus Vespassian (AD 9–79), commander of the II Augusta Legion, a future emperor, was ordered to cross further downstream. They were fighting Caratacos and his brother Togodumnos and it is here that Togodumnos was reported to have been killed.

Squerryes Park, Westerham (TQ 443522) is a triangular fort, which seems to have been erected about 100 BC. Protected by a ditch, its east and west sides are steep. The apex of the triangle is north while across the southern base are a bank, ditch and counterscarp. The main entrance seems to have been at the south-east. Several finds were made here from the Iron Age period.

Before leaving Kent, the **Folkestone Museum** (Folkestone Library, Grace Hill), founded by the Folkestone Natural History Society in 1868, is worth a visit as it prides itself on Romano-British finds from the area. **Maidstone Museum** (St Faith's Street) specializes in local history and **Sevenoaks Museum** (Buckhurst Lane) has an excellent collection of Romano-British discoveries from the area. Those interested in the meaning of place-names will find that Kent has managed to retain many of its original Celtic place-names: perhaps the most interesting is the port of Dover whose name, first Latinized as Dubrae from the Celtic, is still clearly decipherable as 'the place of the waters', referring to ancient streams which met there. A comparison with the Brythonic Celtic words for 'water' is fascinating: *dwfr* (Welsh), *dovr* (Cornish) and *dour* (Breton).

Moving west into Surrey to **Anstiebury**, Capel (TQ 153440) we find a strong fortified hill-fort enclosing 4 hectares and surrounded by two banks and ditches and a counterscarp on the east and west sides. The inner rampart is 10.7m wide and 1.8m high and has a revetted stone face. The entrance is on the east and there is a gateway between the outer and inner ramparts. The fort was constructed around 50 BC and probably left unfinished. Evidence suggests that it was attacked and the inner rampart destroyed not long after its construction. It may well have been attacked during the settlement of the Commios Atrebates from Gaul, who were fleeing from the Roman conquest. They would have been settling in this area during the period of the fort's construction. This would have been a border area of the Atrebate tribe whose main lands were in Hampshire and East Sussex. It is fascinating to note that the fort was reoccupied about the time of the Roman invasion of Britain in AD 43, probably against the south-western march of the II Augusta Legion.

Caesar's Camp, Farnham (SU 825500) stands on a level area encompassing 10.2 hectares. The main construction is defended by the naturally steep slopes of the hill, although on the south-west there is a strong ditch, bank and counterscarp, with a smaller bank and ditch beyond. On the south-east there is a small bank, ditch and counterscarp. There is also a double bank on the north side. The entrance is through the south-west rampart. A pond is encompassed in the fortifications and a spring rises at the north-east corner.

Dry Hill, Lingfield (TQ 432417) is oval in shape, enclosing 10 hectares. There are strong double ramparts and ditches with counterscarps on the south-west and north-east. A single rampart protects the south-east with a ditch and counterscarp. A rampart stands on the north which may have been protected by a ditch which is no longer traceable. There are entrances at the south-west, south and north-west. It is thought that iron-smelting was an occupation here but no material has been found to give an approximate date of occupation, though it is obviously Iron Age.

Hascombe Hill, Hascombe (TQ 004386) is a small promontory hill-fort enclosing 2.4 hectares. The sides are very steep and artificially scarped at the top in order to make them impossible to scale. The ramparts are surrounded by a ditch. To the north-east, where the hill-fort is easily approachable, there is a strong rampart and ditch with a single entrance, comprising an entrance passage some 24m long. Excavations found that it was occupied during the first century BC.

Holmbury, Shere (TQ 105430) is claimed as a Belgic (Atrebate) fortress built in the first century BC. On the west and north, double ramparts and a ditch defend it, while on the south and east, naturally strong slopes, which have been scarped, provide the barriers. The original entrance was in the north-west corner. The outer ditch was about 6m wide and 2.4m deep while the inner ditch was 9m wide and 4m deep.

St Ann's Hill, Chertsey (TQ 026676) is a small hill-fort of 5 hectares, now on a steep-sided wooded hill in a public park. A ditch and counterscarp can be seen on the west and run southwards, but nothing else is now visible.

At **St George's Hill**, Walton-on-Thames (TQ 085618), the hill-fort of 5.7 hectares is almost hidden by houses and a wood which now covers it. It is roughly rectangular, surrounded by a single rampart and ditch, which has been doubled on the north-western side. On the north-east is a semicircular enclosure, probably for cattle. The entrance is here. The original site was built in the third century BC; it was abandoned and then reoccupied in the first century during the Roman invasion.

Moving into West Sussex, keeping in the Atrebate border country, we find **Barkhale**, Bignor Hill (SU 976126), an oval enclosure of 2.5 hectares. Ploughing has destroyed much of the earthwork but ditches can still be seen on the north and north-east with parts of a bank. It is an old site which has even yielded late neolithic pottery.

Chanctonbury, Washington (TQ 139120), is a pear-shaped fort of 1.4 hectares on a dominant hilltop. Protected by a single bank and ditch, with an entrance at the south-western end, it is thought to date from the seventh or sixth centuries BC. Cross-dykes guard the approaches. Excavation in the centre of the hill-fort revealed the foundations of a Romano-Celtic temple, rectangular in shape, measuring 7.3m by 5.2m. Next to it was an oval foundation which has puzzled archaeologists. Both structures were of flint and mortar and date from the second century BC to the late first century AD.

Chichester Dykes: it is worth noting that between Bosham and Bognor, an area of several square kilometres is protected by streams and a line of dykes. These dykes are traceable in places, standing to a height of 3m with a rampart width of 6–8m and a ditch 6m wide. Sections are visible at SU 837080, SU 847080 and between SU 880085 and SU 918086. It is likely that these dykes were a complex of fortifications built by the Continental Atrebates, fleeing from the Roman invasion of Gaul, who settled the area. The purpose, it is supposed, was to protect their capital but where this capital was is a matter of speculation. It may have been near Chichester or Selsey.

It was from here that a chieftain called Verica (c. AD 10–40) struck an abundant amount of gold and silver coinage, styling himself son of Commios of the Atrebates. Verica seems to have been very pro-Roman, making an alliance with Adminios, the renegade son of Cunobelinos, who in about AD 39 tried to persuade the Roman emperor Gaius (Caligula) to invade Britain. In AD 42, Verica himself appealed to the Roman emperor Claudius to interfere in British affairs but, by the time of the Roman invasion in AD 43, Verica appears to have died, or been deposed, and Cogidubnos became chieftain here. Cogidubnos became one of eleven Celtic rulers to submit formally to Claudius after the fall of Camulodunum (Colchester) in AD 43.

Chichester was to become a local capital after the Roman invasion, called Noviomagus Reginorum (The New Place of the

Regini). Cogidubnos was rewarded with the title '*Rex Magnus Augusti in Britanni*' (Great King of the Emperor in Britain) and took the name Tiberius Claudius Cogidubnus. He was allowed to be a 'client king', recognizing the overall authority of the Roman emperors. His tribe then became the Regini (or King's People). Cogidubnus, obviously to protect his own position, was very pro-Roman and a promoter of Romanization among his people. Tacitus records him as one 'who maintained his unswerving loyalty down to our own times', adding, perhaps cynically, that he was 'an example of the long-established Roman custom of employing even kings to make others slaves'. An inscribed stone, giving his title and name, was found in 1723 and is now part of the wall of Chichester Town Hall. The Roman villa at **Fishbourne** (SU 8404) is said to have been built for him. However, following his death, *c.* AD 90/100, the Roman authorities formally annexed the Regini and assimilated them into the Roman province.

Cissbury, Worthing (TQ 137079) is an oval hill-fort enclosing 26 hectares with strong ramparts, 9m wide at the base, with ditch and counterscarp. The ditch is 3m deep with a curious central ridge on its otherwise flat bottom. The ramparts are enlarged on either side of two gates, one to the east and another to the south. Iron Age pottery has been discovered and later Romano-British pottery. About the first century BC, the interior of the fort was ploughed. In the late Roman period, the hill-fort was reoccupied, perhaps as a means of protection against the invasion of the ancestors of the English. Activity at Cissbury goes back beyond the Iron Age for within the fort are flint mines, in the south-east section, in which neolithic pottery has been discovered. An antler picked from one of the eight flint mine shafts gives a radio-carbon date of 3600 BC. In another shaft the skeleton of a young woman was found as if she had accidentally fallen into it head-first; another contained the crouched burial of a young man. The flint mines were worked until the Bronze Age but they were probably forgotten by the time the fort was constructed.

Devil's Dyke, Poynings (TQ 259111) stands 217m above sea-level, and is a promontory fort cut off by a bank and ditch 183m in length and 3.7m high. It is undated although it contained a circular dwelling and three storage pits which produced Iron Age pottery. To the south-west of the fort traces of an Early Celtic farming settlement have been found.

Goosehill Camp, West Dean (SU 830127) is overgrown but it can be seen as an oval enclosure of 0.2 hectares, surrounded by a rampart and ditch of about 1.5m. The ramparts are of chalk and show no signs of timber strengthening. The entrance is on the west with, possibly, a second to the north. A second rampart, the inner ring, is now incomplete on the south-east side, with an entrance at that point. Two dwellings have been found in the inner oval. Pottery dates the site to the end of the third century BC.

Hammer Wood, Iping (SU 845240) is a wooded promontory fort of 7 hectares. On its northern side are two ramparts and ditches, while a single rampart and ditch enclose the other sides, doubling at the southern end. The inner rampart has a stone face and the ditch is 2.2m deep. There is an oblique entrance in the nothern ramparts. Early Iron Age pottery was discovered here.

Harting Beacon, Harting (TQ 806184) is a rectangular hill-fort of 10 hectares, with a rampart and ditch broken on the west side by an entrance. The ditch was flat-bottomed and 1.2m deep. The bank was of dumped chalk retained by wooden fencing. Structures with four and six post-holes have been found in the south-east corner with storage pits. Iron Age pottery has been discovered, together with the remains of an adult male burial, including two gold penannular rings. Because of the slightness of the construction it is thought that this was more a stockade for cattle than a defensive work.

Highdown, Ferry (9TQ 093043) is a small hill-fort of 0.8 hectares, originally constructed in about 500 BC. Chalk and timber-faced ramparts are separated from a flat-bottomed ditch, 1.8m deep, in which a skeleton was found. The hill-fort is rectangular in shape. An additional bank was constructed, with ditches on the south and east sides. One to the west has been filled in by ploughing. The entrance was on the east side. In about the third century BC, new defences were constructed and the entrance was moved 3m to the south. In the interior, a rectangular dwelling was uncovered. Occupation of the site actually goes back to the Bronze

Age. Curiously, the fortress was refortified in the third century AD, during the Roman occupation, when the Saxons, pushing the Celts out of the area, took it over and used it as a burial ground. In the Second World War, it was still used as a defence system, housing a radar station!

Park Brow, Sompting (TQ 153086) is a 'classic' Celtic settlement, set among Celtic field systems, which can be seen over the hillside. Originally constructed in about 1000 BC, some eight huts stood on the hill: they were of the conical thatched-roof type with small storage pits in their floors. In about the eight or seventh century BC, two larger huts were built 180m to the north-east, with deeper storage pits from which have been recovered spindle whorls, weaving combs and items which show clearly that textiles were manufactured here. During the first century BC, the settlement was reconstructed and the houses were rebuilt on a rectangular pattern, with plastered walls and glass in their windows. The settlement was destroyed by fire in the third century AD and not reoccupied.

Thundersbarrow Hill, Old Shoreham (TQ 229084), originally a small agricultural settlement of the fifth century BC, was protected by a low bank and ditch. It was later protected by a triangular hill-fort whose ramparts still stand 2m high. There are signs of damage to the east and west entrances and by about 250 BC the fort was abandoned and not used again. During the first century AD, a Romano-British farmstead was built outside the eastern rampart which was occupied until the Saxon invasion. Many Celtic fields are seen on the hill which gets its name from a bowl-barrow close to the southern gate. There is no record of any finds within it.

The Trundle, Singleton (SU 877110): this hill-fort has a breathtaking view over Sussex and the sea and was originally occupied about 3000 BC in neolithic times: a skeleton of a woman from the period was discovered here. The Celtic hill-fort was constructed about 500 BC, and later ramparts and a ditch, with counterscarp, were erected in 320 BC. It was occupied down to the first century BC when the Atrebates reached the area. In the fifteenth century a chapel to St Roche was constructed here and then a windmill, burnt down in 1733 AD.

Wolstonbury, Pyecombe (TQ 284138) is an oval fort. No entrances can be identified and it is enclosed by a ditch with an external bank, apparently made by throwing the chalk downhill. To the south is a dyke defending an outer enclosure and this is probably where the main entrance was. An oval enclosure was found within the fort. Excavation has produced some Iron Age pottery. There is a record of local children during the nineteenth century discovering various coins at the hill-fort from the Celtic, Roman and Danish periods.

In East Sussex we are in the border country of the Cantii again. **The Caburn**, Glynde (TQ 444089) is on the summit of Mount Caburn, and was originally constructed in about 500 BC. At that time it seems to have been lightly defended with a palisade and entrance to the north-east. Around 150 BC the major defences were constructed with a double line of ramparts and a ditch. The ditch is 1.5m deep and there is a high internal bank. At least 150 storage pits have been found inside the fortifications, suggesting several dwellings, although only two doubtful examples have been discovered. Around 43 AD, with the Roman invasion, the fort was hastily refortified with a box rampart and stout posts at back and front filled with chalk. A new ditch was dug along the north side about 2.5m deep and 9m wide. The entrance was strengthened. The II Augusta Legion, in its march south-west, must have attacked the fort for the gate was burnt and there is evidence that the hill-fort was hastily evacuated. In the twelfth century an adulterine castle was built on the hilltop.

East Hill, Hastings (TQ 833099) is a promontory fort of 14 hectares, with sea-cliffs to the south and natural steep slopes to the north, and a strong bank running north-south. The entrance seems to be at the south end of the rampart where a second bank lies west. It has been eroded by the sea but it has been suggested that the Romans, having driven out the original Celtic inhabitants, used it as an invasion base.

High Rocks, Frant (TQ 561382): above the escarpment of the High Downs Rocks lie the damaged remains of a 10-hectare promontory fort, thought to have been constructed in the first century BC. In the face of the Roman invasion of AD 43, the ramparts and ditch were refortified and to the north and east, a second rampart was constructed. The entrance was at the south end through elaborate outworks.

Hollingbury, Brighton (TQ 322078) is said to be the classic Early Celtic site of Britain. A hill-fort which is square in shape but with rounded corners, it encloses 3.5 hectares, and is defended by a rampart and ditch with traces of counterscarp to the south. Excavation showed that the rampart was composed of two rows of posts 2.1m apart, tied with cross-beams and filled in by chalk rubble forming what is now called, by archaeologists, the 'Hollingbury-type' rampart. The posts were 15cm in diameter and the position of some of them is marked on the site with modern metal posts. The gate to the west is inturned while the east gate is a strange through one. A slight bank 30m inside the fort and parallel to the east side indicates an earlier enclosure and some Bronze Age axes have been found in four bowl-barrows. These, with Bronze Age jewellery, are now in the British Museum.

While at Hollingbury, a visit to the **Brighton Museum** (Church Street) is worth while for their exhibition of local artefacts of the period. The museum has displays of coinage, pottery and other items, including loom weights, combs, brooches, a swan etched pin, a boar figurine and a shale bracelet. The principal sites represented in the collection include Hollingbury, Cissbury, Slonk Hill and Bishopstone.

Long Man, Wilmington (TQ 54309) stands on the steep north face of Windover Hill, overlooking the village of Wilmington. One of the few hill-figure carvings from Celtic times, it is also one of the largest representations of the human figure in the world. The outline stands 69m high, with staffs in either hand, 1.2m higher. The whole is so planned that when seen from the ground below, and foreshortened, the dimensions of the figure are not disproportionate and this indicates that considerable skill was employed in its design and execution – as, indeed, in the design of the Witham shield. The outline we see today is the result of restoration by the Revd de Ste Croix in 1874. The significance of

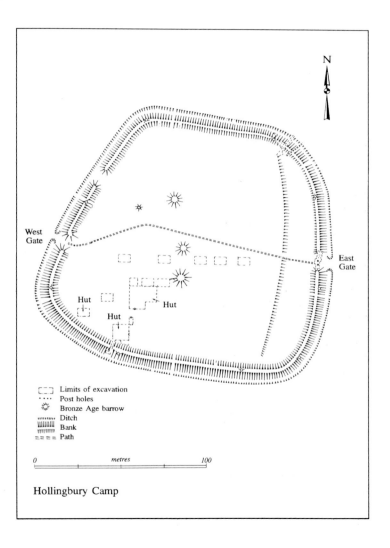

N

West
Gate

East
Gate

Hut

Hut

Hut

☐☐☐ Limits of excavation
···· Post holes
☀ Bronze Age barrow
⫿⫿⫿ Ditch
⫿⫿⫿ Bank
==== Path

0   metres   100

Hollingbury Camp

this piece of Celtic art has not been evaluated. It is generally considered to be a representation of a Celtic god or hero, and bears a similarity to later literary representations of Lugh. The Cerne Abbas figure (q.v.) also seems to be a representation of a Celtic god, so the Wilmington figure would not be unique in this respect.

Ranscombe Camp, South Malling (TQ 438092), 450m west of Caburn, is an unfinished hill-fort, with a 440m length of rampart and ditch laced, according to excavation, by vertical and horizontal timbers. There is a gateway, though no gateposts are present. The site has produced Early Celtic pottery and Roman wares of the second and third centuries AD.

Seaford Head, Seaford (TV 495978): the southern side of this fort has been eroded leaving a triangular fort containing 4.6 hectares, defended by a rampart 2m high and traces of a ditch 2m deep. Three gaps are seen in the ramparts but only the north-west and north-east are thought to be original entrances. Midway along the north-west side is a bowl-barrow which, when excavated, failed to produce a burial although small pits produced carpentry equipment.

Museums with Iron Age exhibits in Sussex, apart from the Brighton Museum include the **Museum of Sussex Archaeology**, Barbican House, High Street, Lewes, the headquarters of the Sussex Archaeological Society, and the **Worthing Museum** (Chapel Road) which has been recently refurbished with a new archaeological gallery.

Chapter 2

South-west England

Berkshire, Hampshire, Isle of Wight,
Wiltshire, Dorset, Somerset and Devon

Starting with Berkshire, probably the best example of a surviving
contour fort in England is **Caesar's Camp**, Easthampstead (SU
863657). The defence works follow the contours of the hill so
accurately along its 122m lines that the overall result is that, from
above, the fort looks like an oak-leaf. The entrance is on the
southern side and the site has not been excavated.

    Grimsbury Castle, Hermitage (SU 512723) is triangular in plan,
its lines based on the contours of the hill. Some 3.2 hectares are
enclosed by its earthworks. There are three entrances: one on the
west, a second to the north and the third to the south-west.
Excavations have placed this fort to the third and second centuries
BC, long before the Atrebates settled in the area.

    Traces of defensive systems can be seen throughout the
Berkshire Downs (SU 546785–570792), although the traces may
not all have been part of one system. Sections of bank and ditch,
stretching over 1km, can be seen east of Beche Farm. On Hart
Ridge, in Brooms Wood and Bowler's Copse, another section is
traceable while yet another stretch, reaching over 1km, is seen
between the Grotto (on the Thames) and Hurdle Shaw. It is
thought that some of the ditches and banks were boundaries rather
than ramparts.

    Standing on the highest chalk hill in Britain, at 297m above sea-
level, is **Walbury**, Combe (SU 374617). Interestingly, the name
'town of the Welsh' (Wealhas, being the Saxon name for the
native British Celts, and meaning 'foreigners') is retained from the
time the ancestors of the English invaded Britain. Combe is the
British Celtic word for 'valley'. The fort enclosed 33 hectares and
it is certainly the largest hill-fort in Berkshire. A single bank and
ditch enclose it, although there are faint traces of an outer

counterscarp bank. There are two entrances, south-east and north-west. Traces of circular dwellings can be discerned within the fort. From the north-west entrance there are some minor earthworks which seem to provide extra defences as they run across the hill spur.

Crossing south into Hampshire, one should make a genuflection to **Silchester** (SU 6462), which is in the extreme north of the county, inside a triangle formed by Newbury, Reading and Basingstoke. Regarded as the most famous of all Romano-British towns, called by the Romans Calleva Atrebatum, the entire town was excavated and provides a fascinating tour with many visible remains and a nearby museum. However, in wandering among the remains, it should be remembered that this was the capital of the Atrebates. Its name Calleva (which Ptolemy gives as Kaleoua) indicates a wood, seen in the modern Welsh *celli*. Before the Roman colonists began to build their town, the Atrebate capital was surrounded by a series of earthworks, which encircled the entire site. The inner earthwork is regarded as the original and was levelled. The outer earthwork (until recently considered Roman) was actually erected in the first century BC. The Roman town was not laid out until the end of the first century AD although some buildings, such as the baths (*c.* AD 55/65), are earlier.

It was to Calleva that the Gaulish Atrebate chieftain Commios came. Commios had, at first, been pro-Roman. Julius Caesar had called him 'King and Friend' and Commios had given help to Caesar on his two expeditions to Britain. But when the conquest of Gaul started in earnest, Commios and his Gaulish Atrebates fought defiantly against the Romans. It is recorded that an Atrebate kingdom had already been established in Britain over which Commios had authority. When defeated in Gaul, Commios and his personal retinue came to Britain and settled at Calleva.

We find Tincommios, Eppillos and Verica describing themselves as sons of Commios on their coinage. Yet *c.* AD 25, Epatticos, thought to be the brother of Cunobelinos, was issuing gold and silver coins from Calleva and Tincommios had fled to the Roman emperor Augustus seeking aid. Previously, Tincommios' brother, Eppillos, had issued coins from Calleva. With the rise of Epatticos, Eppillos appears issuing coins in Kent, interesting bronze, silver and gold coins, some of which show a striking figure of a British Celtic charioteer with victorious emblems. Had Epatticos chased him out of Calleva and had Eppillos then made successful war on the Cantii, becoming their chieftain? Could this disunity among the south-eastern tribes have been the reason why the Roman invasion force was able to land unopposed in Kent a few years later? It is a matter of interesting historical speculation.

Beacon Hill, Kingsclere (SU 458573) is a contour fort. An area of 3.6 hectares is enclosed in a single rampart, ditch and counterscarp. About twenty circular dwellings with storage pits have been traced within the fort. The site was occupied in neolithic times: two slight banks, only visible on aerial photographs, show the presence of a causeway camp. A curiosity is a railed enclosure in the south-east which marks the tomb of Lord Caernarvon (1866–1923) who, with Howard Carter, excavated in the valley of the Kings, Luxor in Eygpt, and discovered the tomb of Tutankhamen in 1922. In the valley south of here are traces of a Celtic field system.

On a small spur above the Lymington River, whose Celtic name signifies a river by elm trees, stand **Buckland Rings**, Lymington (SZ 315968). Enclosing 3 hectares, it is rectangular in shape and defended by two banks and ditches with a counterscarp on the north and south sides. The ramparts were lined in timber on both the inside and the outside. The entrance on the eastern side, a long inturned passage with a gate, has been damaged. The fort appears to have been constructed in the first century BC. Much of it was deliberately dismantled sometime after AD 43, probably by the Romans as they demilitarized the Atrebates in the area. To the east of this fort, at a distance of 360m (where a modern factory now stands) was a small fort beside the river. This was called **Ampress Camp**.

Another fort is beside a stream in **Bullsdown**, Bramley (SU 671583). It enclosed 4 hectares and is oval in shape. The defences are an inner bank, ditch with small counterscarp and a second

bank, ditch and outer counterscarp bank. The fort is on low-lying ground and the banks are now of no great height, though the ditches are still 1.5m deep. The entrance was on the north-east and has been totally destroyed.

Originally constructed in the sixth or fifth century BC, **Bury Hill**, Upper Clatford (SU 345435) was a large fort enclosing 9 hectares with a single rampart and ditch. About 250 BC, the fort was reconstructed and made smaller, enclosing 5 hectares with a new bank, ditch and counterscarp bank, overlying the south-eastern part of the original. The new banks were 2m high and separated by a ditch 6m deep. The entrance, 9m wide, was on the eastern side. The constructions were of dumped chalk and it appears that no timber was used. The second construction appears to have coincided with the destruction of the fort at **Baulksbury**, near Andover, at the valley bottom. Occupation of Bury Hill lasted until the Roman invasion.

Butser Hill, Petersfield (SU 712201) is part of the South Downs, separated from their main mass by a narrow neck of land cut by three cross-dykes. These dykes are thought to have been field enclosures rather than an attempt at fortification. On the north-east spur of the hill, known as little Butser, is the site of the **Butser Ancient Farm Project** (SU 719207). This is a unique attempt to recreate an Early Celtic farmstead and is open to the public all year round. Based on the circular hut excavations, the collection of dwellings have conical roofs. The centrepiece is a dwelling built from 200 trees and thatched. Inside are replicas of Iron Age tools and implements. Outside, the pens contain breeds similar to those the Celts would have maintained before the Roman invasion – Soay sheep and Dexter cattle. Early forms of cereals and herbs are grown here, and there is also a shop on site. The farm can be entered from the A3 Petersfield-Portsmouth road (6.4km south of Petersfield) next to the Queen Elizabeth Country Park Centre (SU 716189).

Three banks and two ditches surround the oval fort of **Castle**

Pimperne House in Butser Ancient Farm. A reconstructed Iron Age house and thatched grain storage pits based on evidence from excavations

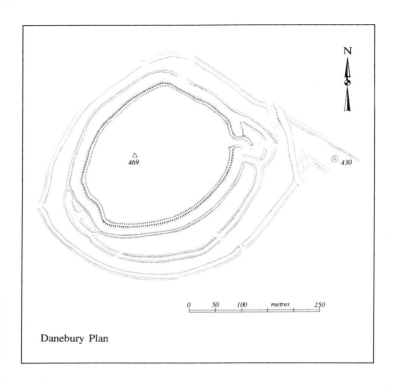

Danebury Plan

Ditches, Whitsbury (SU 128197). The fort encloses some 7 hectares and is remarkably strong with the inner rampart rising to 6m in height on the southern side. The other bank is almost as high. The entrance, on the west, has now been destroyed by farm buildings. There is another earthwork to the south-east, covered by a wood, and a ditch (Grim's Ditch) to the north. These may have been connected with cattle-ranching based on the fort.

Danebury Ring, Nether Wallop (SU 323377) is one of the most interesting hill-forts in England. Containing 5.3 hectares in its interior, it is protected by a rampart, ditch and counterscarp bank. Outside are another rampart and ditch which increase the area

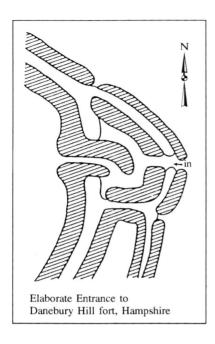

Elaborate Entrance to
Danebury Hill fort, Hampshire

defended to 11 hectares. Between the two ramparts is a
semicircular area most probably built to hold cattle. The original
entrance on the west has been blocked while another has been
constructed on the east. The actual site has been inhabited from
the Beaker period (2500–2300 BC). The Celts constructed the first
hill-fort here in the fifth century BC. Its early ramparts were box-
like (of the Hollingbury type, q.v.) and with a ditch. Inside the
fort were small, square dwellings with four corner posts and
probably raised floors. It has been suggested that they were simply
granaries. Over the following two centuries, many new huts and
dwellings were built, some very large and built along streets,
concentrated mainly in the southern part of the fort. There are
5000 pits in the northern sector.

About 400 BC the gateway was reinforced with **guard chambers** to protect it. Then it was remodelled on a massive scale and the defences extended. Again, in the third century BC, the defences were strengthened and V-shaped ditches were constructed. The cattle annexe was added. Inside the fort the circular dwellings had wattle and daub walls and thatched roofs. Shortly before 100 BC an outer bank and ditch were established.

The remains of animals and the large quantities of granaries and stores show that the Celts of Danebury constituted a rich agricultural community. The large quantities of metalwork and pottery and evidence of trade also show that it was a township of some importance. Around the mid-first century BC, the site was abandoned. Could this have something to do with the settlement, after 50 BC, of the Gaulish Atrebates of Commios in the area? It seems likely.

Before going to see Danebury, I would advise a stop in Andover to visit the **Museum of the Iron Age** (6 Church Close, Andover) which is part of the Hampshire County Museums Service and houses collections from sites such as Danebury, Winklebury, Owslebury and Balksbury. The museum displays what is undoubtedly one of the best reconstructions of Early Celtic life, with its artefacts and accoutrements, in Britain. Some of the main features include a reconstruction of part of the Danebury rampart, the interior of a roundhouse, with its implements, a weaving loom, plough, oven and quern. All show how the Celts of Danebury would have lived until the coming of the Romans. This museum is particularly recommended for children, and school work packs are available, as well as brochures, guides and other materials. After a visit to the museum, a trip to the Danebury site itself is much more rewarding.

The interesting thing about **Ladle Hill**, Sydmonton (SU 478568) is the fact that it was never finished. A ditch was built, about 3m wide and 0.5m deep, to enclose an area of 3.3 hectares. Gaps were left for entrances on the south-west and east. The topsoil and chalk rubble were dumped inside the fort, with hard chalk being kept to construct the ramparts. It was probably under construction when the Romans marched through the area and therefore work was halted. Inside the fort, and to the north and south-east, are Bronze Age barrows.

Lying among Celtic fields is the rectangular enclosure of **Martin Down**, Martin (SU 043201). Enclosing 0.8 hectare, the bank might have supported a wooden stockade. The ditch which surrounds it is 2–3m deep. Entrances are at the south and east. However, it has been suggested that this was merely a cattle pound.

Old Winchester Hill, Meonstoke (SU 641206) is an important hill-fort. The River Meon below it still retains its Celtic name, the main river, related to the Gaulish name Moenus. An oval fort enclosing 5 hectares, it is defended by a single bank and ditch with counterscarp. The rampart still stands 6m high. At the eastern and western ends are entrances. Outside the eastern entrance are two pits, one either side. Several Bronze Age barrows were destroyed when this fort was constructed.

Nearby is **Winchester** itself (SU 4829), which the Romans recorded as being the capital of the Belgae (Venta Belgarum). The Belgae once occupied much of what is now Hampshire and Wiltshire. The Celtic settlement, enclosed in an earthwork called **Oram's Arbour**, was situated on the western outskirts of the modern town. Lying between Clifton Road and Clifton Terrace, it appears to have been a rectangular enclosure of 18 hectares, fairly large, with a gate on the western side, and surrounded by a ditch. Few traces of it can now been seen but excavations in the Castle Yard have helped to date it to the first century BC. A Belgic coin has been found close to Winchester Cathedral. With the Roman conquest, a Roman fort was constructed, part of which was excavated in Lower Brook Street. Now only the name of the city, in part, marks the fact that this was once a Celtic tribal capital. The old Celtic name has been said to derive from the root *ven-*, to love or enjoy, to which the English added *ceastar* for a Roman fort.

Winchester City Museum should be the first port of call in the city for it has an excellent collection of Early Celtic material and its guides will explain the Celtic sites in the city. The museum has an interesting display of coins from the southern tribes, particularly a collection of Durotrigean coins, as well as some iron currency bars, including a hoard of thirteen found at Worthy Down. Bucket mounts, horse-bits, brooches, a remarkable display of other jewellery, farm implements such as a knife and sickle, weaving combs and pottery comprise a fascinating collection.

South of Winchester on **St Catherine's Hill** (SU 484276) stands an oval hill-fort enclosing 9 hectares, with rampart, ditch and small counterscarp. It is now on a tree-clad summit and inside are the remains of a medieval chapel and a maze (said to have been cut by the boys of Winchester College). When the original settlement was built in 500 BC, the site was free of trees. The fort was constructed in about 400 BC and reinforced with a ditch 8m wide and 3.5m deep. The entrance, at the north-east side, was 12m wide. The gate itself was of wood hung in a timber-lined passage. Later the entrance was narrowed to one gate guarded by flint-faced walls. At this time the rampart height was increased. Around 50 BC the gateway was burnt and the site ceased to be occupied. This would coincide with the movement of Commios and his Atrebates into the area, perhaps a sign that not all the British welcomed the settlement of the Gaulish chieftain here. Only the rampart history has been learnt and there is still much to find out by future excavations about the interior occupation.

Woolbury Ring, Little Somborne (SU 381353) is a circular fort of 8.1 hectares, defended by a single rampart and ditch with slight counterscarp. The rampart rises to 3m high but has been destroyed on the east side. The entrance is on the south-west. This fort is particularly noted for its adjacent Celtic field systems running to the south and cattle enclosures marked by three dykes which run up to it from the west and south-west.

Across from the Hampshire coast stands the Isle of Wight, which was part of the Belgae territory. It was called Vectis by the Romans in an attempt to emulate the sound of the original Celtic name, which seems to have meant 'that which rises above the sea', in other words an island. There are few visible Early Celtic remains here although **Brading Villa** (SZ 6086), on the outskirts of Brading, a Roman villa constructed in the first century AD, shows signs of a pre-Roman occupation of the site. Roman villa sites at Newport, Rock and Carisbrooke are of much later construction.

There is a promontory fort at **Five Barrows Camp**, Gatecombe (SZ 483842). This enclosed a fort of 10 hectares. The bank stands 3m high and there is a ditch on the south-western side. The entrance is at the north-western end of the rampart. The defences seem to have been unfinished. Another fort is located at Ventnor (SZ 578778) in the south of the island but there is little to see of it.

Moving back into Wiltshire, we enter a county which is more rich in pre-Roman remains than any other English county. Avebury, for example, is one of the largest henge monuments in Britain and one of the most impressive archaeological sites in Europe, its complex stretching from Silbury Hill (constructed around 2500 BC) across to the world-famous Stonehenge. Avebury was in use for 1000 years from 2600 to 1600 BC, overlapping the neolithic and Bronze Age periods. A museum tells the story of Avebury in great detail.

It is small wonder that the Early Celtic inhabitants of the area continued to build and live here. It is an area of numerous hill-forts and settlements.

Barbury Castle, Wroughton and Ogbourne St Andrew (SU 149763) is said to have been the traditional site of the Battle of Beranbyrg in AD 556, when the Celts tried to turn back the incursions of the Saxons, who were relentlessly carving their new kingdom of West-Saxony (Wessex). According to the *Anglo-Saxon Chronicle* for that year, Cynric, the king of the West Saxons, defeated the British here. Barbury (Bera's burg), whose Celtic name is now lost, is an oval hill-fort of 4.7 hectares, strongly defended by two banks and ditches with traces of sarsen stone facing in the ramparts. Entrances are on the east and west. Inside are traces of circular dwellings. Several Iron Age weapons and agricultural implements, as well as parts of harnesses and chariot fittings, have been discovered here. The fort was probably refortified by the Celts during the westward expansion of the Saxons, just before they suffered defeat here by Cynric.

Battlesbury Camp, Warminster (ST 898456) is the site of a massacre of the Celts. A pear-shaped hill-fort enclosing 10 hectares, Battlesbury overlooks the River Wylye, whose Celtic name meant 'tricky river', or one which was liable to flood. The name is identical with the Gwili in Wales. It had double ramparts separated by a ditch, and an inner ditch with an extra rampart on the northern side; the entrances were on the north-west and south-east. An excavation found Iron Age pottery, quernstones, ironwork and part of a chariot wheel. Outside the north-west entrance a mass Iron Age burial was discovered, the result of a massacre. The most likely explanation for this was an attack by Roman legionnaires. The fort does not appear to have been occupied since.

Bratton Castle, Bratton (ST 900516) is a contour hill-fort defended by a single rampart and ditch. On the east and south, the ramparts are doubled with strong banks and ditches. There is a rectangular annexe outside the entrance to the north-east and a similar rectangular enclosure at the southern entrance. Grinding stones, parched wheat, sling-shots and other items have been discovered, and inside the fort is a barrow in which charred human bones, pottery and animal bones were found. Do not be confused by the Westbury White Horse cut below the fort's rampart. This is not a Celtic hill figure but was cut in 1778.

Traces of the movement of Vespassian's II Augusta Legion, as it moved south-west 'pacifying' the Celtic tribes, can be found at **Bury Camp**, Colerne (ST 818740). This Belgae fortress, enclosing 9 hectares within triangular ramparts, single and with a ditch on two steep sides, and double on the level ground to the south-west, has its main entrance on the north-east. This, together with its long inturned passage, was destroyed by fire. A small rectangular earthwork at the centre of the fort was also laid waste by fire. It appears that the Romans fired the outer gates and pushed through to the interior.

What marks **Casterley Camp**, Upavon (SU 115535) as different from the usual hill-fort is the fact that the site seems to have been a sanctuary for Celtic religious worship before the fort was built. The fort itself is a very large enclosure of 27.5 hectares. Overlooked from the west, it is not really a good defensive site and, indeed, the defences were never completed. Entrances

existed on the north, west and south. In the centre of the fort were
two enclosures (now destroyed by ploughing) which excavation
showed to be from the first century BC. One was oval and the other
was rectangular. The oval enclosure contained a pit in which stood
a post, almost a metre in diameter. Around it were four human
burials and fourteen red-deer antlers. This is an uncommon feture
and hence it has been thought that the site was a religious one.

Castle Ditches, Tisbury (St 963283) is a tree-covered fort,
situated on a lower escarpment overlooking the Nadder valley.
The Nadder still carries its Celtic name – 'to flow'. A triangular-
shaped fort, it encloses 10 hectares within triple banks and ditches.
Entrances are on the west and east, the eastern one being the
more elaborate. Extra ramparts and ditches are placed in front of
the entrances.

Cley Hill, Corsley (ST 839449) guards the Frome gap. Corsley,
below, was a boggy area: its original Celtic name *cors* means 'bog'
or 'fen'. The River Frome also still carries its original Celtic name,
meaning 'fair, fine or brisk', which is identical in meaning to the
Ffraw in Anglesey. The hill-fort, of 7 hectares, defended by a
single bank and ditch and perched on top of the isolated chalk hill,
prevented any surprise movement on the river by potential
enemies. A chalk quarry has now destroyed part of it as well as its
south-eastern entrance. Traces of several dwellings have been
discovered inside, and round barrows of the Bronze Age are
nearby.

The circular fort at **Figsbury Rings**, Winterbourne (SU 188338)
may well have been simply a farmstead with enclosures for cattle-
ranching. It encloses 6 hectares. Although excavations have shown
storage pits with Bronze Age and early Iron Age pottery, no date
has been established. However **Fosbury Castle**, at Tidcombe and
Fosby (SU 320565), an oval fort enclosing 12 hectares within
ramparts and defended by double banks and ditches, is clearly a
fortress and sherds of early Iron Age pottery have been discovered
here.

Perhaps the finest example of Celtic agricultural field systems
found in the country is that of **Fyffield and Overton Downs** (centre,
SU 142710). It comprises a landscape of rectangular fields with

banks and trackways. Stone walls, ditches and banks mark the field boundaries. One of the best visible systems is at **Piggle Dean**, beside the A4 roadway (SU 143688). Farming in this area was continuous from 700 BC through to the Roman occupation.

A fort of some interest, though not for the period under discussion, is **Liddington Castle**, Liddington (SU 209797). It is an oval hill-fort, enclosing 3 hectares in a single rampart, ditch and counterscarp, and dates from about the sixth century BC: excavations have revealed pottery from the period and traces of Romano-British pottery. Liddington is famous as being the supposed site of the Battle of Mons Badonicus in which, around the beginning of the sixth century AD, the Celtic prince Arthur and his warriors were said to have checked the westward push of the Saxons. It is one of twelve battles in which Arthur is said to have fought. Other sites have been claimed for the event, however, including Bradbury Hill.

A large rectangular fort of 13 hectares is sited overlooking the Vale of Pewsey at **Martinsell**, Pewsey (SU 177639). It is defended by a single rampart and ditch with an entrance to the north-east. An Atrebate rubbish pit was found to the north. What seems to be an added protection for this fort is found south-west along the escarpment in the shape of a small promontory fort called **Giant's Grave**, which is protected by a rampart with outlaying banks and ditches. Pottery has been discovered here.

Said to be an agricultural centre rather than a hill-fort in the proper sense, **Ogbury Camp** stands at Durford (SU 143383). It is comparatively large, enclosing 25 hectares in ramparts which still stand 2.4m high.

Oldbury Castle, Calne (SU 049693) is a rectangular fort enclosing 4.8 hectares. It has a single rampart and ditch. Although the site was disturbed in the nineteenth century, some Early Celtic pottery was discovered here. Do not be confused by the White Horse which was cut in 1780 by Dr Christopher Alsop of Calne. The name Calne, incidentally, retains its Celtic form, being 'the place of the roaring river'.

Dominating the Avon Valley to the west is the site of **Old Sarum**, Stratford-sub-Castle (SU 137327). The site itself is marked by a Norman castle motte, but the surrounding earthworks are from the Iron Age, enlarged during the Middle Ages to form an enclosure of 11 hectares with an entrance to the east at the point where the Normans built their fort. Some Iron Age material has been recovered from here.

Another fort of interest for a much later event than the period under discussion is **Oliver's Castle**, at Bromham (SU 001646). It encloses 1.2 hectares in a single bank and ditch. The interior produced Iron Age pottery. To the south-west are Bronze Age barrows which revealed cremations and material from that period. The site overlooked that of the English Civil War battle called 'Bloody Ditch'.

Ryebury Camp is a small fort enclosing 1.5 hectares at All Cannings (SU 083640). It actually overlies a neolithic camp. The entrance is on the south-east and the ramparts do not appear to be strong.

A more interesting fort is that at **Scratchbury Camp**, Norton Bavant (ST 912443), which is a contour fort of 15 hectares enclosed in a single bank and ditch with counterscarp. There are three entrances, one north-west and two south-east. The interior fort, a small circular earthwork, dates back to 350 BC. It is thought that some parts of the fort date from the Roman occupation. There are indications of an agricultural system nearby and inside the fort to the north are two small barrows which contained a bronze dagger, a bronze pin, an amber ring and beads.

A triangular promontory fort stands at **Whitesheet Castle**, Stourton (ST 804346), enclosing 5.6 hectares. The site is unexcavated.

Another promontory fort at **Winkelbury Hill**, Beriwick St John (ST 952218) is actually unfinished but is of some interest. It was first erected in about 300 BC, with two ramparts and ditches enclosing 6 hectares, and a new rampart was begun fifty years later but was not finished. In 50 BC the Atrebates reduced the fort in size to 1.8 hectares by a curbed rampart and ditch with an entrance at its eastern end. Were these British Atrebates trying to withstand the arrival of Commios of the Gaulish Atrebates?

Another fortification constructed at the same time, 50 BC, is

Yarnbury Castle, Steeple Langford (SU 035404). This is a circular fortification enclosing 10.5 hectares. It has two banks, 7.6m high, and deep ditches. There are traces of a third outer rampart. The inturned entrance is on the east, 9m wide with elaborate outworks. The interior, however, is earlier than the outworks, even as early as the seventh to the fifth centuries BC. This earlier work encloses 3.7 hectares. Another fortification on the western side of the fort was added during the Roman occupation. From the eighteenth century until 1916 an annual sheep fair was held here and some of the ridge markings are due to this rather than to the original occupation.

The name of Dorset originates from the Durotriges, 'the kings of the strength', whose main tribal lands covered the area, touching into Wiltshire and Somerset. They were a rich trading tribe whose ships sailed to Gaul. They produced their own coinage, including silver, bronze and pure struck bronze. The countryside was rich agriculturally and also minerally; they had natural supplies of iron. They had several powerful hill-fort centres, especially within Dorset itself; this seems to bear out their tribal name.

Abbotsbury Castle, Dorset (SY 555866) is a triangular fort of 2 hectares, surrounded by two ramparts and ditches except to the south-east where they increase to four. The north-east rampart holds the entrance. Circular dwellings have been traced there.

Another settlement is found at **Badbury Rings**, Shapwick (ST 964030), which is much depleted. There are two strong inner ramparts and a weak outer rampart enclosing 7.3 hectares. Traces of field systems, Bronze Age barrows and four Roman roads stand beside or near this fort.

Perhaps the largest hill-fort in Britain, enclosing 114 hectares, stands at **Bindon Hill**, Lulworth (SY 835803). The ramparts actually enclose Lulworth Cove and run along the coastal strip for

Cerne Abbas Giant, standing 55 m high, is thought to be what Caesar described as the *Dis-Pater* or Father of the Gods. In British tradition this was *Cernunnos*. The figure is thought to date no later than the 1st century AD

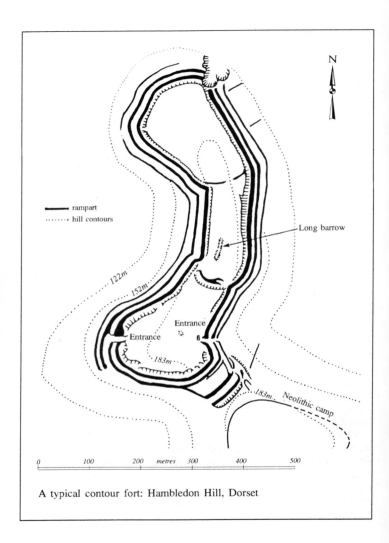

N

rampart
hill contours

Long barrow

122m
152m

Entrance

Entrance

183m

183m Neolithic camp

0   100   200 metres 300   400   500

A typical contour fort: Hambledon Hill, Dorset

some 2375m with an inturned entrance 1800m from the eastern end. It has been suggested that this was a protected trading port of the Durotriges. The Celtic name merely signifies it is 'the place inside the fort'.

Buzbury Rings, Tarrant Keyneston (ST 919060), which is an enclosure on the side of a hill, is a cattle enclosure rather than a hill-fort as such. This was probably the centre of a prosperous farmstead.

The **Cerne Abbas Giant**, Cerne Abbas (ST 667016) is a famous hill-figure carving some 55m high and 51m wide. Professor Stuart Piggot has seen the carving as a representation of Hercules and claimed that it must date to the reign of Commodus (AD 180–93) when there was an attempt to revive a cult of Hercules. The Cerne Abbas figure is almost a replica of a carving found at Costopitum (Corbridge, Northumberland), now in the Newcastle upon Tyne Museum of Antiquities, which is also claimed to be Hercules. However, many Celticists see the Cerne Abbas Giant as a representation of a Celtic god and not an import from Rome or Greece. Later Irish literary references portray the Irish 'father of the gods', The Dagda, as carrying a club in the manner of the Cerne Abbas figure. The Dagda had his equivalent in Brythonic Celtic tradition – Caesar called him the Dis Pater, whose name in Brythonic Celtic seems to have been Cernunnos. He was not only the father of the gods but the ancestor of the people. Contrary to Professor Piggot's contention that the figure represents Hercules, it is argued that there is no reason to think that the figure is anything other than a Celtic hill-figure carving. Above it on the hillside are numerous earthworks dating from Iron Age times. The name Cerne signifies 'rock or stones' while Abbas represents the later fact of an abbey in the area.

Chalbury, Bincombe (SY 695838) is a triangular hill-fort of 4 hectares in the middle of a field system. The fort is defended by a single rampart and ditch and there are traces of some seventy dwellings and storage pits. Two of the circular dwellings have been excavated and human remains were found scattered on the floor. Pottery, an iron knife, ornaments and milling equipment were found.

In **Dorchester** (see Maiden Castle) there is the Dorset County Museum (High West Street), which contains many finds from the period including the finds from Maiden Castle itself.

One of the most striking hill-forts is that at **Eggardon Camp**, Askerswell (SY 541948). It encloses 8 hectares on a spur of Eggardon Hill. Three ramparts and ditches surround it except on the south-west where the ramparts were destroyed in Iron Age times by a landslide. Some 500 storage pits have been identified and five were excavated: only a few flint knives and scrapers were found.

One of the most important hill-forts in the area, and a must for any enthusiast, is **Hambledon Hill**, Child Okeford (ST849122). The site was originally occupied in about 3500 BC: there are signs of a neolithic enclosure of 8 hectares. The fort has been built and rebuilt several times. The Celtic hill-fort is on a massive scale with imposing earthworks, banks and ditches and counterscarp. The defences are doubled to the south-east where the fort could be more easily attacked. Traces of circular dwellings have been found and it is thought that some 200 houses were protected here. The fort had three entrances, north, south-east and south-west. So far no extensive excavation has been carried out on the hill.

An important centre of the Durotriges was **Hengistbury Head**, Bournemouth (SZ 164910). It stands on a headland jutting westward across the south side of Christchurch Harbour. Unfortunately its seaward side has been eroded while the harbour side has silted up. Today the fort encloses 70 hectares but at the time of the Roman conquest it was twice as big. Two close-set lines of rampart and ditch, the former still 7m high, protect the western end of the spur. Three entrances were recorded in 1777. Hengistbury was occupied throughout the entire Iron Age (700 BC onwards). That this port of the Durotriges was a major trading centre before the coming of the Romans is confirmed by the discovery of large numbers of continental pottery types and imported wine amphorae, coins from the Gaulish Celtic tribes. More than 3000 coins have been excavated here including Roman coins and coins minted by the Durotriges themselves. It is thought that Hengistbury was the main mint for the tribe in the area.

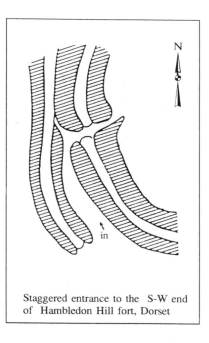

Staggered entrance to the S-W end
of Hambledon Hill fort, Dorset

Thirteen round barrows have been excavated here. One of them
produced two gold coins, a halberd pendant, amber beads,
flintwork and an incense cup with a cremation in an inverted urn.

Hengistbury doubtless fell to the II Augusta Legion, as did **Hod
Hill**, Stourpaine (ST 857106), another major fortress of the
Durotriges, which stands 100m above the River Stour, 'the
powerful river'. Two great ramparts enclose the 22 hectares of this
rectangular fort except on the west side where a single defence
system suffices. Two of the five gates are Early Celtic while the
north-west and east gates are of Roman construction. The fort was
originally built in four stages throughout the Iron Age. Of the
buildings inside the fort only forty-four still survive in the south-
east quarter, measuring on average 3.5m across. Others have been
destroyed by ploughing. One of the houses that remain stood in its

Maiden Castle in Dorset: an aerial view from the west. Maidun, the fortress of Mai, was a major hillfort of the Durotriges

own enclosure and excavation has shown that this doubtless the chieftain's dwelling, was attacked by iron ballista bolts fired by Roman siege artillery. This is obviously one of the twenty forts that Vespassian is recorded as attacking. No cemetery has been found and it has been supposed that the bodies were removed, for the Romans took the unusual step of building their own fortification in the north-west corner where it can still be seen.

No visit to the Celtic hill-forts of Dorset can be complete without a visit to the most famous of them all – **Maiden Castle**, Winterborne St Martin (SY 669885). This is the fort of Mai – Mai's

dun. It was the site of an almost continuous occupation from 3000
BC when the earliest earthworks were built. It was not until 350 BC
that the Celts constructed their fortifications with a single rampart
and ditch. Another hundred years passed before the fort began to
be extended to its present 19-hectare enclosure with new ramparts.
A human burial of the time was found at the southern point.

Around 15 BC the defences were again rebuilt by the Durotriges.
Double ramparts were constructed on the north side and triple on
the south. The inner rampart was made more impregnable: from
ditch bottom to top was a vertical barrier of 15m. The ramparts
were reinforced with blocks of limestone, which were provided by
internal quarries. At the east and west entrances elaborate
barbicans were constructed to guard the gates. Inside, the dwelling
houses were circular in shape.

Around 100 BC the defences were again remodelled and the
entrances developed to the complex structures we see today. One
guard chamber had a pit which contained 22,260 sling-shots (a
weapon effective to a range of 130m) ready to repel any attack.
Until AD 44 the defenders of Maiden Castle continued to repair
their impressive fortress, which dominated the countryside across
the Frome valley.

Then in AD 44, Vespassian, one day to be emperor, with his
brother Sabinus, led the II Augusta Legion down from the chalk
hills across the Frome, by the site of the modern town of
Dorchester. Three km away the great multiple ramparts of the
fortress stretched against the skyline. The legion marched to
attack, Vespassian ordering an attack on the weaker eastern gate.
Ballista artillery soon rained down on the defenders a barrage of
machine arrows – a weapon perhaps they had never seen. Then
the dwellings at the eastern gate were set alight. Under cover of
the smoke, the legionnaires charged, scaling the ramparts under
cover of their shields. Some thirty-eight defenders were killed by
the western gate . . . or at least thirty-eight were buried there. The
gates, east and west, were burnt down. Men and women and
children were slaughtered, the wounds of the skeletons showing
that they were struck by many blows when one would have been
sufficient. The dead were buried in hurried, shallow graves, the

corpses tumbled in instead of being carefully placed according to custom. One woman was buried with her arms pinioned behind her, her skull smashed in by three death-dealing blows. Most of the skulls recovered were scarred with sword cuts. The legion moved on relentlessly. The inhabitants appear to have continued to live there for a further twenty years before they moved down the hill to the site of Dorchester – Dorcic, 'the bright place' – where the Romans had erected a fort earning the suffix *ceaster*. It was not the end for Maiden Castle: in the fourth century a temple was built in its ruins, with a house. Perhaps a druid continued to worship there for a while? The finds from the site are displayed in the **Dorchester Museum** (High West Street), and include the skeleton of a defender whose vertebra has been pierced by a Roman machine arrow (a ballista bolt).

Pilsdon Pen, Pilsdon (ST 413013) is an oval fort of some 3 hectares with two ramparts and a ditch with counterscarp. There are signs of circular wooden dwellings here and one of them may have been a gold-worker's shop since a crucible and traces of gold have been found. The fort is noted for an unusually long – 32m – rectangular wooden building with a central courtyard. Cobblestones were laid at the centre of the enclosure. The only significant find, however, was the head of a Roman ballista arrow.

Poundbury, Dorchester (SY 683912), on a hill west of the town, was used by the Romans as a cemetery. Originally it was a rectangular hill-fort enclosing 5.5 hectares with two banks and ditches. It has been dated to the sixth century BC. Excavation shows that it was built with timber facing; in the first century BC it was reinforced with limestone and a second bank and ditch constructed. The entrance was on the eastern side. A Roman aqueduct to the north and a railway tunnel passing underneath have damaged it.

Occupied from the third century, **Rawlsbury Camp**, Stoke Wake and Hilton (ST 767057) is a contour fort enclosing 1.6 hectares. The ramparts are of two banks and ditches, and the main entrance, an elaborate passage, is to the east. Signs of dwellings in the fort have been noticed. Outside, cross-dykes indicate cattle enclosures or tribal borders.

A victim of a Roman attack: a Celtic defender of Maiden Castle with a Roman *ballista* arrow lodged in his vertebra

Ringmoor Settlement, Turnworth (ST 809085) is a settlement set among a Celtic field system. The village was built within a small oval enclosure surrounded by a bank and a ditch.

Another site of a Roman attack is **Spetisbury Rings**, Spetisbury (ST 915020) where some 120 people were slain. The hill-fort overlooks the River Stour enclosing 2 hectares with a rampart and ditch. The defences seem to be unfinished, particularly to the north-east. Perhaps the defenders were still trying to get ready when the II Augusta Legion burst upon them. They were buried, probably after the legion passed on, with Celtic grave goods and even some Roman weapons.

Somerset is a border territory between the Dumnonii to the south and the Dobunni to the north and also the Durotriges to the south-east. **Brent Knoll** (ST 341510) is fairly typical of the isolated hill-forts in the area. This one encloses 1.6 hectares with a single rampart and ditch. However, it has been scarped on the west and south to increase its defensive position. While damage has been done by quarrying, some Roman coins and pottery have been discovered here.

Charterhouse (ST 5056), on the border of Somerset and Avon, was the centre of the Mendip lead mines. Some scholars have remarked on the ability of the Romans to start exploiting the mines within six years of the conquest. They forget that the native Celtic population was already working them before the Roman arrival and that the Romans simply took over their administration. Among the lead ingots to have been discovered, one now lost, was dated to AD 49. Mendip ingots read BRIT:EX.ARG.VEB – 'British lead from Veb . . .'. Little can now be seen of the Early Celtic or, indeed, the Roman occupation, although finds from Charterhouse are displayed in the Bristol and Taunton Museums.

Cheddar Caves (ST 466539) are of interest in that the outer part of Gough's Cave was occupied during the Iron Age and after the Roman occupation. It was first used by palaeolithic man. It may have been used by Celts hiding from the fearsome Roman invaders.

Cow Castle, Simonsbath (SS 795374) is an attractive oval fort enclosing 1.2 hectares in a stone rampart, 2m high. There are entrances at the north-east and south-west.

At 333m above sea-level **Dowsborough**, Holford (ST 160392) is one of Somerset's highest hill-forts. Oval, enclosing 3 hectares, it is defended by a rampart, ditch and counterscarp. The entrance is at the east. It seems likely it was the centre of cattle-ranching with **Dead Woman's Ditch** (ST 161381) forming a territorial boundary.

On the summit of the Brendon Hills is an unfinished fort called **Elworthy Barrows**, Brompton Ralph (ST 070338). The fort has not been excavated and no explanation has yet been put forward as to why it was not finished. Whether it was being built as the Romans pushed into the area is a matter of conjecture.

Glastonbury (ST 492409) and **Meare** (ST 446423) are two Early Celtic marsh villages which only exist as humps in fields. The museums at Glastonbury and Taunton contain information on them. **Ponter's Ball Dyke**, Glastonbury (ST 533377) seems to be the boundary mark of the tribe who lived in the Glastonbury marsh village. Iron Age pottery has been discovered there.

Perhaps the most important site in the county is that of **Ham Hill**, Stoke-sub-Hamdon (ST 484164). It has been called the capital of the Durotriges. It is one of the largest fortifications in the country, enclosing 85 hectares and with a perimeter of 4.8km. The site is roughly L-shaped and the defences are double ramparts and ditches with triple ramparts on the north-west and south-west. From accidental discoveries it has been confirmed that the site was in occupation from about the seventh century BC into the Roman period. A wide range of pottery, chariot fittings, currency bars and silver/bronze coins of the Durotriges have been found here, together with a stylized bull's head of bronze. Also discovered was a Belgae cremation burial in a pit and an infant burial containing an iron ring-headed pin. Remains of a Roman villa have been found in the south-east of the fort.

The Durotriges were known to have a good trade with Gaul and while the Roman conquest of Gaul upset their trading economy they nevertheless continued as a wealthy group until the Roman conquest of Britain. They had developed a splendid coinage which was issued until the Roman conquest. But several other areas in Dorset may well have been a position of equal importance, and without detailed excavation we will not know which was the tribal capital.

Another impressive fort of the Durotriges is that of **Maesbury Castle**, Dinder and Croscombe (ST 610472), which is oval and encloses 6 hectares.

Read's Cavern, Churchill (ST 468584) was the site of a tragedy around 100 BC. A number of people were in this single large cavern when a massive roof fall occurred, killing them. Amongst the contents of the cave were a set of shackles and bronze bands from a tankard.

Dating to the beginning of the first century AD is **Small Down**,

Evercreech (ST 666406), an oval fort with a single rampart, ditch and counterscarp enclosing its 2 hectares. There is a second rampart and ditch on the eastern side. The entrances are to the east and south-east. This fort contains four round barrows, whose burials are dated to the same period. Taunton Museum exhibits the finds.

Perhaps one of the most romantic hill-forts is **South Cadbury Castle**, South Cadbury (ST 628252): romantic, because it is suggested that it was the Camelot of Arthur and his Celtic warriors during their struggle against the invading Saxons. Certainly a late occupation between AD 400 and 600 gives some credence to the idea. However, the earliest known occupation of the hill was in 3300 BC. It was occupied during the Bronze Age and afterwards until the Celts built a fortress here in the middle of the fifth century BC. New ramparts were constructed in 400 BC and ditches cut deep into the rock of the hillside. It contained an enclosure of 8 hectares.

By 200 BC all four ramparts had been rebuilt and strengthened and ditches and counterscarp made. The gateway on the south-west had two semicircular guard chambers. Inside the fort round and rectangular timber dwellings almost jostled each other in a closely built township. Refuge pits were found to be filled with a wide variety of Iron Age pottery.

In the early parts of the first century AD the Durotriges rebuilt the fortifications. Then came Vespassian's II Augusta Legion, remorselessly taking the Roman conquest south-west. Evidence shows that the Romans attacked the fortress, probably soon after the attack on Maiden Castle: the bodies of men, women and children were found scattered in the entrance passage. Many had been gnawed, after death, by scavenging animals. The gateway was pulled down by the Roman troops and the hill was deserted by the time they moved on.

Trendle Ring, Bicknoller (ST 118394) is a small enclosure of 0.8 hectare, with an entrance on the north-east side. There is nothing to suggest this was any more than a main cattle enclosure, connected with stock-rearing.

We move south-west into Devon. The name is identical with
Defnas, people of Devon, from the tribal name of the Dumnonii,
the original inhabitants, which name was transferred to the Saxon
conquerors. The Welsh still call Devon Dyfnaint from the same
root. The Dumnonii were the people living in Devon, Somerset
and Cornwall. During the westward expansion of the Saxons, the
battle at Mons Badonicus halted the invaders and allowed the
kingdom of Dumnonia to appear as a political unit for some
centuries. Its eastern border, however, was in a constant
transitional stage as Saxon and Celt engaged in bitter border
warfare. Inevitably, the Saxons pushed westward. By the eighth
century the Saxons were at the River Tone, which still retains its
Celtic root *tan*, the roaring river. Here they captured the Celtic
fortress and renamed it the *tun*, or fort, by the Tone – Taunton.
They pushed into the north of Devon and soon the 'West Welsh'
(*weahlas*, foreigner, the name the Saxons called all Celts) were cut
off from their fellow Britons in the north. The modern borders of
the countries of Britain were beginning to appear. The Saxons
were even launching raids deep into the west. In about 721/2 the
Britons managed to inflict a defeat on the Saxons during such a
raid at Camel. A battle in Devon in 838, at Hingston Down, saw
their defeat by Ecberht of Wessex (802–39). It was not until 936
that Athelstan of Wessex (925–39) fixed the Tamar as the border
between the Celtic kingdom of Cornwall (land of the Kernweahlas) and Wessex, which had now absorbed Devon and whose
Celtic language was either quickly absorbed or, more likely, lost
because the Celtic inhabitants were pushed out or eliminated.

Sitting astride a narrow ridge at Southleigh is **Blackbury Castle**
(SX 187924), an enclosure of 2.6 hectares, oval in shape. It is
protected by a single rampart and ditch. The entrance is on the
south. Limited excavation has only uncovered one dwelling in the
enclosure.

More spectacular is **Bolt Tail**, Malborough (SX 669397), from
which there is a commanding view across Bigbury Bay. The steep
rock cliffs are a defence to this promontory fort, enclosing 5
hectares, in addition to the stone-faced rampart which stands 4.5m
high and is 275m long. There is an inturned entrance with a

semicircular outwork from which a hollow leads to a second small fort which overlooks Hope Bay and guards a fresh water supply for the main fort.

Burley Wood, Bridestow (9SX 495876) is an interesting site enclosing 6 hectares in cross-ridge dykes above the River Lew, the brilliant river, cognate with the Welsh *lliw*. It is oval in shape with a inturned entrance protected by a single rampart, ditch and counterscarp. It is obviously the centre of an agricultural settlement. North-east of the hill-fort sits a medieval motte-and-bailey castle.

Burridge Camp, Roxborough (SS 569352) is an oval hill-fort of 1.2 hectares defended by a single rampart and ditch. This is an example of a multiple enclosure fort, but it has been damaged and would appear to have been reused during the period of the Saxon expansion into Devon.

Another interesting fort is the oval fort of **Cadbury Castle**, Cadbury (SS 914053). Excavations here have revealed pottery, bones and ashes, twenty metal and four shale bracelets, rings, beads and an iron knife. The fort contained 1.6 hectares in massive ramparts, still rising 6m high on the south-east and south-west. A steep slope added to the north-west defences. The original entrance is to the south-east.

Clovelly Dykes (SS 311235) are a set of field boundaries meeting at a defence work which was probably the centre of an agricultural and cattle-ranching settlement. The earthworks are overgrown today but the ramparts are quite massive at what was the entrance.

A coastal promontory fort stands at **Countisbury**, Lynton (SS 741493), lying between the sea and the East Lyn River. The neck of a spur of Wind Hill is cut by a strong rampart 0.4km long and 9m high.

It is thought that the circular hill-fort at **Crankbrook Castle**, Moretonhampstead (SX 738890) was built at two separate periods. The first defence work encloses 4 hectares and rises to a height of 1m. A second line of rampart and ditch was begun but left unfinished.

Dumpdon Great Camp, Luppitt (ST 176040), overlooking the River Otter, is actually a small camp enclosing 1.2 hectares in a diamond shape. Double ramparts and ditches are on the north side while elsewhere the defences are single with a trace of a counterscarp. There is an interesting entrance.

At **Exeter** (SX 9192) lies the capital of the Dumnonii – or so the Romans designated it, building a fort to contain the people there in around AD 50. They called the spot Isca Dumnoniorum. The second name obviously derives from Dumnonii but the first is the Celtic river name which simply means 'water'. It is also cognate with Axe, Esk and Usk and Isch (on the Continent). Compare the modern Irish, Manx and Scottish Gaelic words for water: *easc, ushtey* and *uisg*. Interestingly, this form for 'water' does not occur in Brythonic Celtic and the name seems to be a survival of Goidelic, thus supporting the argument that Goidelic was the earlier form spoken in Britain. There is nothing to see of the pre-Roman settlement here but a visit to the **Royal Albert Memorial Museum** (Queen Street, Exeter) is worth while, especially for its collections of local archaeology.

Standing amongst a group of Celtic fields is **Foale's Arrishes**, Widecombe (SX 737758), a group of six circular huts between 5.5m and 9m in diameter. Once the settlement was surrounded by an enclosure but there are now no traces of this. It is similar to **Grimspound**, Manaton (SX 701809), named after the synonym for Odin. This was merely a cattle enclosure and dates from the Bronze Age period.

Hembury, Payhembury (ST113031) is an impressive and important hill-fort. The original occupation of the hill took place in neolithic times and finds of pottery, charred wheat and other items such as axes, dating from 4200 to 3900 BC, have been made. The Celts restructured the site into a hill-fort around the third century BC. About 50 BC the Dumnonii added two banks midway across the fort with ditches on the south. It would seem, therefore, that the southern end of the fort was used as a stock enclosure while the northern end was used by the people. Only one rectangular dwelling has been traced here. However, there is some evidence that the fort was still in use, or reused, during the period of the Saxon conquest of Dumnonia.

Kestor, Chagford (SX 665867) is the site of two dozen dwellings

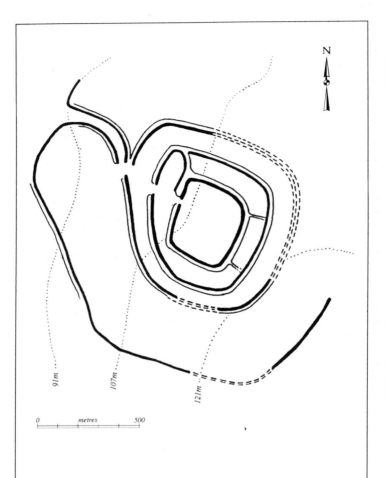

N

91m

107m

121m

0   metres   500

Multiple-enclosure or hillslope fort in Milber Down Camp, Devon

which are placed by Celtic field systems that are marked by lines of upright stone slabs. There are traces of two sunken roads of the period running from north-east to south-west. One of the huts, 11m across, showed traces of an iron-smelting furnace. The other huts are 6–10m in diameter.

Milber Down, Haccombe (SX 884699) was abandoned at the time of the Roman conquest. It was more a cattle ranch than a hill-fort, for it stands on the slope of the hill and could not, therefore, have been easily defended. Such sites as this, and there are many near the coast, may well have been gathering points for the collection and export of cattle to Gaul. Excavation has shown that this site was built in the first century BC.

Prestonbury Castle, Drewsteignton (SX 746900) stands overlooking the River Teign, which Celtic name seems cognate to the Welsh *taen* meaning 'a sprinkling'. The inner enclosure is oval with a rampart surrounding it. There is an entrance on the east.

There is some argument whether **Shoulsbury Camp**, Challacombe (SX 706391) is actually a Roman legionary marching camp or was built by the Dumnonii. It is very regular in shape and seems to contain a mound that may have been used for a signal tower.

A double rampart and ditch surround 4.4 hectares at **Sidbury Castle**, Sidbury (SY 128913), which is almost pear-shaped. The main entrance is to the north.

Stanborough Camp, Halwell (SX 773517) is a small circular fort looking eastwards over Start Bay and enclosing 1.4 hectares by a single rampart and ditch.

Chapter 3

Cornwall (Kernow)

including the Scilly Isles

Cornwall still belongs to Celtic Britain rather than to England and
for this reason it stands apart from South-west England. The
Saxon conquest of the isle of Britain was still incomplete at the
beginning of the tenth century AD. In 937 Athelstan of Wessex
fought one of the last major battles between the Celts and Saxons
for the supremacy of the island. Athelstan was a grandson of
Alfred who became king in 925. An alliance of the Scots, the
Strathclyde British, the Cumbrians, the Welsh, the Manx, some
Irish and the Cornish met Athelstan in Northumberland.
Brunanburgh, the site of the battle, cannot be identified but is
believed to be on the coast of Yorkshire or even Lincolnshire. A
poem called *Armes Prydain Ffawr* (Prophecy of Great Britain), of
which 199 lines are still extant and claimed for Welsh literature,
calls upon the Celts to unite and drive the English out of Britain.
But it was not to be. The *Anglo-Saxon Chronicle* tells us that it
was the bloodiest fight since the English people had first come to
Britain to conquer the Celts. The victory now allowed Athelstan to
consolidate his borders.

In 936, Athelstan finally cleared up the fudged border of what
had been Dumnonia and Wessex. He is recorded as expelling that
year all the Celts, or West Welsh, from the parts of the town of
Exeter which they inhabited and from the surrounding
countryside. Henceforth the River Tamar, whose name ('sluggish
river') was cognate with the Thames, Thame, etc., would be the
border between the English and the Celts of the south-west. This
was the land which the Celts called Kernow and which henceforth,
to the English, would become Kernweahlas – the land of the
foreign Kerns, Cornwall. Native chieftains continued to rule there,
under English suzerainty, until after the Norman conquest, when
Cadoc, the last of them, married the daughter of Reginald, son of

Henry I (1100–1135). Cornwall remained a distinct political unit apart from England until Tudor times, when laws had to be passed *in Anglia et Cornubia*. In addition, King John granted a charter to the mining communities of Cornwall in 1201 which recognized their separate identity in the holding of a Stannary Parliament. In 1337 Cornwall's independent position was further recognized when it was made a Duchy, with the eldest son of the ruling English monarch appointed as Duke. The Stannaries of Cornwall had their own courts, laws and taxation. In spite of Tudor centralist policies, which provoked Cornish uprisings against English rule in 1497 and 1546, the Stannary Parliament continued and was granted a power of veto over the Parliament in London in 1508. The last time this power of veto was confirmed was in 1753. The Stannaries fell out of use until 1974 when they were reconvened, but they are not recognized by the current UK government.

The Cornish language developed from the common British Celtic when Cornwall became isolated from the rest of the British population. Its literary remains are sparse and the bulk of them are centred around medieval religious plays and poetry. One of the main causes of the 1546 uprising was the imposition of English in religious worship. However, the language died as a generally spoken means of communication at the end of the eighteenth century, although a native knowledge lingered on until the beginning of the twentieth century when the current revival of the language began. It is, of course, closely related to Welsh and Breton, and less closely to Irish, Manx and Scottish Gaelic.

Cornwall was almost the first part of Celtic Britain to emerge into recorded history. There is evidence of early trading with Europe centuries before the Romans thought about invading Britain. In the second half of the fourth century BC, Pytheas, a Greek explorer from Massilia (Marseilles), made a voyage to Britain and his work has been quoted by Strabo, Diodorus Siculus and Pliny the Elder. Pytheas noted the existence of the Bristol Channel: 'a stormy strait separates the shores of Britain, which the Dumnonii hold, from the Silurian island'. According to Diodorus Siculus, a Sicilian Greek historian (*c.* 60–30 BC):

The inhabitants of that part of Britain which is called Belerion
[Land's End] are very fond of strangers, and from their
intercourse with foreign merchants are civilized in their
manner of life. They prepare the tin, working very carefully
the earth in which it is produced. The ground is rocky, but it
contains earthy veins, the produce of which is ground down,
smelted and purified. They beat the metal into masses like
astragali and carry it to a certain island lying off Britain called
Ictis . . . here, then, the merchants buy the tin from the
natives and carry it over to Gaul and after travelling overland
for about thirty days, they finally bring their loads on horse to
the mouth of the Rhone.

Such trade has been confirmed by archaeological evidence. It is
often thought that the Romans did not come to Cornwall to any
great extent, halting their westward conquest at Exeter where
Vespassian sent cohorts of his II Augusta Legion northward into
Somerset, Gloucester and also South Wales. The fact was that
military invasion was not really necessary, although twenty-four
legionary marching forts and five Roman 'milestones' have been
found in Cornwall. A villa in the Romano-British style was found
at Magor (Illogan) and another site at Gwithian. Finds in Cornwall
show much evidence of communication with the Roman occupiers
of Britain. There seems to be no record of resistance in Cornwall
and therefore no permanent garrisons were necessary.

The Celtic tribe who inhabited Cornwall is generally believed to
have been the western branch of the Dumnonii. However, the
Ravenna Cosmography places the Cornovii here, and mentions a
town called Duro-Cornavis (the fortress of Cornovii). It is believed
that Kernow derives from the name Cornovii. However, there are
two other tribes in Britain which seem to share this common name
of Cornovii – one in the Shropshire area and another in northern
Scotland. Some scholars have believed that the Romans, using the
word *cornu* in its Latin sense of 'horn', meant it to refer to a
people who dwelt on a peninsula. This is blatantly nonsensical in
terms of the Shropshire Cornovii (q.v.). Professor Charles
Thomas, of the Institute of Cornish Studies, has made an excellent

argument for some Celtic tribal names deriving from totemic animals. Perhaps this could be the case with the Cornovii.

Bodrifty, Madron (SW 445354) is a fourth century BC settlement of circular huts. In about the second century BC they were enclosed by a wall which does not seem to have been made as a fortification but more as a simple enclosure to safeguard animals. Inside the wall an area of 1.2 hectares contained eight huts. The largest has an external diameter of 14m. They had central fireplaces. The walls were faced with stone and filled with rubble, some standing a metre high; the roofs were thatched. On the hillside overlooking the village traces of fields can still be seen. From the site have come many items of undecorated pottery, spindle whorls, showing that wool was spun here, and evidence of slings-shots.

Boleigh Fogou, Boleigh (SW 437252) was once enclosed within an earthwork. It now stands on its own as a long passage 1.5m wide, running south-west to north-east for 12m in the direction of the prevailing wind. On the western side there is a short L-shaped side passage with an air-shaft hole in the roof. The western door jamb, of uneven stone, has been claimed by some to represent a figure. Fogous are now generally accepted to be cold stores or cellars. The word comes from the Cornish *fogo* or *fougo* meaning a subterranean chamber. Similar constructions are found in Scotland and Ireland where they are called souterrains.

Cadson Bury, St Ives (SX 343674) is a small hill-fort perched on an isolated hill overlooking the River Lynher. Enclosed within its now low banks is an area of 2.8 hectares. The bank does not rise beyond 2m and the ditch is relatively shallow. The entrance was on the east; its remains suggest the former presence of guard chambers. Seen on the approach to the hilltop, the hill-fort gives an impression of impregnability because of the steepness of the climb.

Camelford contains the **North Cornwall Museum** (The Clease), a small, private museum covering Cornish history.

Carn Brea, Redruth (SW 686407) is a large Iron Age hill-fort which now stands between a medieval castle on the eastern summit and a monument to Sir Francis Basset on the west. The hill-fort is thought to have been built in three stages: firstly, an enclosure around the area of the Basset monument; secondly, an expansion of the fortifications on the central saddle of the hill; and thirdly, the final outer circle. Excavations have shown a dozen circular Iron Age huts inside. The inhabitants produced pottery and cordoned ware. A hoard of Kentish staters was found here, which suggests trade contacts. The stone wall round the castle on the eastern summit indicates that the construction is much older than Iron Age, dating to the neolithic period. Irregular huts in this area have been dated by carbon-14 to between 3109 and 2687 BC, which would make this settlement the oldest in Britain. Claims that the entire site could be neolithic in origin have also been made.

Carn Euny, Sancreed (SW 403288) was built about 400 BC. It then consisted of a group of timber dwellings which were later rebuilt in stone. The group now consists of four courtyard houses and a few smaller buildings which are dated to the first century BC. The Celts who dwelt here were farmers and stock-breeders, and were also involved in the local tin trade. Excavations have uncovered pottery, of the cordoned type, grinding stones and spindle whorls. One interesting feature is the fogou, entered through an underground passage 20m long, with a low passage at the west end and a circular corbelled chamber. It seems that this elaborate cellar, used for food storage, was the first building to be constructed.

Castle-an-Dinas, St Columb Major (SX 946623): there are two hill-forts of this name, which is tautological, meaning 'castle of the fort'. The English, not understanding Cornish but recognizing a fort or castle, merely added the word 'castle' to the Cornish word for fort. The first of the two forts is 3.2km east of St Columb Major, on top of a hill rising 214m and placed at a remarkably strategic position, commanding the surrounding area. It is worth the climb for the view which extends from the Bristol Channel to the English Channel across the Cornish peninsula. There are three main ramparts of differing dates protecting the circular fort, which is 229m in diameter. There are two rings of massive stone-built ramparts, protected by ditches and counterscarp banks. The inner ring has an additional ditch outside the counterscarp. Between the two rings are traces of a third rampart and ditch which might not have been completed. The original entrance seems to have been at the south-west although there are other gaps in the ramparts. The hill-fort had its own water supply feeding a pond in the centre around which a number of hut circles have been traced.

Castle-an-Dinas West, so called to distinguish it from the one near St Columb Major, is 5km north-east of Penzance on the summit of a hill rising 233m. The summit gives an excellent view over Mount's Bay. It is a mile west of Chysauster (q.v.). It has three concentric ramparts faced with stone. The tower standing by the west rampart of the fort was built in about 1800 by the landowner. Called Roger's Tower, after the worthy, it is classed as a 'folly'.

A hill-fort which is one of the largest in Cornwall, some 800m in diameter, is **Castle Canyke**, Bodmin (NG 086658). The great ditch and bank are best preserved in the north-west segment, immediately beside the road.

Castle Dore, St Sampson, Golant (SW 103548) is 1.6km inland. The name prefixes 'castle' to a Cornish name thought to mean 'waters or stream', deriving from the British *dubra*. It is one of the most romantic circular hill-forts because legend has it that it contained the palace of King Mark of Cornwall, to which Tristan brought Iseult. Initially built in about 150 BC, it was certainly still in use in the sixth century AD. It consists of two asymmetrically constructed ramparts and ditches. The inner circle enclosed 0.5 hectares with a counterscarp bank on the eastern side. The outer circle forms a strong defence to the west while on the east the defence diverges around a crescent-shaped enclosure through which the fort was entered by a barbican-like passage. Excavations place the initial construction to 150 BC with later work in 50 BC when the inner ramparts were rebuilt. At least five round-houses were associated with the earlier constructions and a further four with the second phase of building. There are also the remains of three rectangular buildings attributed to the early medieval period, perhaps being the palace of Mark of Cornwall in the sixth century. A large amount of pottery, much of it the highly decorated 'Glastonbury Ware', was excavated from the site. It was the centre of a rich agricultural community which was also involved in the working of tin and iron.

A distance of 2.4km from the earthwork, at a road junction
about 1.5km from Fowey, towards Par, near the disused entrance
to Menabilly House, stands the 'Castle Dore stone' which has
provoked much speculation. The stone was actually found within
the earthwork itself. The now accepted reading of this sixth-
century memorial is *Drustaus* [or Drustanus] *hic iacit Cunomori
filius* (Here lies Drustaus [or Drustanus] son of Cunomorus).
Drustanus has been linguistically identified as Tristan while Mark
was known as Marcus Cunomorus. Urmonek, a monk of
Landévennec, Britanny, writing his *Life of St Pol de Leon* in the
ninth century, points out that King Mark's other name was
Cunomorus. Pol was his chaplain. Incidentally the name Mark is
not from the Latin *praenomen*, Marcus, but from the Celtic
March, a horse; Cunomorus means 'hound of the sea'. Béroul's
famous version of the legend (in the thirteenth century) refers to
Mark as having 'horse's ears'. So the final reading of the stone is
given as 'Here lies Tristan, the son of Mark.'

This puts a different complexion on the famous love story of
Tristan and Iseult. In the legend, Tristan is said to be the nephew
of Mark. How much more poignant would be the tale if he eloped
with his stepmother! There are several hundred different versions
of the Tristan legend which the scholar Joseph Bédier traced back
to one twelfth-century French poem. It is accepted that the story
made its way from Cornwall, the land of its provenance, into
Brittany and from Breton versions into French.

Cunomorus is regarded as one of the Dumnonii kings rather
than just a king of Cornwall and his influence also exerts itself in
Brittany. His other son (if we accept the stone making Tristan a
son) was Custeinnin (which comes down in Latin as Constantinus),
whose name is found in Gildas' sixth-century writings as a king of
Dumnonia. Custeinnin's son Erbin had a son named Gereint who
also appears in the list of Celtic heroes assembled against the
Angles of Catterick in the famous attack of the Gododdin: *Gereint
rac deheu* (Geraint for the south). There are also traces of a heroic
Celtic saga of a Geraint who fell in battle against the English at
Llonborth – perhaps Langport in Somerset. However, this Geraint
was not the son of Erbin, the hero who rode with the Gododdin of

what is now Edinburgh. The Geraint who fell at Llonborth is recorded in the *Anglo-Saxon Chronicle* as fighting against Ine, King of Wessex in AD 710; five years earlier 'Geruntius, king of Domnonia' was the recipient of a long letter from Aldehelm, West Saxon Abbot of Malmesbury and first Bishop of Sherborne.

Chun Castle, Morvah (SW 405339): the word Chun is a contraction of the Cornish *chy-an-woon*, the house on the moor. This hill-fort, which stands on a hill frequently shrouded in sea mist, is circular with its outer wall, 85m in diameter, broken on the south-west by its entrance. There is an inner dry-stone wall 2.5m high which is entered through two massive gateposts, 1.5m apart, and inturned. The gate to the inner fort is not opposite the one on the outer rampart and so anyone trying to enter would have to present their right flank to the defenders. There is a well within the fort and a number of roughly rectangular enclosures. On the evidence of pottery, the fort was occupied between AD 550 and 650. A furnace seems to belong to the latter period. Traces of a dozen circular dwellings are to be found in the interior with pottery and materials dating habitation to the third and second centuries BC. In the nineteenth century, part of the site was ruined when a pulpit-like feature was established on the main rampart for outdoor Methodist services.

Although they do not belong to the period under review, there are many interesting ancient monuments nearby such as the Men Scryfa (written stone) which is 2.5m tall and was set up in the sixth century AD to *Rialobrani Cunovali Fili* (Rialobran, son of Cunoval), thought to be a Cornish chieftain. The names mean 'Royal Raven' and 'Worthy Fame' respectively. Also in the vicinity are the stone circle of the Nine Maidens and the Men-an-Tol (stone with the hole). Other stones complexes are the Lanyon Quoit, Chun Quoit and Mufra Quoit.

Chysauster, Madron (SW 472350) is one of the best preserved Early Celtic villages. The village was built about the first century BC and was occupied throughout Roman times. There seems to have been a peaceful abandonment of the village in the fourth century AD. There are eight houses, four on either side of a village street, while down an alleyway lies a ninth house. They tend to be

oval in shape, with an entrance passage often 6m long, leading into a courtyard out of which a series of doors lead into circular and rectangular rooms. The floors were paved. Some of the rooms were for living in, others may have been for working in. Fireplaces and corn-grinding querns, as well as large quantities of pottery and much domestic rubbish, have been discovered. One house at least had underfloor drainage. It is thought that the roofs were corbelled or thatched and the courtyards were left open to the sky. Under one of the houses at the south-eastern corner of the village, about 100m from the rest of the dwellings, is a fogou about 15m long. Terraced and wall 'garden' plots lie behind the dwellings. The inhabitants seemed to specialize in stock-rearing and some arable farming. Traces of a field system can be seen nearby. A track also leads to a nearby stream where tin-working was carried on.

Giant's Castle, St Mary's, Isle of Scilly (SV 924101) is a small promontory fort whose inner rampart used natural rock outcrops; the outer defences are of stone-built ramparts and rock-cut ditches. Since the eighteenth century many of its stones have been taken to use for local building.

Gurnard's Head, Zennor (SW 433387) is situated on a massive rocky headland and is a fort of 3 hectares, with two banks and ditches 60m long. The inner rampart consisted of a stone wall about 3m wide and still 2m high in places. The back of the wall was stepped. Two ditches guarded it. There is another ditch, separated from the main group and 3.5m wide. Traces of thirteen circular dwellings can still be seen. Pottery finds here have been dated back to the beginning of the first century BC.

Halligye Fogou, Mawgan-in-Meneage (SW 712238) is an impressive stone-lined passaged 16.5m long. A cross-passage joins it at the eastern end and is likewise lengthy. There is a short passage at the western end which runs south. A block of rock 0.6m high lies across the floor of the main passage. The fogou was the cold storage place of a small settlement since destroyed.

The paved entrance to a courtyard in Chysauster, a Celtic village near Madron in Cornwall built during the second century BC and occupied from then until the third century AD when it was abandoned

Harlyn Bay, near Padstow (NG 877754) is particularly worth a visit for it is one of the few examples of an Early Celtic (Iron Age) burial ground. Dated to the fifth century BC, over 200 skeletons have been discovered. They were buried in crouching positions, with their knees to their chins, and many had their skulls smashed after death. Each was accompanied by personal jewellery. A museum, attached to the Lower Polmark Hotel (open only in summer), displays the grave goods as well as five of the open graves under protective glass. This is all of particular interest because the Iron Age saw an innovation in burials: bodies were placed in individual graves under level ground, not cremated and placed in barrows as in the Bronze Age. Many burial sites of the period are consequently unrecognizable as they are beneath level fields. Finds such as the Harlyn Bay site have been few.

Helsbury Castle, Michaelstow (SX 083796) is a circular hill-fort containing 1.4 hectares. It is defended by a single strong rampart and ditch. To the east there is a rectangular annexe covering another 0.6 hectare. The entrances to both enclosures are on the east and in line.

Lawrence House Museum (9 Castle Street, **Launceston**) has a good local history collection.

Maen Castle, Sennen (SW 347257), the 'stone castle', is the most western promontory fort in Britain. The interior is less than one hectare in size and there are no signs of dwellings though some early Iron Age pottery has been discovered. It is protected by a ditch and granite wall 60m long and 3.5m thick. The entrance consists of a stone-lined passage with post-holes visible at the inner ends.

Old Block House, Tresco, Isles of Scilly SV 896155) is, in fact, a defensive work from the English Civil War period, but it has been built on an old Celtic promontory fort whose semicircular rampart cuts it off. Lower down the hill slope are two further banks. The entrance appeared to be on the other side.

One of the best examples of a promontory fort is Gurnard's Head cliff castle, West Penwith, Cornwall. This is defended by ditches and banks across the neck

Pendeen Vau, Pendeen (NG 384355) is a fogou which lies in the grounds of Pendeen House, between Morvah and Pendeen. It is an interesting Y-shaped construction built partly underground and partly in the thickness of a Cornish stone hedge. One of the arms is a low-entranced side chamber while the main angled passage is about 16m long.

Another fine example of an Early Celtic village can be seen at *Porthmeor*, Zennor (NG 434371). It is a courtyard village which resembles Chysauster in many respects. The houses have paved pathways and an efficient drainage system. There is also a fogou which, unlike other structures of this kind, was built above ground. It consists of a curving passage about 6m long and 1.5m wide from which, unfortunately, the roofing stones have vanished. The passage continued to a room which is 7.5m square with drains under the floor. This inner chamber was corbelled but the roof has long since collapsed. The houses, which are scattered and surrounded by field systems, were first erected about the first century BC and occupied until the fourth or fifth centuries AD. In about the second century AD, the entire village was enclosed within a protective wall. The inhabitants were farmers and miners: there is evidence of a furnace and the working of tin and iron.

At the south-west end of **Rough Tor**, St Breward (SX 141815) there are a number of hut circles surrounded by a small oval enclosure and on the summit of the tor are two rock outcrops constituting the walls of a small hill-fort. Two ramparts can be traced on the west but little remains on the east. Hut circles can also be found inside the fort. Dates vary to as early as 700 BC.

The Rumps, Pentire Head, Polzeath (SW 934810) is a good example of a cliff fort, protected by three ramparts and ditches which cut off an area between two rocky headlands. The entrances were lined with timber and dry-stone walls. Within the fort a number of hut circles were found and pottery included not only Celtic items common to Cornwall in the first century BC but also some Mediterranean wine amphorae of the period, reinforcing ancient writers' comments on trade between the Continent and Cornwall. An unusual find was a wooden structure considered to be part of a loom, an indication of an advanced form of weaving.

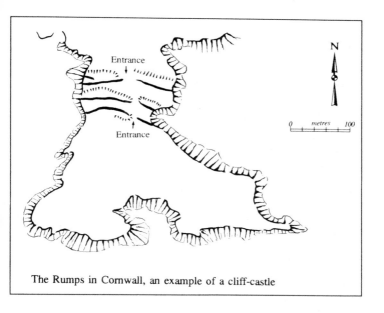

The Rumps in Cornwall, an example of a cliff-castle

Five ramparts with ditches make **Treen Dinas**, Treen (SW 397222) into a strong cliff castle, set on a rocky headland with its naturally rocking Logan Rock. There are many stock rocks in Cornwall: these are stones which are naturally based so that they rock. In 1824 a Lieutenant Goldsmith of the Royal Navy took a party of sailors and overthrew the rock from its pivot. Such was the widespread anger this aroused that the Admiralty ordered Goldsmith to put back the rock at his own expense. It took several months but, since then, the rock has never rocked on its pivot again.

Two widely spaced concentric circles form the ramparts of **Tregeare Rounds**, St Kew (SX 033800), while ditches provide an added defence. This hill-fort enclosed 2 hectares. There is a crescent-shaped annexe to the south-east. The inner enclosure is defended by a bank 10m wide and 3m high; the outer bank is 16m by 3m. The main entrance to both enclosures is on the south-east.

Pottery excavated from the fort is dated to the first century BC.

Trencrom, Ludgvan (SW 517363) is a small fort of 0.4 hectare, enclosed by a single dry-stone wall consisting of stone slabs and a natural outcrop of rock. There is no additional ditch, the ground being too rocky. There are entrances on the east and west. The remains of a dozen circular dwellings within the fort contained pottery which is dated to the second century BC.

The finest of all Cornish cliff forts is **Trevelgue Head**, Newquay (SX 827630). Perched on a headland, separated from the mainland by a chasm, the fort was originally defended by six main ramparts, three of which are still massive. Finds suggest that the site was inhabited during the neolithic and Bronze Ages, two Bronze Age bowl-barrows being discovered here. The remains of two dwellings contained finds which place occupation of the fort itself from the end of the third century BC onwards into the Roman period. Iron, mined from the nearby cliffs, was smelted inside the fort: a furnace was found. Bronze was also smelted and used here. It was estimated that half-a-ton of metal and slag was discovered. Some twenty spindle whorls indicate weaving. Waste pits displayed the remains of cattle, sheep, goats, pigs, birds and shellfish. The horns of deer were also used as implements. The evidence suggests that Trevelgue was a very important site.

In **Truro** there is the **Royal Institution of Cornwall County Museum** (River Street), which has an excellent exhibition of items from the period.

Warbstowbury, Warbstow (SX 202908), is a strategically placed hill-fort with extensive views in all directions except the south-west. It is contained within two concentric circles of ramparts with ditches and counterscarps. The inner rampart is about 4.4m high. Entrances are at the north-west and south-east.

Chapter 4

Mendips, Cotswolds and Chilterns

Avon, Gloucester, Hereford and Worcester, Oxfordshire and Buckinghamshire

Avon is a common river name in England. The reason is that it is simply the Celtic word for a river. It is now also the name of the new county of Avon, which marks the south-western territory of the Dobunni, stretching from the Mendip Hills. The Dobunni seem to have divided into two septs, one with its chieftain in Avon and the other in Gloucestershire. The original Celtic form of the Mendips is still recognizable and cognate with the Welsh *mynydd*, a hill. On one border is the Bristol Channel, once the channel or sea of the British, into which the Severn flows. The Celtic name of the river was the Sabrina, an ancient Celtic river name whose meaning is unclear. It is also found in the old name of the stream at Bedford, the Seuerne, and in the Sabrann, which was the ancient name of the Lee in the south of Ireland.

Blaise Castle, Bristol (ST 559784) is an oval fort of 2.8 hectares, on top of Blaise Hill. It has been dated by pottery and brooches, found in storage pits, to the third century BC. Unfortunately, nineteenth-century landscaping has destroyed much of the original ramparts, banks and ditches. Just 0.4 km to the south-west is **King's Weston** (ST 557782), a tiny promontory fort of 0.4 hectare. Much early Iron Age pottery was discovered here.

At Cromhall is **Bloody Acre Camp**, (ST 689915), a diamond-shaped fort now covered with trees, enclosing some 4 hectares within double banks and ditches to the north-west and triple banks and ditches to the south-west, and protected on other sides by steep natural slopes. Its entrance was at the north-eastern end.

Another fort, pear-shaped in plan, is **Bury Hill Camp**, Winterbourne Down (ST 652791). While quarrying has damaged its western defences, excavations have produced Romano-British material including a dwelling enclosed in a long mound in the centre of the fort. There was a well south of the north-west gate.

A fort that was in occupation prior to the Roman invasion and during the earliest years of it is **Cadbury Camp**, Tickenham (ST 454725). It is an oval fort of 2.5 hectares with double ramparts and ditches. It has dry-stone walls. The entrance is on the northern side.

No fewer than three promontory forts guard the Avon Gorge, known as the **Clifton Promontory Forts**, Bristol. The Clifton Down Camp (ST 566733), the Burwalls (ST 563729) and the Stokeleigh Camp (ST 559733) vary from 1.2 to 3 hectares. The inner rampart at Stokeleigh is quite impressive, rising 10m above the bottom of its defensive ditch.

On the northern edge of the Mendips stands **Dolebury**, Churchill (ST 450590) enclosing 7.5 hectares. It has ramparts of limestone, a ditch and counterscarp bank. The entrance is on the west. There is evidence of lead-mining within the fort.

Another promontory fort is that at Horton, known both as **The Castles** and **Horton Camp** (ST 765854). While the south and west are defended by natural slopes, ramparts and ditches defend the north and east. The entrance was at the south-east corner. It enclosed some 2 hectares.

One of the finest multivallate hill-forts in the area is to be found at **Sodbury Camp**, Little Sodbury (ST 760826). Rectangular, it enclosed 4.5 hectares. It has double ramparts and ditches on all sides with the exception of the west. The main gate on the east side has been burnt down, probably in the Roman westward expansion.

'The most perfect specimen of Celtic antiquity still existing in Great Britain,' boasts a notice at the entrance of a barrow at **Stoney Littleton**, Wellow (ST 735572). The notice was put up to commemorate the restoration of the barrow chamber in 1858. The barrow belongs to the Bronze Age and while it is now beginning to be accepted, as explained in the introduction, that this was a Celtic period in Britain, the notice has been considered by some to be jumping the gun somewhat. However, the chamber, in which many human bones, pottery and other items were discovered in 1816, is worth a visit. It measures 20m long and 15m wide, with an

entrance at the south-east and a western door leading to three
pairs of side chambers and a further chamber. The gallery is 16m
long and just over 1m high.

Worlebury, Weston-super-Mare (ST 315625) is of particular
interest. The fort is placed on a narrow ridge of land with a steep
drop to the sea to the north, and a substantial stone rampart with
an external ditch to the south. The rampart curves eastward and
there is an additional rampart 40m further on protected by four
ditches. Excavation confirms the walls to be 10-11m thick, and
they are more than 3m high. It had a strong inturned entrance on
the south. Within the oval area of the fort were ninety-three
storage pits. Excavations showed late Iron Age pottery, spindle
whorls and sling-stones. The area produced numerous skeletons,
indicating that the fort was attacked by the Romans and
destroyed.

Keeping in Dobunni territory and moving north-east into
Gloucestershire we find, in the county name, an echo of the
original Celtic place-name of Glevum, the bright or splendid place,
to which the English added *ceaster*, indicating a Roman fort.
Glevum is cognate with the Welsh *gloiu, gloew, gloyw*. Where
better to start than at the 'bright place' itself with the **City of
Gloucester Museum**, Brunswick Road, Gloucester. The most
significant group of artefacts of Early Celtic interest is the Birdlip
Grave Group, containing the famous Birdlip mirror. There is some
Dobunnic coinage on display, and currency bars from
Salmonsbury as well as pottery. Perhaps most intriguing is a
southern Italian column of the seventh or sixth century BC.
Whether this is an ancient import or an antiquary's loss is a matter
of debate. It could well be a sign of the early trade with Europe.
However, undoubtedly the pride of place goes to the Birdlip
mirror, one of the finest surviving examples of British Celtic art. It
is an intricately worked piece of bronze which is unparalleled
outside national collections, and it was found in an Early Celtic
grave with the skeleton of a woman aged about thirty. This woman
had at some time undergone surgery for impacted wisdom teeth,

which indicates that there was a high degree of medical training among the Early Celts. She obviously held high rank among the Dobunni, and was buried with two males in about AD 50. The graves also contained other items, such as jewellery, bowls, even a pair of tweezers, demonstrating the sophistication of the art of the period.

At **Bagendon** (SP 018064) there is an important site which was the capital of the Gloucester Dobunni (and perhaps Ptolemy's Corinion). According to Dio Cassius, Cunobelinos was regarded as suzerain monarch over the Dobunni, thus reinforcing the contention that there existed a system of High Kings, in southern Britain at least. Bagendon is an area of 81 hectares, defended by earthworks on three sides and a forest on the fourth. It is low-lying, so it is not a hill fort, but, like Verulamium, it is an enclosed settlement of large proportions. The Celts had a mint here before the Roman conquest and there is evidence of much coinage being produced round AD 20-30. Finds such as pottery from the Mediterranean and brooches of Continental origin indicate that Bagendon was the centre of a flourishing trade in the years before the Roman conquest.

Following the defeat of the south-eastern tribes, after Caratacos had fled westward, the Dobunni became active against Rome and it was not until Ostorius Scapula (AD 47-52) established a permanent garrison of the II Augusta Legion in Glevum (Gloucester) that the area was pacified. From Dobunni coinage, however, we find that the southern sept of the tribe, whose ruler stamped his coins CORIO, seemed anti-Roman, the coins being traditionally Celtic in design, while the northern ruler, whose coins were stamped BODVOC, introduced the Romanized types. The Dobunni coinage became extinct just after the Roman conquest of the area (c. AD 50).

A few scholars are of the belief that **Cirencester** was the Dobunni capital because the Romans built a fort there soon after Ostorius' conquest. But the name indicates that it was associated with another tribe. The fort was badly sited, being on marshy ground by the River Churn, a river name which still reflects its Celtic root but whose meaning is not certain. So a second fort was

Discovered in 1879, the Birdlip Grave Group, now in Gloucester City Museum, contains one of the finest surviving examples of British Celtic art, the Birdlip Mirror. The items were buried in the grave of a woman, perhaps a chieftainess, of the Dubonni about AD 50

built on the site of the modern town. Within a few years the town that grew up around the fort became a flourishing trading centre and the second largest town of Roman Britain after London. It was named Corinion, according to Ptolemy, but this was a mistake for Durocornovio, the fort of the Cornovii, a tribe whose territory was just to the north. The shortened form Cornion developed to Ciern when the Saxons took over and they also added *ceastar*, to indicate a Roman fort, hence the development into Cirencester. While there is little indication of a pre-Roman settlement, the town is worth visiting for the **Corinium Museum** (Park Street) which has one of the best collections of mosaics from the Roman occupation period. A particular school of Romano-British mosaic artists became established here.

Hailes Abbey boasts a small fort called **Berkbury Camp** (SP 064299). The southern and eastern approaches are protected by a rampart 2m high and a ditch. Steep slopes on the north and west provide natural defences here. The entrance was to the south-west and on the eastern side of the fort a dry-stone outer wall shows evidence that it was burnt, perhaps during Ostorius' 'pacification' of the area.

Brackenbury Ditch, North Nibley (ST 747949) is a small triangular hill-fort of 1.6 hectares. It is covered by trees. However, the rampart stands 3m high and a ditch is 13.5m wide. There is an oblique entrance passage 3m wide at the south wall.

Cleeve Cloud, Southam (SO 985255) is a promontory fort of 0.8 hectare defended to the west by a cliff while two sets of banks and ditches protected it on the other side. Dwellings have been found, circular and 8m in diameter. Early Iron Age pottery has been discovered here. Unfortunately, the making of a golf course has done much damage. Indeed, on the same hill, close to the A46, is a circular bank and ditch enclosure called **The Ring** (SO 984266). This is being used as part of the golf course but is of ancient construction. Also part of this complex, 0.5km to the north (so 985263), is a dyke running east to west, with a ditch on the south side facing the fort. It could mark a territorial boundary with the nearby **Nottingham Hill**, Gotherington (SO 984284), which is of considerable size. It covers 49 hectares, but does not seem to have strong defences, so may be simply an enclosed settlement. A single bank and ditch protect three sides of a steep promontory while two higher banks and ditches protect the south-eastern side only. No entrance is discernible. Three leaf-shape swords have been found here and it has been reputed that coins and coffins have been found in the past but nothing has been published in this respect.

Crickley Hill, Coberley (SO 928161) is an ancient site, originally inhabited about 3500 BC. It continued to be occupied into the Celtic period. In 700 BC the first fortifications were built there and a ditch cut into the limestone. Finds of rectangular dwellings and store huts have been made. At some stage around the sixth century BC, the fortress was burnt down: evidence is clearly shown at the gates and the dwellings. Not long afterwards, the ramparts were repaired and massive new gates were designed with a stone barbican. A large round-house was built with several smaller round dwellings. The style of pottery now changes, suggesting that the inhabitants were newcomers, perhaps from the south-east of Britain. Alternatively, of course, the natives could merely have adopted a new style. The site was a wealthy agricultural one. Around 500 BC the fortress was burnt down once more and abandoned.

A formidable promontory fort is that at **Haresfield Beacon**, Haresfield (also called Ring Hill) (SO 823090). Surrounded by a rampart, but no ditch, it enclosed 4 hectares. There are four possible entrance gaps, and it is surrounded by several ditches and dykes which may have been cattle enclosures. Another promontory fort is that of **Leckhampton Hill** (SO 948184) enclosing 3.2 hectares. This has been damaged by quarrying and it is impossible to complete the original circuit. The ramparts were built with dry-stone and timber lacing. The entrance was on the east with two semicircular guard chambers on either side of a 3m entrance passage. No huts have been discovered inside but traces of the fort having been burnt are evident.

Of particular interest is a promontory fort of the first century BC at **Lydney Park**, Lydney (SO 616027). It is on a steep-sided spur jutting south towards the Severn. It encloses 1.8 hectares, protected by a bank and ditch. It was later strengthened. During the second and third centuries AD, under the Roman administration, iron was mined inside the fort. On the west side a bath-house was built. Soon after AD 364 Romano-British buildings were erected and enclosed within a stone wall with a south-east gate where the hill-fort gate had probably stood. There was a temple 26m by 20m dedicated to the Celtic god Nodens. To the north was a large house; there were more baths to the west and a long dormitory building. This had clearly become a sanctuary which was connected with healing. It could well have been a spot sacred to early druidic worship. Nodens corresponds etymologically to the Celtic hero/gods Nudd and Nuada. In both

Irish and Welsh literature, the hero/god finds his kingdom
threatened from outside and defends it through seeking the aid of
the god Lugh/Llefelys. There is a private museum in Lydney Park
House in which finds from the site are exhibited.

One of the most fascinating earthwork complexes is the
Minchinhampton Common Earthworks (SO 858010), a series of
banks, enclosing much of the modern town of Minchinhampton.
The Cross-dyke (SO 852012 – 853014) and the Low Banks may be
parts of former defence works or simply cattle enclosures. Much
Iron Age pottery has been found within the works. Do not be
misled by Amberley Camp and Pinfarthing Camp for they are
more recent constructions.

Large-scale quarrying and the *coup de grâce* of a golf course
construction have destroyed much of **Painswick Beacon**, Painswick
(SO 869121). Yet from a distance, silhouetted against the skyline,
the hill-fort looks quite imposing. Massive double ramparts and
ditches, with a counterscarp, and the steep incline all added to its
impregnability. The entrance was at the north-west corner. There
is a circular hollow 6m in diameter in the centre of the fort.

While **Salmonsbury**, Bourton-on-the-Water (SP 175208) does not
look as imposing, it has produced many interesting discoveries. It
encloses 23 hectares within double banks and ditches. There seem
to have been two entrances, one on the west and the other on the
north-east side. A stream crosses the fort. The original construction
was in the third or second century BC. The ramparts then were of
gravel revetted with dry-stone walls. A number of a circular
dwellings and storage pits date from the first century BC. One of the
pits contains human remains, including two infants. There are signs
of new huts being built during the first century AD, and a new wall
was constructed across the main entrance: fragments of imported
pottery date from the same period. A hoard of 147 iron currency
bars was found on the north-west side of the camp in 1860.

Uley Bury, Uley (ST 784989) is, without doubt, the best
example of a Cotswold promontory fort. Except at the northern
corner, the hill falls steeply 100m to the valley below. A rampart
and two ditches enclose 13 hectares. There is another rampart,
constructed of dry-stone walling, and a ditch lower down the hill.

The passage of the southern oblique entrance was lined with timber. The site has not been excavated but a gold stater of the Dobunni, now in the Gloucester Museum, was found there. A crouched burial has been discovered, and a rubbish pit containing two iron currency bars was revealed in 1976 when a pipe was laid across the site.

Windrush Camp, Windrush (SP 182123) is a good example of a circular fort enclosing 2.6 hectares. It stands on level ground above the Windrush valley with a single bank and ditch. The entrance is on the west.

Crossing into Hereford and Worcester, we find several hill-forts of interest. **Aconbury Hill**, Kingsthorne (SO 504331) was occupied from the first century BC until into the Roman period. It is an oval-shaped fort enclosing 6.9 hectares with a single rampart and ditch. The entrances are on the east and west.

Of much interest is **Bredon Hill**, Bredon's Norton (SO 958402). Bredon retains its Celtic name, meaning 'fort on the hill', which precisely describes it. The name is from the compound *briga*, a height (cognate with Welsh *bre* hill) and *dun*, a fort. It was first built in about 300 BC, a dating for the outer ramparts, while the inner rampart was built in 150 BC and the inturned entrance around 100 BC. There are signs that this was remodelled in about 50 BC. It is a square-shaped promontory fort, with the north-east and north-west defended by precipitous slopes. To the south-east and south-west, ramparts and ditches afford protection. Dry-stone walls and timber breastworks have been uncovered. The fort was attacked in the first century AD, presumably by the Romans in their western march. The gate was burnt down and the bodies of more than sixty young men, hacked to pieces by the evidence of the sword marks on the bones, were left on either side of the inner entrance. Some have argued that the attack was made by another Celtic tribe as a row of skulls were set on poles above the gate where the defenders had fallen. It is pointed out that Celts revered the heads of their enemies. Nevertheless, this was also a Roman practice, designed to strike fear into the population.

Capler Camp, Fownhope (SO 593329) is a narrow oval hill-fort of 4 hectares above the Wye (which still retains its Celtic form, although the meaning is obscure. It is cognate with Wey.). The fort is protected by double banks and ditches with a steep scarped slope on the north.

Conderton Camp, Conderton (SO 972384) was built in the third century BC as a small oval fort on a south-facing spur of Bredon Hill. Steep slopes protect it on all sides except to the north. Originally it was defended by a single stone rampart and ditch, but in the first century BC it was refortified with dry-stone walling and a central inturned entrance with double gates. The northern area became the site of a village with traces of a dozen circular dwellings, storage pits and working hollows. Pottery indicates that it was abandoned before the Roman conquest. The name Conderton, incidentally, is Anglo-Saxon for the 'tun' or fort of the Kentish men, indicating a movement of Saxon settlers from Kent at the period when the Celts were being driven from this area.

Looking over the plain of the Teme, a river whose Celtic name is cognate with Tame, Thames and Tamar, meaning 'sluggish river', stands **Coxall Knoll**, Buckton and Bucknell (SO 366734), a hill-fort of 5 hectares. The fort is now badly mutilated but the ramparts, ditches and, in parts, a counterscarp can be seen.

One of the largest contour forts is that of **Credenhill Camp**, Credenhill (SO 452445), which encloses 20 hectares. It is protected by a single rampart and ditch. Two entrances, one in the east and another at the south-east, are guarded with long inturns and chambers. Nine square or rectangular huts have been traced in rows, each apparently having been built several times. The buildings seem to have had raised floors. It has been suggested that the entire fort was covered by such houses and that the population may have been as high as 4000.

Croft Ambrey, Croft (SO 444668) was first built in about 550 BC, enclosing 2.2 hectares. A triangular fort, it is protected by a steep escarpment on the north and on the south and west by ramparts and ditches. Inside, rows of four post buildings have been traced. In about 390 BC a ditch was dug outside the defences and a massive new rampart was erected enclosing another 3.6

hectares. Gates were made at the south-west and east. By 80 BC bridges had been built over the old gateways and an annexe of 4.8 hectares was added for animal storage. A circular mound, thought to have been used for Celtic religious purposes, was built in the early first century BC. The occupation of the fort ended when the Romans moved into the area in about AD 50. Dr S. C. Stanford, who excavated it, believed the fort was a stronghold of the Deceangli, although this would place them much farther south than is normally credited. Indeed, the Cornovii territory intervenes. However, Dr Stanford believes that in about AD 48 Ostorius reduced the Celts of this area and they abandoned the fort. He worked out that between 500 and 900 people lived here.

Dinedor Camp, Dinedor (SO 524364) is a rectangular hill-fort of 5 hectares with prominent ramparts on the eastern side. It seems the ramparts were stone-faced. The Celtic name Dinedor tells us exactly what the place is: a fortified hill.

On a low hill between the Malverns (a Celtic name which means 'bare hills') and the Severn, stands a contour fort. This is **Gadbury Bank**, Eldersfield (SO 793316). The hill is not steep but the only defences are a single rampart and ditch. **Garmsley Camp**, Stoke Bliss (SO 620618) is another oval fort enclosing 3.6 hectares with a rampart, ditch and counterscarp. The entrance is on the western side.

Herefordshire Beacon, Colwall (SO 760399) is probably one of the finest examples of a contour fort in Britain. The ramparts and ditches closely follow the lines of the hill. Today the hill is crowned by a medieval castle dating from the twelfth century but the original fort would seem to date back to the third century BC, enclosing 3.2 hectares. There were four entrances. The remains of many circular dwellings have been discovered and it is estimated that the population before the Roman conquest was some 1500–2000.

A triangular fort stands at **Ivington Camp**, Leominster (SO 484547), enclosing 9 hectares. It has double ramparts and a ditch, although it is also protected by precipitous slopes. In the north-west corner of the fort is an earthwork of 3 hectares which is thought to date from an earlier period.

Midsummer Hill, Eastnor (SO 761375) was a fort begun in about 400 BC and covering two hilltops, enclosing them with ramparts, ditch and counterscarp in an area of 12 hectares. It is irregular in shape and the ramparts are stone-faced. The entrance is on the north-west and excavation shows at least seventeen rebuilding operations. Some 250 dwellings have been traced, most about 3.5–4.5m in diameter. The buildings were laid out on a regular plan with streets between them. The fort was burnt down by Ostorius Scapula in AD 48 in his attack against the Celts of this area who were still fighting with Caratacos.

A triangular hill-fort enclosing 3.6 hectares stands on a steep hill at **Pyon Wood**, Amnestry (SO 424664), protected by a bank, ditch and counterscarp. The entrance is at the south-east. When the Saxons invaded and settled this area they found it 'gnat-infested' (*pyon*).

Risbury Camp, Humber (SO 542553) is a low-lying fort of 3.6 hectares. It is noted for its massive earthworks between 7.6m and 9m high. It is rectangular in shape with double ramparts and ditches on the west and treble defences on the other sides. The ramparts are faced with stone. To the south-east and south-west are several dykes and ditches which may have been used for animal husbandry.

The oval-shaped hill-fort of **Sutton Walls**, Sutton St Nicholas (SO 525464) was built in about 100 BC and enlarged in about AD 25, its ramparts revetted with timber and dry-stone walling. It was attacked by Ostorius in about AD 48, and its Celtic defenders were slaughtered. The remains of two dozen inhabitants were found, their bodies having been dumped into the defensive ditches at the eastern entrance. Most had battle wounds, discernible by sword marks on the skeletons, while others were decapitated. The ramparts were pulled down on to the slain. It is thought that other bodies may be buried in this fashion in other parts of the fort but we shall never know for much of the interior of the fort has been removed for gravel and the quarry which remains is now used as a dump for toxic waste. It was found, however, that the fort was reoccupied until the third century AD.

Wapley Camp, Staunton-on-Avon (SO 345625) is a triangular

fort of 10 hectares overlooking the valley of the river Luff, the
bright river, cognate with river names such as the Llugwy and
Lligwy in Wales. The ramparts are now covered with pine trees
but the interior of the fort is unplanted. It is protected by four
ramparts and ditches except on the west where the number
increases to five. A 'ritual shaft' and mounds are placed inside the
fort.

Another fort of interest is the kidney-shaped earthwork at
Woodbury Hill, Great Witley (SO 749645). It encloses about 10
hectares with strong ramparts, ditch and counterscarp. The
entrance is on the north-west.

At **Wychbury Hill Camp**, Hagley (SO 9208818), on the north-
west facing spur of Clent Hills, overlooking the Stour (the
powerful river), is a triangular-shaped hill-fort. There is an annexe
on the south-west. Two lines of ramparts, ditch and counterscarp
stand on the south-west. There is little need for defence on the
west and there are only indications of a bank on the north.
Excavations have uncovered an Iron Age knobbed terret, an iron
dagger and a bronze ring.

Oxfordshire is an area where the tribal territories of the Dobunni,
Atrebates and Cassivellauni met and there are several forts in the
area reflecting this. **Alfred's Castle**, Ashby (SU 277822) is a small
hexagonal defence work of 0.8 hectare enclosed in a single
rampart and ditch. The entrance is on the north-west. Some Early
Celtic and Romano-British material has been found here. Some
later Saxon material has also been discovered which might confirm
that the site was the spot where Ethelred, King of Wessex, and his
young brother Alfred, who was eventually to succeed him,
gathered an army in 871 to successfully face a Danish army at
nearby Ashdown.

A fort initially built as a stockade camp in the sixth or fifth
century BC stands at **Blewburton Hill**, Blewbury (SU 547862). In
the fourth century BC it was expanded to enclose 4 hectares within
ramparts which were faced with timber, strengthened with
crossbeams, and filled with chalk rubble. It has a gate to the west

11m wide. The whole was protected by a ditch, bridged at the gate. It then seems to have been deserted for a while but reoccupied in about 100 BC, the ramparts being rebuilt and the defences strengthened. Within fifty years it was abandoned again, probably because of the settlement in the area of the Atrebates, who were fleeing from the Roman conquest of Gaul. The skeletons of ten horses were found by the entrance to the fort.

A large fort of 22 hectares is to be found at **Bozedown Camp**, Whitchurch (SU 643783), which overlooks the Thames valley to the south. However, this once impressive circular fort has been damaged by cultivation and few traces of its ramparts, ditch and counterscarp can be seen. Some scraps of pottery and part of a bracelet from the Iron Age were found there.

Fort or simple cattle corral? Experts are undecided on the precise function of the **Castleton Camp**, Castleton (SP 259283), which is circular and contains 1.2 hectares. For a corral, however, the walls are substantial, being 6m wide and 3.6m high in places. The inner face of the wall was of large stone blocks. There are two entrances, one to the east and the other to the north-west. The question arises because excavation has failed to produce visible signs of dwellings. However, hearths and paving have been found and a considerable amount of pottery.

Built around the first century BC **Cherbury Camp**, Kingston Bagpuize (SU 374963) was originally constructed on an island in a marsh and enclosed 3.6 hectares. The marsh is now drained. It is an oval fort which protected a settlement with three ramparts and ditches of dry-stone walling. A well-laid road led across the marsh to the gate. The fort was occupied until the Roman conquest and pottery from the site is now in the Ashmolean Museum, Oxford.

Another large site is the 46-hectare enclosure between the Thames and the Thame at **Dyke Hills**, Dorchester-on-Thames (SU 574937). Built on low-lying ground and on a promontory formed by a loop in the rivers, the earthworks were levelled in the nineteenth century, though here and there they still stand 3m high. Aerial photographs show the site is crowded with dwellings, pits and gullies; it must therefore have been a considerable Celtic town. An excavation in 1870 produced some pottery, both of the hand-thrown variety and wheel-turned.

Grim's Ditch was a name given by the Anglo-Saxons to many Celtic earthworks in several parts of the country. In Oxfordshire there are no fewer than three Grim's Ditches. *Grima*, in Old English, meant 'a mask person' and it was a synonym for Odin. Therefore, the superstitious Saxons believed that the god Odin had built the Celtic earthworks. There is a Grim's Ditch at East and West Hundred (SU 423845–542833) and another at Mongewell (a good viewing point is at SU 636606 and another at SU 669869). This one seems to be part of the Grim's Ditch of the Chilterns. The last Grim's Ditch is in North Oxfordshire, with the best sections at Blenheim Great Park (SP 427183), Glympton Farm (SP 423197), Out Wood and Berrongs Wood (SP 413 208), Home Farm (SP 402215) and Model Farm (SP 383209). This complex in North Oxfordshire seems to have been erected during the first century BC when the Atrebates were settling the area. It seems to be a series of boundary dykes.

Knighton Bushes, Compton Beauchamp (SU 300830) marks the centre of an Early Celtic settlement with something like 800 hectares of Celtic fields and no fewer than three Celtic villages which existed into the Roman occupation. One settlement is west of Knighton Bushes Plantation (SU 298831), the second between Woolstone and Uffington Down and the third at SU 302853. A quantity of Romano-British material has been discovered here.

Another earthwork thought to be a cattle corral rather than a fort is **Lyneham Camp**, Lyneham (SP 299214), which is a circular earthwork of 2.6 hectares surrounded by a single stone rampart and ditch. The rampart is 1.8m high. The entrance is at the north.

At **Madmarston**, Swalcliffe (SP 386389), an important site has been all but destroyed. It enclosed 2 hectares within treble ramparts and ditches to the south and west and double on the other sides. The gate was at the south. Some pottery put the initial occupation at the third century BC and it was discovered that the site was reoccupied in the fourth century AD.

Do not pass by the City of Oxford without a visit to the **Ashmolean Museum**, which is open every day. The museum houses one of the best national collections in the country and among its better-known artefacts are the Wittenham and Standlake swords. Found at Standlake, in the Upper Thames, the two bronze scabbard plates are excellent examples of Celtic basketweave design and are dated to *c*. 300 BC. The museum also has some iron currency bars from Salmonsbury, Gloucester, and an interesting display of coins of Tascionvanos, Eppillos and Verica.

Segesbury Camp, Letcombe Regis (SU 385845) is one of the largest forts in Oxfordshire, enclosing 10.5 hectares. It was defended by a single bank and ditch with counterscarp. The bank was faced with sarsen stones, many of which were removed for local building purposes. Pottery, part of a shield, and human bones have been discovered.

Sinodun Camp, Little Wittenham (SU 570924) is a well-sited fort on a steep-sided hill. Kidney-shaped, it encloses about 4 hectares in ramparts and ditches. Finds of Iron Age pottery have been made here. The fort appears to retain its Celtic name, with *dun* indicating a fort – hence Sino's *dun*.

Uffington Castle, Uffington (SU 299864) is not especially interesting in itself. The fort encloses 3.2 hectares within two banks and a ditch, with an entrance on the north-west. The banks were originally faced with sarsen stones. What makes the place interesting is the nearby **Uffington White Horse** (SU 302866), a typically Celtic mythological animal measuring 112m from tail to ear carved into the turf to chalk-level. The horse has an interesting similarity to horse designs on British Celtic coins from before the Roman occupation, for example the horse on the gold coin of the Aulerci (first century BC). It is thereby believed that this is one of the earliest surviving Celtic hill-figure carvings and dates from the Iron Age. When the Saxons moved into the area, renaming it the *tun* or fort of Uffa's people (Uffington), they developed numerous legends about the horse, including one that it had the power to grant wishes. Another legend was that St George slew the dragon here – indeed, the area immediately below the horse is called Dragon Hill. It became a regular practice for local villagers to clean up the carving, with several days of festivity marking the event. Today it is done by workmen from the Department of the Environment. So persistent was the belief that the horse was

The Uffington white horse is 365 feet from nose to tail and one of several Celtic hill figures to survive. It is dated between the first century BC and the first century AD and is thought to be a product of Belgae craftsmanship

carved by the Saxons that in 1990 a team made a scientific dating of the carving which proved that it belonged to the Celtic period.

Crossing to Buckinghamshire, we are in Cassivellauni territory, again with the remains of several hill-forts and sites. The tribe is also referred to as Catuvellauni but it is generally believed by Celticists that the tribe took its name from its ruler (or vice versa) Cassivellaunos (lover of Belinos), who led the British tribes against Caesar. The tribal territory extended for about 130km northwards from the Thames and 100km east-west between the valleys of the Lea and Stort in the east and that of the Cherwell in the west. When Caesar refers to the Belgic tribes of Britain he does not list the Cassivellauni among them. It has been suggested

The Iron Age House, the Chiltern Open Air Museum. This is a reconstruction based on archaeological evidence of a farmer's house dated *c.* 700–600 BC found in 1976 at Puddlehill on the Chiltern Range

that this people did not exist as a separate tribal unit before the coming of Caesar and that perhaps a group of smaller tribes confederated under Casivellaunos and took their name from him.

During the period 50 BC–20 BC the Cassivellauni grew wealthy and powerful, perhaps as a result of their trading treaty with Rome. Around 20 BC the Cassivellauni seem to have achieved domination over their eastern neighbours, the Trinovantes, and the whole area betwen Essex and Oxford attained political unity with the Cassivellauni chieftains moving their capital to Colchester (Camulodunun). By the time of Cunobelinos (hound of Belinos) their power is said to have extended over southern Britain.

Boddington Camp, Wendover (SP 882080) enclosed 7 hectares in a lemon-shaped promontory fort. The ramparts were of dumped chalk; a single bank and ditch entered on the south-west. There was an interior enclosure but any hope of excavation has been obliterated by tree-planting.

The largest hill-fort in Buckinghamshire is **Bullstrode Camp**, Gerrard's Cross (SU 994880). Enclosing 9 hectares in two banks without ditches except on the west and north-west sides, it is oval in shape. Excavations have failed to date the site but it is thought that the north-east gap would have been the original entrance.

While you are examining the remains in Buckinghamshire, I recommend a visit to the **Chiltern Open Air Museum** (Newlands Park, Chalfont St Giles, Buckinghamshire). This museum was opened in 1976 with the aim of rescuing buildings which would otherwise have been demolished and re-erecting them on its 18-hectare site. One of the attractions of the museum is its 'Iron Age House', constructed from the evidence of an archaeological excavation at Puddlehill, near Dunstable, Bedfordshire of a building which dated from the seventh century BC. This circular, timber-framed Celtic homestead is typical of the type of house generally found in southern Britain during the period. It was recreated by members of the Manshead Archaeological Society of Dunstable between November 1978 and April 1981. The museum now employs an 'interpreter-in-residence' at the house to explain its construction to visitors. The museum also runs classes for adults on Early Celtic (Iron Age) pottery, metalwork and building techniques. An information pack is available from the museum bookshop.

Cholesbury Camp, Cholesbury (SP 930072) is a small oval fort of 4 hectares, defended by a single bank, ditch and counterscarp with a second ditch and counterscarp on the southern side. Pottery from the site dates it to about the second century BC.

At **Danesborough**, Wavendon (SP 9223448), part of the extensive earthworks have been vandalized and destroyed without record by the construction of a golf course. The hill-fort, enclosing 3.4 hectares, is roughly rectangular in shape and defended by a bank, ditch and counterscarp except at the north-east where the rampart appears to have been destroyed. Iron Age pottery has been discovered. It appears to have been the centre of a large cattle ranch.

One of the oldest hill-forts in England is that on the rounded spur of **Ivinghoe Beacon**, Ivinghoe (SP 960168). It encloses 2.2 hectares in a single rampart and ditch, forming a pear-shape. To the southern and western sides, a second line of ditch faces the ancient roadway, the Icknield Way, running south of the hill. The entrance, at the eastern end, is 3m wide, and the entrance passage was lined with posts. The ramparts were of two lines of timbers filled with chalk rubble, and were fronted by a chalk-cut ditch 3m wide and deep. Both circular and square buildings existed in the interior, as indicted by post-holes. Most of the pottery discovered here was from 500/400 BC, although a bronze razor and pieces of sword could be dated to the eighth century BC.

At **Pulpit Hill**, Great Kimble (SP 832050) is an oval fort of 1.6 hectares defended by a double rampart and ditch. The steepness of the hill to the north-eastern and south-western sides allows for only a single bank and ditch. The main entrance is to the east. A series of banks and ditches nearby are probably connected with the cattle-ranching activity of the occupants.

A circular fort of 1.2 hectares lies at **West Wycombe Camp**, West Wycombe (SP 827949). Although its ramparts are now covered with trees, they still rise 3.5m on the north-east side and the ditch is 15m wide and still 1.6m deep. However, the south-east defences were destroyed to make way for the mausoleum of Sir Francis Dashwood (member of the notorious Hell Fire Club), which was built in 1763–5 by John Bastard on the lines of Constantine's Arch in Rome.

Chapter 5

East Anglia

including Hertfordshire and Bedfordshire,
Norfolk, Cambridge, Suffolk and Essex

Hertfordshire was the central homeland of the Cassivellauni. It was here that the tribal capital was situated until Tascionvanos' rise to power. He was laying claim to Trinovantian territory, to the east, by 15 BC when he issued some coins with the mint mark of Camulodunum. He died in about AD 10 when his son Cunobelinos was established at Camulodunum, either by a dynastic marriage or by force of arms. Around that time the Cassivellauni and the Trinovantes appear to have been united. Dubnovellaunos, the last independent Trinovante chieftain, is reported to have fled to Rome. However, Cunobelinos had good relations with Rome and Strabo tells us that he sent embassies to the emperor Augustus and won his friendship. The Romans must have respected the power and influence which Cunobelinos enjoyed. Cunobelinos was to die in AD 40, giving the Romans the opportunity to launch their invasion three years later.

It was the dynastic struggle, in fact, which gave the Romans the excuse to invade. Cunobelinos had established one of his sons, Adminios, as chieftain in Kent. His brother Epaticcos was controlling the Atrebate kingdom from Silchester. In AD 39 Adminios fell out with his father and fled to Gaul to seek the help of the Roman emperor Gaius Caligula. Caligula did not invade but made much of Adminios' plea for help. It reawoke Roman interest in Britain. After Cunobelinos' death in AD 40, the kingdom was ruled, apparently jointly, by his sons Caratacos and Togodumnos. The political domination of the Cassivellauni caused the Atrebate chieftain, Verica, to go to Rome in AD 42 to ask the new emperor, Claudius, to intervene in British affairs. The result was the Roman invasion of AD 43.

The power of the Cassivellauni was quickly destroyed by Rome.

Togodumnos was killed fighting the Romans in Kent while his brother Caratacos, defeated at Camulodunum, fled to the western tribes and continued to fight the Romans for a further nine years before he was betrayed by Cartimandua, ruler of the Brigantes, to whom he had appealed for sanctuary after his final defeat in battle. Caratacos and his family were taken in chains to Rome where the Celtic chieftain made an eloquent speech before Claudius, who gave him and his family freedom to live within the confines of Rome for the rest of their natural lives. Some traditions have it that Linus, who became leader of the Christians in Rome after the death of Peter, was actually a son of Caratacos.

While Strabo provides a list of the British exports to the Roman world in the period of the chieftaincy of Tasciovanos and Cunobelinos, there is evidence of a wealth of imported goods found in Essex, Hertfordshire and Bedfordshire, including Italian wine amphorae, bronze and silver vessels, jugs, bowls, strainers and goblets. The last decades of the first century BC and opening decades of the first century AD saw a wide range of goods being imported, demonstrating the valuable trade between southern Britain and the Roman Empire: amphorae from Spain containing olive oil, fish-sauce and tableware from the Celts of Gaul, glassware from southern Italy and jewellery from other parts of the empire.

The extent of the trade implies that the British Celts had excellent merchant shipping: indeed, one of Cunobelinos' coins shows a high-sided, flat-bottomed vessel with mast, yard and stays.

Arbury Banks, Ashwell (TL 262387) is a fortified farmstead not far from the Icknield Way, which was a Celtic roadway later remodelled by the Romans. It stands on an oval plateau and encloses about 5 hectares within a single bank and ditch. The bank is now damaged and the ditch filled in. A single circular dwelling was discovered within the banks, together with storage pits, quantities of pottery and the bones of domestic animals.

Another such fortified farmstead is at **The Aubreys**, Redbourn (TL 095113), which is thought to have been used for cattle and pig husbandry. Enclosing 7.3 hectares, it is defended by a double bank and ditch except on the west side where a single bank suffices.

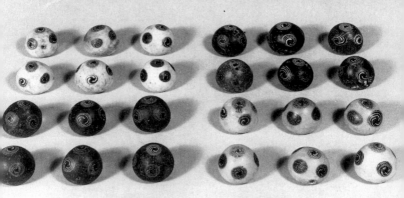

A set of glass gaming pieces from a burial excavated at Welwyn Garden City, Hertfordshire (first century BC). The pieces were found together with a much decayed gaming board

Entrances are on the west and north-west.

The early capital of the Cassivellauni, which was reduced by Caesar's legions in 54 BC, was at **St Albans**, which the Celts called Verulam(ium). The Celtic township lay just west of the Roman city, in Prae Woods. From Verulam the Casivellauni rulers minted their own coins. Tasciovanos (*c.* 30 BC–10 AD), who was to change his capital to the Trinovante city of Camulodunum (signalled by the mint-mark CAM on his gold staters), also produced coins marked VER on his early gold pieces. Bronze and silver coins were also produced. A fragment of a coin mould can be seen in the **Verulamium Museum**, St Michael's, St Albans. Coins from the Verulam mint were produced indicating the names of rulers such as Tasciovanos, Addedomaros, Dubnovellaunos and Cunobelinos, who had changed his mint to Camulodunum.

Verulam before the Roman conquest was, therefore, a Celtic

capital of considerable importance and there are indications that Tasciovanos welcomed ambassadors from the emperor Augustus to his court there. With the Roman conquest, a Roman military post was established here but, within a few years, they began to build their own city, a *municipium*, according to Tacitus. This was destroyed during the Boudiccan uprising (in AD 60/61); and did not recover for ten or fifteen years. The remains of the Roman town are certainly worth taking time to examine.

If one is in search of the pre-Roman Celtic remains then one needs to go to **Prae Woods**, St Albans (TL 123068), where a semicircular earthwork with banks and ditches still survives. Unfortunately it is overgrown, on private land, and visitors are seldom admitted. But these earthworks form part of the defences of the Celtic fortified town which Julius Caesar's troops stormed in 54 BC. The defences were found to extend eastward for 1km to the western wall of the Roman town and much of the site has been built on. Two cemeteries have been found within the complex and excavations have found pottery and ovens with baked clay coin moulds.

Beech Bottom Dyke, St Albans (TL 155093), a huge ditch with banks on the north and south sides, 27m wide and 9m deep, is thought to be an extension of the massive system protecting the Cassivellauni capital. It is similar to the **Devil's Dyke**, Wheathampstead (TL 186133), which stands some 4.5km to the north-east. This is an enormous dyke some 460m long, 12m deep and 40m wide at the top. On the eastern side a bank rises 2.5m high and another 2m high on the western edge. The dykes seem part of a complex which cut off and protected the area between the Ver and Lea valleys.

There is one part of this complex at **Devil's Ditch**, St Albans (TL 123084), near Mayne Farm on the Gorhambury Estate. This stretch of ditch is 15m wide and perhaps constituted the northern boundary of the land connected with the Cassivellauni capital, estimated by some to have enclosed 36 hectares.

A more traditional hill-fort, and one that some archaeologists favour as that which Cassivellaunos defended against Caesar in 54 BC, is **Ravensburgh Castle**, Hexton (TL 099295). It is certainly the largest surviving hill-fort in eastern England. Rectangular, enclosing 9 hectares, it is defended by steep-sided valleys on three sides. It is protected by a single bank and ditch, doubled on the western side. The ditch is 6m wide and 3.6m deep. The rampart on the east still reaches to a height of 6m. It was constructed in about 400 BC, the rampart being reinforced by stout posts, front and rear, with horizontal crossbars. It appears to have been deserted for a while and then during the first century BC it was reoccupied and refortified. Excavations indicate that the principal activity of the inhabitants was cattle-ranching.

Moving into Bedfordshire, still in the land of the Cassivellauni, **Caesar's Camp**, Sandy (TL 179490) presents us with a promontory fort enclosing 3 hectares. It stands on a sandy spur overlooking the valley of the Ivel, which still retains its Celtic name meaning 'the forked river'. It is protected by steep slopes on all sides except the north. Some of its ramparts have been destroyed or weakened.

Maiden Bower, Houghton Regis (SP 997224) is a hill-fort of some interest because, in about the third century BC, it was the scene of a battle in which sling-shots were used in large numbers and slaughter ensued. The fort encloses 4.4 hectares within a single bank and ditch. The rampart remains 2m high in places. The interior is now ploughed. The entrance was on the south-east side.

Another promontory fort in the Chilterns stands on a north-facing spur at **Sharpenhoe Clapper**, Sharpenhoe (TL 066302). A rampart partially cuts off the spur at its neck. A footing trench for a timber palisade was built in about 300 BC with a possible external ditch. The surviving ramparts, however, were erected in medieval times.

Turning into East Anglia proper we start in Norfolk. Norfolk was the heartland of the Iceni tribe whose chieftain, Prasutagos, surrendered to the Roman emperor Claudius in AD 43, after the Roman victory at Camulodunum (Colchester). Prasutagos became a 'client king', recognizing Roman overlordship. P. Ostorius

The Snettisham torc, found in a hoard in Norfolk during 1948–50, is dated to the mid-first century BC and is made of electrum

Scapula, who became governor in AD 47, ordered the Iceni to disarm, in spite of their relationship as free allies of Rome. The Iceni rose in revolt and occupied, according to the Roman historians, their hill-forts. This is interesting, as hill-forts are very rare in East Anglia. Scapula could not spare his veteran legionaries and so dispatched his auxiliary cavalry. They had to dismount to storm the hill-forts and despite strong resistance, they secured a victory. Curiously, the treaty between the Iceni and Rome appears to have continued in effect. On the death of Prasutagos, in AD 61, his widow, Boudicca (Victory), known to the Romans as Boadicea, became ruler of the Iceni. The emperor

Nero, whose policy was unfavourable to the continuance of 'client kingdoms', ordered their abolition and establishment of direct rule. Prasutagos had attempted to secure the status quo by making the emperor co-heir of the kingdom. However the emperor's procurator, Decianus Catus, not only enforced the emperor's orders but sent troops to the Iceni capital where Boudicca and her two daughters were raped and flogged. The Iceni rose with Boudicca at their head. The rising spread to the Trinovantes and doubtless members of the Cassivellauni.

Camulodunum was besieged and the centre of Roman administration in Britain went up in flames. The IX Hispana Legion, marching from Lincoln, was annihilated with only 500 cavalry making good their escape. Decianus Catus, whose zeal had started the uprising, fled to Gaul. The town of London, once a Trinovante trading town, now an important Roman port and centre, also fell to the Celts, because the acting commander of the II Augusta Legion refused to march to face the Celts, presumably having learnt of the fate suffered by the IX Hispana. Boudicca's army marched on Verulam (St Albans) where, once more, the former capital of the Cassivellauni, and now another major Roman settlement, fell to them. The new governor, C. Suetonius Paulinus, with the XIV Gemina and XX Valeria Victrix, chose a battleground north of St Albans and in a piece of astute generalship won a tough battle over the Celtic army. Boudicca and her daughters were reported to have taken poison. The Roman administration exacted a heavy tribute on the Iceni and Trinovantes. It broke independent Celtic power in this corner of Britain for the rest of the Roman occupation.

Caistor St Edmund (TG 2303), some 5km south of Norwich on the Ipswich road, was named as the capital of the Iceni by the Romans. Having put down Boudicca's uprising they began work on a town they called Venta Icenorum. It is uncertain whether this was, in fact, Boudicca's capital or simply designated as such by the conquerors. The town seems to have been laid out in about AD 70 and it is worth spending some time examining it, although there is nothing to indicate any pre-Roman settlement here.

One cannot leave this area without a visit to the **Cockley Cley**

Iceni Village and Museum (5km south-west of Swaffham, Norfolk).
Cockley Cley stood on the Icknield Way. Part of the East Anglian
Historical Museum, it contains a unique reconstruction of an Iceni
settlement of the first century AD, on a site which is believed to
date from the time of Boudicca. It contains a typical Early Celtic
timber-framed circular house with rectangular buildings in a
palisade enclosure, with watch tower. A ditch and moat guard the
palisade. For those in search of the Early Celts, a visit to the Iceni
Village is undoubtedly a must to give one a feeling of life and
technology in this period.

Holkham Camp, Holkham (TF 875447) encloses 2.4 hectares.
Until 1722 it was separated by the mainland by a tidal marsh. It is
protected on the south and east by ramparts and ditches, with
traces of a second bank on the south. The steep scarp and water
afforded natural protection on the north and west. The entrance
was on the southern side. Though some Iron Age pottery sherds
have been found the site is still unexcavated.

Tasburgh (TM 200960) is situated on a low spur of the River
Tas, and the single rampart and ditch enclose 10 hectares. Much of
the site has been mutilated by roads and buildings but in view of
its large size it could well have been the pre-Roman tribal capital
of the Iceni. Boudicca's palace might have been situated here.

Warham Camp, Warham St Mary (TF 944409) is situated on a
hill overlooking the River Stiffkey. This is undoubtedly the finest
Celtic fort in Norfolk, and is laid out with mathematical precision.
It is circular; its ramparts are 3m high, and its ditches 3m deep.
The complete circle covered 3.6 hectares. When the canal was
built from the river in the eighteenth century, the south-eastern
side was levelled and the original entrance, facing east, was
destroyed. The site has failed to produce much early Celtic
material, although some Roman material has been discovered.
The fort dates from the first century BC.

A life-size model of a Celtic warrior of the 1st century BC at the Museum of
the Iron Age, Andover. The accoutrements are replicas of items found at
archaeological sites in Britain

Cambridgeshire formed part of the territory of the Iceni and, like Norfolk, produces few fortresses. At **Belsar's Hill**, Willingham (TL 423703) is an oval fort which is unusually placed on a slight island at the edge of the Fens. It consists of a single rampart and ditch, broken by an entrance to the west and, possibly, one to the east. Identification has been made difficult by ploughing and the land is now under pasture. It is linked by a causeway through the marshes to the Isle of Ely, 14.5km to the north-east.

Wandlebury, Stapleford (TS 493534) is a fort which dates back to the fifth century BC, at which time it had only one outer rampart and ditch, the rampart being 4m wide and faced with timber both inside and out. The external ditch had steep sides and a flat floor. In the fourth century BC, after a period of some disuse, the ditch was recut and material was dumped outside to form a counterscarp. The original rampart was replaced and strengthened by an inner rampart. This was given a stronger outer facing of timber. The interior of the fort was occupied until 250 BC. More recently, in the eighteenth century, much of the fort was demolished in the interests of landscape gardening and many visible features have been destroyed.

Crossing into Suffolk, there is only one Celtic fort worth noting. **Clare Camp**, Clare (TL 768458) is a hill-fort overlooking a tributary of the River Stour. The fort has a double rampart and ditch surrounding a rectangular area of 2.6 hectares. It has been damaged by the building of houses on the south and east and the entrances are not certain. It is thought that Clare marked the northern extent of the territory of the Trinovantes.

Southern Suffolk and Essex made up the teritory of the Trinovantes. The Thames provided the southern border while the Stort valley formed the western border. Celtic coinage appeared in this area with the importation of Belgic coinage from the Continent. Archaeologists have therefore leapt to the conclusion that the Trinovantes were Belgic Celtic settlers. The Trinovantes made their first historical appearance in Caesar's account of his invasions of Britain when he relates how a Trinovante named

Mandubratius fled to him for protection. Mandubratius told
Caesar that he was the son of the Trinovante chieftain,
Imanuentios. Their western neighbours, the Cassivellauni, had
defeated and killed Imanuentios in battle and Mandubratius
wanted Caesar's help to take revenge and become ruler of the
Trinovantes. Fascinatingly, the name Caesar records is a stigmatic
name – Mandubrad, the Black Traitor. Later British tradition
records the real name of this Trinovante as Avawry. He gave his
services to Caesar against his fellow Britons and, as a reward,
when Caesar left, Mandubratius was established as ruler of the
Trinovantes and the Cassivellauni were bound by treaty not to
molest the Trinovantes.

Some archaeologists have therefore argued that the rise of
Cunobelinos marked a rise of Trinovante power over the
Cassivellauni and that Cunobelinos was a Trinovante chieftain and
not a Cassivellauni ruler. This does not seem to fit the
contemporary references of the Roman writers. When Tasciovanos
died c. AD 7–10, Cunobelinos drove out Dubnovellaunos,
described as a king of the Trinovantes, and established himself at
the Trinovante capital of Camulodunum. One must, however,
point out that Dubnovellaunos has also been referred to as having
dominion over the Cantii of Kent. Some have argued that at this
time coins issued by chieftains with names such as Sego, Rues,
Andoco and Dias were issued from the Cassivellauni capital of
Verulam while Cunobelinos was issuing his coins at
Camulodunum. However, these would appear to be sub-chieftains.
From AD 10 Cunobelinos ruled over both the Cassivellauni and the
Trinovantes.

Southward then, into Essex, one is in the main territory of the
Trinovantes, whose dispute over the succession to their chieftain
Imanuentios gave Caesar an excuse to invade Britain in 55 BC.
There are more surviving forts in this area.

Ambresbury Banks, Epping Forest (TL 438004) is a plateau fort,
shield-shaped and enclosing 4.5 hectares. It is surrounded by a
single rampart and ditch with traces of a counterscarp bank. The

rampart is between 1m and 2m high. The ditch has been shown to be 3m deep and 6.7m wide. There is an entrance on the western side. The apparent entrance on the north-east was made in medieval times. A stream rises inside the fort, providing it with water.

Colchester Dykes (TL 995253 to the town centre): Colchester was to become, for a brief while, the capital of the Roman province of Britain. Before it fell to the emperor Claudius in AD 43, it had originally been the capital of the Trinovantes. Tasciovanos and the Cassivellauni had claims over the centre but it was Cunobelinus who established it *c.* AD 10 as the capital of his unified territory.

Though little is now visible of the old Celtic capital, Camulodunum, fortress of Camulos (a Celtic war god), excavation has discovered that the capital was enclosed within a large promontory of some 34km², bounded on the north, south and east by rivers. The western defences were supplied by a series of dykes: these are extremely complex and were formed in a series of six phases. The Celtic rulers of Camulodunum were very rich and influential, as already described,, and this was a trading centre and mint for coinage. When the Victorian suburb of Lexden was built some Celtic graves and later Roman ones were found. One of the graves was surrounded by an earth tumulus, still to be seen in Foxwalter Road. This was partially excavated in 1924 as tumuli of this nature rarely occur in Britain. A burial of exceptional richness was discovered. Sadly, there was evidence that the grave had been opened before and some of the richest grave goods removed. However, there was evidence of an iron-bound chest, iron chain mail, and leather items. Other finds included silver ears of barley and animals and a medallion of Augustus struck in 17 BC. While some romantics thought the grave might have been that of the great Cunobelinos himself, Dr D. Peacock, working on the amphorae, dated the burial to about AD 1: this might place its occupant as the chieftain Addedomaros who is thought to have died here at that time.

The centre of the Celtic town is on the gentle slope of Sheepen Hill, which rose above the Colne valley marshes and commanded the ancient ford across the river. It was conveniently supplied by the Sheepen springs to the west. Excavations have been carried out in this area. In 1930, underneath what is now the North-east Essex Technical College, were found the remains of an important dwelling which had been destroyed at the time of the Roman invasion. That it was singled out for this treatment points to it being the home of someone of importance. Its rubbish pits, six of which were found, included a remarkably high number of expensive imported items, Roman glass, pottery, Arretine ware and other items. It has been suggested that this might have been the home of Caratacos himself. Remains of larger buildings have been found and in 1970 further excavations were made, confirming the wealth of some of the inhabitants of pre-Roman Colchester. One interesting find is a bronze bust of the emperor Gaius (Caligula) in a Colchester Celtic grave. Could it have been the grave of Adminios, Caratacos' brother, who betrayed his family to ask Gaius' help to overthrow his father, Cunobelinos? Adminios returned to Britain with the Roman invasion. Did he bring a bust of his Roman patron Gaius, now dead, with him? It is a romantic speculation.

Danbury, Chelmsford (TS 779052) is a small oval fort, poorly preserved, with a single bank and ditch. It is unexcavated and the position of the entrance is unknown.

Loughton Camp, Epping Forest (TQ 418975) is another oval hill-fort, with an extensive view. It encloses 2.6 hectares with a single bank and ditch. A stream rises in the south-east corner. No original entrance has been discovered and much has been destroyed by a road on the western side. Loughton belongs to a string of hill-forts – Loughton, Ambresbury Banks, Wallbury (q.v.), Little Hadham, Barkway and Littlebury (q.v.), many of which are barely visible now – which dominated the Lea and Stort valleys and, so it is argued, marked the disputed territory between the warring Trinovantes and Casivellauni. These forts fell out of use when the tribes united.

Pitchbury Ramparts, Great Horkesley (TL 966290) consists only of a remaining north-western rampart standing 3m high with a ditch 15m wide. Most of it has long since been ploughed away.

Some Celtic pottery has been found here and it seems to have been occupied until Roman times. It is considered to be a bivallate fort but so little remains that it is dificult to estimate its size. According to Professor Hawkes, it was simply part of the defences of Camulodunum.

Ring Hill, Littlebury (TL 515382) is another oval fort in the 'frontier area' mentioned above. It consists of 6.7 hectares defended by a bank, ditch and counterscarp. Both banks have been levelled by construction so that only the ditch remains prominent. It is about 15m wide and 4.6m deep. The site is now completely covered by trees.

Wallbury Camp, Great Hallingbury (TL 493178) is a pear-shaped hill-fort enclosing 12.5 hectares. On the east is an inner rampart rising 3m high and the ditch is 3m deep. Excavation has shown the ditch originally to have been 6m deep. On the west, the defence was a single rampart. This was because of the steep slope down to the River Stort. The original entrance is thought to be that on the eastern side, about 100m north of the modern entrance drive.

The **Norwich Castle Museum** is the main East Anglian museum exhibiting artefacts of this period. Both the **Chelmsford and Essex Museum** (Oaklands Park, Moulsham Street) and **Colchester Castle** are worthy of a visit while on the trail of the original Celtic inhabitants of the area, especially the latter, which was built on the foundations of a Romano-British temple. Its Romano-British collections are of great importance.

Chapter 6

The Midlands

Cheshire, Salop (Shropshire), Staffordshire,
West Midlands, Warwickshire, Northamptonshire,
Leicestershire, Derbyshire, Nottinghamsire
and Lincolnshire

This tour takes us from the lands of the Deceangli and Cornovii in
the west across the northern borders of the Dubunni and
Cassivellauni in the south to the country of the Coritani in the
east. Most of the Deceangli territory lies in North Wales.

Starting out in Cheshire, we are in the border country of the
Cornovi. Unlike the tribes to the south, little is known about this
people prior to the coming of the Romans. They left no coinage
but we are certain of their tribal name thanks to a dedication on a
building to the emperor Hadrian by the Civitas
Cornoviorum (the tribe of the Cornovii). However, there are two
other tribes in Britain, widely separate, which have the same
name: one given by Ptolemy in north-west Scotland, and the other
given west of the Tamar in the Ravenna Cosmography. There are
several suggestions as to what the name meant. Dr Anne Ross
attributes the uses of the word *cornu*, horn, to Celtic horned
deities. Another argument is that *cornu* indicates dwellers in a
peninsula – but that could hardly apply to the people of Cheshire
and Salop. The tribal capital was at Wroxeter, Salop which was
recorded by Ptolemy as Viroconion. This would have been 'the
town of Virico' (a personal Gaulish Celtic name), which might give
us the name of the chieftain who defended the fort at Wroxeter
against the Romans. Professor Kenneth Jackson believes that the
name was Urioconon, changed by the Romans for ease of
pronunciation. But that leaves us with an obscure meaning. The
Romans built a fortress at **Wroxeter** (SJ 5608) around AD 58,
recognizing it as the tribal capital of the Cornovii.

   Commencing our search for the Cornovii through Cheshire we
start with a fort at Eddisbury Hill: **Castle Ditch**, Delamere (SJ
553695). Built in the second century BC, it was destroyed at the
time of the Roman conquest. Enclosing 4.5 hectares in double
ramparts and a ditch, it was built in four distinct stages and
eventually faced with stone with timber lacing. The entrance was
at the east; within the fort only one dwelling has been found, just
inside the entrance. Interestingly, during the Saxon expansion in
the tenth century, the fort was reoccupied and strengthened.
   While little remains of Romano-British **Chester** (SJ 4066) and
nothing of any pre-Roman occupation, it is worth noting that the
Romans constructed an earth and timber legionary fortress here
shortly after AD 50. This was later expanded until Chester became
a site of strategic importance, one of two forts which held the key
to the subjugation of the area which is now Wales. The II Adiutrix
Legion were the first troops to be permanently garrisoned here
after their move from Lincoln; they were replaced around AD 87
by the XX Valeria Victrix. Whether there was originally a Celtic
fort here is difficult to say because of the extensive over-building.
But it is interesting to note that in Roman times Chester was called
Deva, the name surviving in the River Dee by which the town
stands. It is believed to have meant 'the goddess river' or 'holy
river'. In Welsh the river is called Dyfrdwy, *dyfr* meaning 'water'
or 'river' (as in Dover).
   An oval fort of 3 hectares stands at **Kellsboro' Castle**, Kelsall (SJ
532675), in a single bank and ditch. The entrance is to the east.
   The third fort of interest in Cheshire is a rectangular
promontory fort of 0.5 hectare called **Maiden Castle** (again, Mai's
dun) at Bickerton (SJ 497528). This was built in the first century
BC. Protected by steep cliffs to the west and north, it has double
ramparts on the south and east. Over a period of time it was
improved and faced with stone and timber lacing. The entrance
was to the east and of an inturned type with a passage 12m long.
Parts of the fort were burnt, probably in the first century AD and
therefore most likely by the Romans.

Moving into Salop (Shropshire), we are in a county which has no
fewer than fifteen noteworthy hill-forts. Indeed, almost every
hilltop in Shropshire seems to carry a Celtic fort on it. There is still
a strongly 'Celtic flavour' to western Shropshire and we must
remember that some areas of the county were part of Wales until a
new border was arbitrarily set in Tudor times (at the time of the
Acts of Annexation). Thus Welsh-speaking communities straddled
the border, as they did in Hereford, and there is the seeming
anomaly of being a native Welsh-speaker of Shropshire and
Herefordshire. Shropshire is the area in which, tradition has it,
Caratacos last held out against the Roman conquest, being
defeated by Ostorius Scapula and then fleeing north to the
Brigantes where their ruler, Cartimandua – the Sleek Pony –
betrayed him and had him sent in chains to the Romans. This area
is regarded as the heartland of the Cornovii.

The Berth, Baschurch (SJ 429237) enclosed 2.5 hectares on a
small hill in a single bank and ditch. The fort was not strong.
Excavation has revealed some Iron Age pottery, a brooch and
some Roman ware.

A stronger fort is found at **Burrow Camp**, Hopesay (SO
382831), an oval defence work enclosing 2 hectares and encircled
by double rings of banks, ditches and counterscarp bank. There is
an additional bank with ditch on the west. There seem to be four
entrances.

Bury Ditches, Lydbury North (SO 327837) is a small fort
enclosing 2.5 hectares within two banks and a ditch. There are two
complex entrances on the north-east and the south.

Bury Walls, Weston-under-Redcastle (SJ 576275) is a
promontory fort of 5.5 hectares with univallate defences on all
sides except to the north where there are two banks and ditches
and one of the most impressive ramparts to be seen anywhere – it
is 11m high above the ditch. There are traces of dwellings and an
interior roadway.

The first hill-fort associated with Caratacos in the area is **Caer
Caradoc** (Caratacos' fort) at Church Stretton (SO 477953). Visible
for many miles, it clings precipitously to a windswept rocky ridge.
It is a long, narrow fort of 2.5 hectares. It not only uses the natural

incline for defence but has an outer ditch and counterscarp bank. It occupies one of the most impressive and impregnable positions of any hill-fort.

The other **Caer Caradoc**, that at Clun (SO 310758), is only 1 hectare in extent. It has commanding views in all directions and is protected by rampart, ditch and counterscarp. There are entrances on the east and west.

There is a rectangular fort at **Caynham Camp**, Caynham (SO 545737), enclosing 4 hectares and standing over a tributary of the Teme. The fort seems to have been built in four stages and is now protected by a single rampart and ditch to the north; on the other sides these defences are doubled. Storage pits, signs of dwellings and evidence of occupation have been found but the site has proved difficult to date.

The Ditches, Shipton (SO 545737) constitute an oval fort of 2 hectares defended by three ramparts and ditches. The rampart stands 4.5m in places.

Enclosing 1.2 hectares, **Earl's Hill**, Pontesbury (SO 408046) is oval in shape and sits on a rocky escarpment, which faces east. The entrance is at the northern end. Nearby are cross-dykes and a small oval earthwork probably used for cattle.

Nordy Bank, Clee, is a D-shaped fort enclosing 1.6 hectares on the west-facing spur of Brown Clee Hill. It is protected by a rampart, ditch and counterscarp. There is an outer rampart to the north and north-west. The entrance is on the south-west. To the south is Clee Burf (SO 593740) and to the north is Abdon Burf (SO 595866), two other hill-forts.

Norton Camp, Culmington (SO 447819) is a circular fort enclosing 5.2 hectares. There are two banks and ditches with entrances at the east and south-east.

Perhaps one of the most complex of the hill-forts is that of **Old Oswestry**, Selattyn (SO 296310). It has as many as seven ramparts protecting its 5.3 hectares. Dating to the third or second century BC, a group of circular timber dwellings were originally constructed and later encircled by ramparts. They were faced with stone and accompanying ditches. Later the huts were reconstructed with stone. Further changes took place as, over the years, the fortifications were extended and developed.

At Lydham, **The Roveries** (SO 325925) was a kidney-shaped fort of 4 hectares with a single rampart of dry-stone construction. It had a massive gate. Across the valley, opposite the entrance at the north-eastern corner, a small fort of 0.4 hectare, an outpost which gave warning of surprise attack, has been destroyed by forestry clearance.

One of the largest, and certainly one of the highest, hill-forts, stands at **Titterstone Clee**, Bitterley (SO 592779), 533m above sea-level. The fort encloses 28.8 hectares within an earth rampart. There are two entrances, at the south and the north. Timber reinforced the ramparts and later stone guard chambers were built. The whole was flint-flaked. Dwellings were traced on the eastern side of the fort. There is now a radar installation here which prevents the viewing of the fort.

The Wrekin, Wellington Rural (SO 630083) was built about 300 BC. It encloses 8 hectares on a long, narrow, rocky ridge. Stone ramparts, double in places, and stone guard chambers protect the inner fort, which enclosed 2.8 hectares. Rows of square dwellings have been found here and storage pits with pottery.

Crossing into Staffordshire there is a small oval contour fort of 2.8 hectares at **Berry Ring**, Bradley (SJ 887212) which is now covered in trees. **Berth Hill**, Maer (SJ 788391) is a triangular fort enclosing 3.6 hectares surrounded by bank, ditch and counterscarp, strengthened on the north/north-east side where it is vulnerable. A spring rises within the fort to the north-east side.

Bury Bank, Stone Rural (SJ 880359) is an oval semi-contour fort enclosing 1.5 hectares. It overlooks the River Trent, whose Celtic name means 'trespasser' or 'river liable to flood'. The fort has weathered badly due to the soft soil here and it has not been excavated to date.

Castle Ring, Cannock (SK 045128) stands in a commanding position overlooking Cannock Chase. It is an oval fort enclosing 3.5 hectares, defended by four banks and ditches to the eastern side and two banks and ditches to the north and south-west.

Cannock is a Celtic hill name.

Situated on a hill over the Stour, **Kinver Hill-fort** (SO 835832) is naturally protected by steep slopes on every side except the south-west/south-east. Here the rampart, with interior and external ditches, rises 3–4.5m. The Celtic name is thought to mean 'royal hill'.

At Wetton, **Thor's Cave** (SK 098549) is worth a visit. Sited high up in a jagged peak on the eastern bank of the River Manifold, it has an enormous entrance facing north-west. Inside are a number of small passages, and a second entrance facing west. The cave seems to have been originally inhabited in the palaeolithic period but was also used in the Iron Age and then during the Roman occupation (200 BC-AD 300).

The West Midlands has only one oval hill-fort worthy of inspection, that at **Berry Mound**, Solihill (SP 095778). Surrounded on three sides by water, the fort contains 4.5 hectares. A single bank and ditch survive on the southern side, although it seems there were three originally. The entrance was probably to the east.

In Warwickshire there are several interesting forts and an entire village. At **Burrow Hill**, Corley (SP 304850) is a square fort of 3 hectares overlooking Coventry. It was occupied betwen 50 BC and AD 50 and was built of strong dry-stone ramparts backed with timber-laced banks of earth. Unfortunately it has been damaged on the west and at the entrance on the south-west.

Meon Hill (named after the nearby Celtic-named River Meon), Quinton (SP 177454) is interesting in that a hoard of 394 currency bars was found here. These are now in the museums at Gloucester and Stratford-upon-Avon and in the Ashmolean, Oxford. They were sword-shaped and are believed to have been used in place of coinage. The fort itself is surrounded by a double rampart and ditches except to the north-west where the natural terrain makes only a single rampart necessary.

Nadbury Hill, at Ratley and Upton (SJ 390482) has been badly damaged by a modern road and by ploughing. It was a fort of 7 hectares and oval in shape, its entrance to the west. There are the remains of a bank, ditch and counterscarp. A rectangular fort at **Oldbury Camp**, Oldbury (SP 314947) is in better shape although the south-east rampart is destroyed. Excavations here suggest a date of 600 BC. It originally enclosed 2.8 hectares.

One of the most fascinating sites in the county is **Wappenbury** (SP 377694) where an entire village lies in a rectangular earthwork. The site is dated to the first century BC and was occupied until the Roman conquest. it is low-lying and would indicate an agricultural community which was not particularly bothered about fortification.

Crossing into Northamptonshire there are four forts of interest. The small circular fort at **Arbury Camp**, Chipping Warden (SP 494486), protected by a single rampart and ditch, with an entrance at the south-east, was also used by medieval farmers.

Unfortunately the **Borough Hill**, Daventry (SP 588626) hill-fort his been made inaccessible by a wireless station and a golf course. It was originally a fort of 1.8 hectares and later an additional 6.5 hectares were enclosed. A Romano-British cemetery was sited on the hill. There are traces of a Romano-British bath-house. It has been suggested that the inhabitants were removed to Bannaventa (Whilton Lodge), a small Roman settlement.

A centre of agriculture, metalwork, weaving, and pottery was sited at **Hunsbury**, Hardingstone (SP 737584). The remains of this fort have been badly damaged by ironstone workings, and trees and bushes now cover the 1.6 hectares, originally enclosed by ramparts, ditch and counterscarp. Half a dozen dwellings were found here and 300 storage pits. It was occupied until the Roman conquest. A word of warning: the interior of the fort was lowered by several metres giving the ramparts a more imposing appearance but this was done in the nineteenth century during the ironstone working.

Perhaps one of the most interesting excavations of recent times took place at **Rainsborough Camp**, Newbottle (SP 526348). This oval hill-fort encloses 2.6 hectares in double banks and ditches. It was a strong and complex fort of stone, with stone-built semicircular guard chambers beside an entrance passage some 18m long. A double gate hung between three posts. The fort was first constructed in 500 BC and in 400 BC it was modified and strengthened. Sometime afterwards, however, the fort was attacked and the gateway burnt down. The skeleton of a defender was found in the guard chamber. The fort was then deserted until the second century BC when it was refortified, although it would appear that the refortification was not completed. In the fourth century AD a Romano-British building was erected outside the gate. Some of the fort was destroyed by landscaping in 1772.

North into Leicestershire we find two forts of interest. The first is at **Bulwarks**, Breedon-on-the-Hill (SK 406234), at a place which, by its Celtic name (Breedon), clearly indicates a hill-fort. Bulwarks encloses 9.2 hectares in a pear-shaped fortification. Unfortunately a lot of this has been destroyed by quarrying. Excavations have discovered that there were two periods of construction, with limestone and timber. Iron Age pottery has been discovered here.

The second fort is at **Burrough Hill**, Burrough-on-the-Hill (SK 761119), which encloses 5 hectares and was protected on three sides by ramparts and ditches, as well as by the natural fortification of a steep incline. The fourth side was protected by a dry-stone wall rampart. There is a massive inturned entrance at the south-east, some 45m long. This would have been a Coritani fortress, for we are now in their country. They built strong stone guard chambers at the inner ends of the entrance. Pottery here dates from the second century BC and evidence shows that it was occupied until the Roman invasion. A number of rotary querns were found, indicating the grinding of grain on this site.

North again into Derby, promontory forts seem a feature of the landscape. The first is at **Ball Cross**, Edensor (SK 228691) above the River Wye. This fort was permanently occupied from the Bronze Age until the Roman occupation. The Romans levelled it towards the end of the first century AD.

Castle Naze, Chapel-en-le-Frith (SK 054784) was inhabited in the second century BC, and is a triangular fortification. **Castle Ring**, Hartill (SK 221628) enclosed 0.4 hectare in an oval defence system but much of the interior has been damaged. Another promontory fort stands at Fin Cop, Ashford-in-the-Water (SK 175710), enclosing 4 hectares. On the east and south it is protected by a rampart and ditch.

Mam Tor, Castleton (SK 128838) was occupied as early as early as 1180 BC. A large fort of 7 hectares, originally built as a timber palisade, it was then rebuilt with stone walls, a ditch and counterscarp. Items from the late Bronze Age, including an axe, have been discovered here.

Yet another promontory fort stands at **Markland Grips**, Clowne (SK 511752). It has been badly damaged but three lines of ramparts, faced with limestone slabs, can be seen. While little material from the Iron Age has been found here, substantial Romano-British finds of the second and third centuries AD have come to light.

East into Nottinghamshire we find only one fort, at **Oxton Camp**, Oxton (SK 634532). It is small, only 0.6 hectare, with a single rampart, ditch and counterscarp. A hoard of Roman coins was found here and a later Saxon burial.

East again into Lincoln, we reach the heartland of the Coritani. The Coritani occupied the Trent basin, Lincolnshire and the northern areas of the Midland plain. The southern boundary of their territory would have been between the Welland and the Nene while the northern and western boundaries are rather uncertain and were, perhaps, fluid. It is difficult to place the capital of the Coritani. Excavations at the Jewry Wall, in the centre of Leicester (1936–9), show that a principal settlement of

the tribe existed here. A visit to the **Jewry Wall Museum and Site**
(St Nicholas Circle) is recommended. As well as Celtic finds, the
museum includes part of the Roman wall and bath site and a fine
group of mosaics.

I would argue, however, that old Sleaford in central
Lincolnshire is more likely to have been the tribal capital as it
seems to have been the site of the Coritani mint, for the tribe
produced its own coinage before the coming of the Romans. Some
3000 fragments of clay moulds in which coin-flans were cast have
been discovered here. This then must have been the residence of
the tribal ruler. Nearby at Ancaster where the Romans built a fort
(Anna's *ceastar*, or fort), another prominent Coritani site has been
discovered with coinage and pottery finds. As well as Ancaster and
Old Sleaford, there is a third large Celtic settlement at Dragonby
where numerous finds have been made, including much pottery.

North-west Lincolnshire abounds in iron deposits and it may
have been this metal which provided the Coritani with their
wealth. At South Ferriby and Grimsby several hoards of Celtic
coinage have been found, which might point to merchant activity
across the Humber. It is from Coritani coinage that we have a few
glimpses of this Celtic tribe before the coming of the Romans. The
early coinage bears no inscriptions but the later series, from the
end of the first century BC, are inscribed. On some of these coins
the reverse carries two names (AVN:AST, ESVP:ASV, VEP:CORF, etc.)
and it has been suggested that the tribe was ruled by two
chieftains. The abbreviations are difficult to interpret. Later,
names appear on the obverse as well as the reverse, for example
DVMNO/TIGIR SENO. Dumno and Tigirsenos are acceptable Celtic
names and it could be that this was a coin of Tigirsenos son of
Dumno. Later still, coins appear with VOLISIOS/DVMNUCOVEROS,
VOLISIOS/DVMBOVELLAV and VOLISIOS/CARTIVEL. So there emerge the
names of several leaders including Volisios, who might have been
followed by three sons who struck coinage; an alternative
suggestion is that Volisios was the paramount chieftain while the
others were sub-chieftains.

It has also been pointed out that few of the Coritani Volisios
coins have actually been discovered in Coritani territory: most

were found in the south Yorkshire hoards. This, so it is argued, may be because Volisios, having been chieftain at the time of the Roman invasion, removed his capital across the Humber and took refuge with the neighbouring Parisi, yet still struck his own coins. The Coritani were subdued by the IX Hispana Legion. Unfortunately, there is no reference to them in Roman annals during the first thirty years of the Roman occupation and therefore we do not know whether they resisted the Romans or submitted after Camulodunum.

Lincoln (SK 9771) must have been an important Cornovii settlement for it was here that the Romans chose to construct a small fort which they extended in about AD 60 into the legionary headquarters of the IX Hispana. In AD 70 the IX moved into the territory of the Brigantes in Yorkshire and they were replaced by the II Adiutrix who, in AD 77, were moved to Chester. Thereafter, Lincoln developed as a Roman *colonia* or colony. The title *colonia* was added to the original place-name of Lindum which is cognate with the Welsh *llyn*, a lake. The Coritani settlement had been by the river Witham, the river by the forest, where it broadened out and could be regarded as lake-like.

There are only two surviving forts in this area. That of **Careby Camp**, Careby (TF 040157) is an oval fort measuring 225m by 255m. **Honington Camp**, Honington (SK 954424) is a rectangular fort enclosing 0.6 hectare and overlooking the River Witham. The entrance is on the eastern side. It is recorded that bits of weapons and horse bridles were found here in the seventeenth century but the fort has not been properly excavated.

Another museum worth visiting in this area is the **Scunthorpe Museum**, Oswald Road, South Humberside, which has some good Celtic exhibits. From 3 August 1991 until 26 January 1992, the museum put on an exhibition of the Celtic period which they hoped to be the first of several. The exhibition was an extensive one, with items borrowed from other museums, showing Celtic society and its technology before the coming of the Romans, looking at religion and ritual, communications, industry and warfare.

Chapter 7

Northern England

Lancashire, South Yorkshire, West Yorkshire,
Humberside, Cleveland, North Yorkshire,
Durham, Northumberland and Cumbria

The powerful Brigantes dominated all northern England, with the
exception of the Parisi of the Humberside, up to the border of
Caledonia, marked by the Romans with Hadrian's Wall. It is
assumed that the Brigantes, whose territory was the largest in
Britain, were in fact, a confederation of smaller tribes which had
been formed before the Roman invasion. The name meant 'High
Ones', sometimes thought to indicate 'Hill Dwellers'. That several
tribes existed before being united as Brigantes is argued from the
names for sections of the tribe, such as the Sentantii of the Fylde,
the Carvetii of Eden valley, the Gabrantovices of East Yorkshire,
the Tectoverdi (or Textoverdi) and Lopocares of Northumberland
and Latenses of Leeds. There is some argument whether the
Gabrantovices were, in fact, a sub-division of the Parisi. The
name, according to Professor K. Jackson, could mean
'cavalrymen', or, being a diminutive, be 'colts' or 'young fighters'.

When they emerge into history, just after the Roman invasion of
Britain, they are ruled by a woman, Cartimandua (the Sleek
Pony). This is, of course, not unusual for a Celtic people: in Celtic
society, women were equal with men, could be elected to any
office in the tribe, could lead the tribe in war, and hold full
property rights. Cartimandua decided to ally herself with the
Romans, becoming one of their 'client kings'. It has been argued
that her capital lay in the Vale of York and the most probable site
suggested is that of the large hill-fort at **Barwick in Elmet**, Leeds,
West Yorkshire (SE 39833749). However, this is a matter of
speculation.

When Caratacos was defeated by Ostorius, he fled to

Cartimandua with the intention of seeking her support, and probably intending to continue his resistance against the Roman invasion in the north. But Cartimandua had him handed over in chains to the Romans.

Within a few years her husband Venutios, who was estranged from her, received the backing of the major part of the Brigantes to take a stand against her pro-Roman policy. He led an attempt to overthrow her. Aulus Didius Gallus, the governor from AD 52–57, had to send legions into the territory and succeeded in keeping Cartimandua on the throne. Friction continued to simmer and finally came to a head in AD 69 when Cartimandua divorced Venutios in favour of his charioteer, Vellocatos. Venutios was acclaimed chieftain by the tribe and once more Cartimandua sent to the Romans for help. Vettius Bolanus, the governor, sent an army north. However, Venutios was so popular and so much in control that all the Romans could do was rescue Cartimandua and her new husband and leave the area in the hands of Venutios. Cartimandua and Vellocatos disappear from history, leaving Venutios undisputed chieftain of the tribe – but at war with the Romans. Venutios was pushed back in AD 72 by the new Roman governor, Petillius Cerialis, towards the Eden valley. He is said to have been defeated at Stanwick (q.v.), North Yorkshire, which is the biggest hill-fort in Britain. But there is some contention about this and nothing definite is known about his end. Certainly, the territory of the Brigantes, with the exception of Cumbria, was not fully garrisoned by the Roman occupation forces until the period of AD 78–84, during Julius Agricola's governorship. The Brigantes did not settle easily under the *pax Romana* and throughout the occupation there were several uprisings, for example in *c*. AD 118 and again in *c*. 155, when a serious revolt of the Brigantes caused heavy Roman casualties; another revolt *c*. 193–7 caused the Romans to send a new governor with heavy reinforcements and brought about a new political division of the Roman colonial administration in Britain.

There is no evidence to suggest that the Brigante confederation issued coinage, and coins from the Calder valley, originally thought to be Brigante coins, have now been shown to be

Coritani. An iron currency bar found at Sewell's Cave, near Settle, is unique and perhaps a remnant of cultural contacts with the southern tribes. However, it is unlikely that some form of currency did not exist, as many luxury imports are found within the Brigante area. It is impossible to establish whether a system of barter or some other method of exchange was used. During the Roman occupation, cattle were accepted as payment for taxes.

The main occupation of the Brigantes seems to have been pastoral farming; the majority of farms were situated on steep hill slopes, high above sea-level, presumably for ease of access to upland pastures. Cereal farming on a grand scale is not in evidence. Piggot and Wheeler have argued that the Brigantes may have been nomadic but the modern evidence is clearly against this. Hill-forts, settlements and other centres show that they were a settled people long before the coming of the Romans. Stanwick, for example, as previously mentioned, is the largest hill-fort in Britain and regarded as Venutios' capital. Items excavated there reveal some of the most magnificent pieces of Celtic metalwork.

Moving north into the Brigante territory of modern Lancashire, **Castercliffe Camp**, Nelson (SD 885384) shows signs of destruction by burning. It is an oval hill-fort of 0.9 hectare with entrances on the east and west sides. The ramparts and ditches and counterscarp are impressive. From the signs of destruction, it could be that the fortress was attacked during the period when Venutios was pursuing his successful uprising against his wife Cartimandua.

Portfield Camp, Whalley (SD 745355) is a triangular fort of 1.5 hectares. To the south-east and south-west it is protected by natural escarpments and a single rampart surrounds the whole, with extra defence lines to the south-east. A triple bank and ditch to the north-west complete the fortifications.

Warton Crag, Warton (SD 492727) is a triangular fort of some 6 hectares, defended by three ramparts with precipitous drops to the south-west and south-east. The inner defences have no ditch. The entrance is at the eastern end.

Moving into southern Yorkshire, in the Sheffield and Rotherham area, there are three forts which are worthy of note. On a rocky outcrop of millstone grit, high on Hathersage Moor, above Burbage Brook, stands **Carlwick**, Sheffield (SK 260815). It is a rectangular fort of 0.9 hectare whose only easy access is from the west. Traces of stone walls have been found. It has not been dated.

Scholes Wood, Rotherham (SK 395953) is oval in shape, protected by a single rampart enclosing 0.4 hectare. There is a ditch and counterscarp. The bank stands 1m high. The entrance is on the north-east. Because the site is overlooked by high ground on most sides, it is thought that this was built more as a cattle enclosure than a fortification.

There is no doubt that **Wincobank**, Sheffield (SK 378910) is an oval fort of 1 hectare. There were ramparts, ditch and counterscarp on all sides. The entrance was to the north-east. It was found that the ramparts were of stone reinforced by timbers. At some stage, this fortress was destroyed by a fire so fierce that the stones fused in places. Across the River Don (an old Celtic river name found in many places and probably cognate with the Celtic Danube) the Romans built a legionary fort 2.5km away.

It is worth noting that a line of earthworks, called **Roman Rig**, stretches from Sheffield to Mexborough, from the northern side of the Don as far as the River Dearne. It has been suggested that this might have been part of some frontier fortifications built by the Brigantes to keep out the Coritani, or even the Romans. Much of the course has been built on but some points can be seen east of Wincobank hill-fort to Hill Top (SK 397927). Another section can be seen 1km east of Scholes Wood to Wentworth Park.

Moving into West Yorkshire, one of the most interesting hill-forts is **Almondbury Castle Hill**, Huddersfield (SE 153141), which was mostly obliterated in 1150 when Henry de Laci built his castle there. This early Brigantian fortress, dating back to the eighth or seventh century BC, occupied 1.1 hectares in the south-western end of the hill. The entrance was originally a wooden guard chamber but this fell into decay when a group of undefended round-houses were built there. Early in the seventh century BC, a univallate fort was built with a ditch and a counterscarp bank. Stone ramparts were topped by a wooden fence. The ramparts were later extended to the whole hilltop, enclosing 2.2 hectares. Around 550 BC the ramparts were increased in height and the fortress strengthened. A rectangular annexe was added and a bank was thrown up enclosing 13 hectares at the foot of the hill. There is evidence of some other buildings here. In about 500 BC there was a fire in the fortress after which it was abandoned and not reoccupied.

South Kirkby Camp, South Kirkby (SE 435105) is a small oval fort of 1.8 hectares on sloping ground, protected by a bank and a ditch. The entrance is on the north side. As a fortress, it is not sited in the best defensive position.

Wendell Hill, Barwick in Elmet (SE 399376), in spite of being marked as a motte and bailey castle on the Ordnance Survey map, was originally a hill-fort of 6 hectares, extending north across the village street. The surrounding outer rampart and ditch belong to the hill-fort, though they were probably enlarged in medieval times.

Coming into Humberside, we leave the territory of the Brigantes for a while, and move into that of the Parisi, a tribe which was either the same as, or shared a name with, the Celtic tribe which gave its name to the French capital – the Parisi of the Seine valley. The Celtic name Humber, which is used for a number of streams in England and is cognate with Amber, seems to have meant the 'good river'.

Although this area has a long and unbroken record of occupation from the Late Bronze Age, it has been argued that the Parisi were a Belgic Celtic people who settled the area. According to some archaeologists, the Parisi are differentiated from the rest of the British Celts by what is now called the 'Arras culture'. In

This war-chariot burial was discovered at Garton Slack in East Yorkshire, the country of the Brigantes. The grave is dated to the second century BC

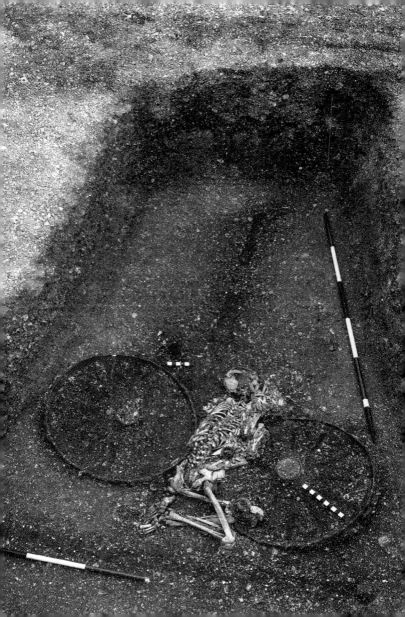

archaeological terms, striking cultural changes took place in this area. These are characterized by the method of burial, which was inhumation under a small barrow surrounded by a square ditch. The culture takes its name from the burials found at Arras near Market Weighton. The most important site is that of **Arras**, Market Weighton (SE 930413). It consists of a second-century BC cemetery originally containing at least a hundred graves of which only three are now visible. Three of the graves were chariot burials. In one, the King's Barrow, the skeletons of an elderly man and two horses, together with the wheels of a chariot, were found. Another grave, the Charioteer's Barrow, contained a skeleton and chariot wheels but no sign of horses. The Lady's Barrow contained a skeleton, a chariot and an iron mirror. Another grave, the Queen's Barrow, produced a female skeleton and much jewellery, including a necklace of blue and white glass beads, an amber ring, a gold finger ring, two bronze bracelets and a brooch and a pendant decorated with white coral. Pig bones were found in almost all the barrows. According to Dr I. M. Stead, the burials at Arras were peculiar to the Parisi and not found in other parts of Britain. His excellent book *The Arras Culture* is an essential guide to the burials and the subsequent finds. In this respect a trip to the **Yorkshire Museum**, Museum Gardens, York, is an essential part of the itinerary in this part of the world. The **City of Kingston upon Hull Museum**, Town Docks Museum, Queen Victoria Square, Hull, is another important point of reference. A new 'Iron Age' gallery was opened here in March 1991, and artefacts from Garton and Wetwang Slack were placed on display. The museum was preparing a guidebook to introduce people to the items.

It has been difficult to locate the capital of the Parisi. Ptolemy names two 'towns' which are at the southern and eastern extremities of the territory. The Antonine Itinerary and Ravenna Cosmography name three more 'towns': Derventio, Petuaria and Delgovicia. Derventio is identified with Malton, the only Roman military site on the River Derwent, from which the town took its name. The Celtic name means 'river by the oaks'. Petuaria, modern-day Brough (*burg* means 'a fort' in old English), is on the Humber. This became a Roman administration centre for the area and its Celtic name means 'a fourth'. It has been argued that the Parisi were split into four septs of which the fourth had its capital here. Delgovicia is thought to have been placed north of Brough and south of Malton. The name means 'fighters with thorns for spears' and, therefore, it is argued that it was the name of a sept of the Parisi. The Gabrantovices have been claimed as the fourth sept of the Parisi.

Dane's Dyke, Flamborough (SE 216694) is an area of 8km² delineated by a massive dyke system that runs north to south across the headland from coast to coast. The bank stands nearly 6m high with a ditch on the western side 18m across with traces of a counterscarp bank. It is unusual to find this type of earthwork so far north.

Another 'Arras culture' burial ground is found at **Scorborough**, Leconfield (TA 017453). This contains some 120 barrows or graves, the largest 15m in diameter. Only a few of them have been opened but they have been poorly preserved. They contained 'contracted' burials and no grave goods.

There has been speculation about the role which the Parisi played during the war between the Brigantes and the Romans around AD 69–74. Tacitus says Venutios called in aid from other tribes and it may well be that the Parisi were one of these. Roman legionary marching forts have been discovered on the River Went, and certainly the direct route to Venutios' fort at Stanwick lay through Parisian territory. By the governorship of Agricola it is safe to say that the Parisi had fallen to the *pax Romana*.

Leaving the Parisi territory, we return to that of the Brigantes in Cleveland where there is only one site of interest. This is **Eston Nab Camp**, Eston and Wilton (NZ 567183), a semicircular promontory fort on a steep cliff. It is well sited on the north-west of the Eston Hills and enclosed by a rampart, ditch and counterscarp. The rampart, stone-walled, is 4.5m thick. Inside the fort a palisade enclosure has been found by excavation, together with some Bronze Age pottery which clearly predates the fort.

Moving into North Yorkshire proper, **Boltby Scar**, Boltby (SE 506857) is considered worthy of note in terms of Celtic territorial divisions. It is a semicircular cliff-edge fort, defended by a single rampart and ditch and probably enclosing 1 hectare. The steep cliffs protect it to the west. Three Bronze Age barrows have been found inside the fort.

A small Brigantian hill-fort, protected by stone ramparts, a ditch and a counterscarp bank, is found at **Castle Steads**, Gayles (NZ 112074). Standing on a north-facing spur, it encloses 1.6 hectares. Its entrance has not been identified.

Castletown Rigg, Westerdale (NZ 682041) seems to date from the seventh century BC. The earthworks cut across a narrow spur and were stone-faced. Between the two walls are traces of circular dwellings, tilled fields and barrows.

A settlement enclosed in an irregular wall some 240m by 400m lies at **Crown End**, Westerdale (NZ 668075). Within the enclosure there are traces of a scattering of several circular dwellings. There are also 200 small cairns nearby. Excavation has failed to produce burials.

Danby Rigg, Danby (NZ 710065) lies among traces of Celtic fields. It is a complex of earthworks (which might indicate a fort), a grave (which was enclosed in a circular bank of earth and stone some 18m in diameter) and some small stone cairns. A series of 300 small cairns nearby have been interpreted as burial mounds but no burials have been discovered. It is suggested that the site was occupied continuously from 1700 BC to the first century AD.

Grassington (SD 995655–SE004654) is the site of a series of Iron Age boundaries and hut circles. These lie on the moors north of Grassington and formed a Celtic settlement which was occupied into the Roman period. The best settlement site is at the north end of Lea Green, where the fields measure 90m by 150m.

The highest hill-fort in England stands 716m above sea-level at **Ingleborough**, Ingleton (SD 742746). This windy and desolate spot seems unsuitable for permanent occupation yet the fort, which is pear-shaped, enclosed 6 hectares in which traces of several circular dwellings have been found. Its single rampart is still 4m thick, made of millstone grit. The main entrance seems to have been on the south-western side. Parts of the walls have been vandalized to construct a modern cairn on the top of the hill.

Roulston Scar, Hood Grange (SE 514816) is the largest promontory fort in Yorkshire, enclosing 2 hectares. The south-west rampart is 3m high with a ditch on the north-east side.

Selside, Horton (SD 77772) is interesting as an extensive area of Celtic fields surrounding traces of circular dwellings, each about 6m in diameter, and each within a walled enclosure. There is a pond nearby and several springs rise amongst the fields across the hillside.

Although the largest hill-fort in the whole of Britain, **Stanwick**, Stanwick St John (NZ 180115) is not the most impressive. Most of it is masked, as it is sited in low-lying ground. According to Sir Mortimer Wheeler, this was the capital of Venutios, the estranged husband of Cartimandua of the Brigantes. The complex is centred on a smaller fort, called locally The Tofts. Sometime around AD 50, the fort was extended so that 50 hectares were added to its northern side. The new rampart was 12m wide and 3m high. It was fronted by a dry-stone wall of limestone slabs. A flat-bottomed ditch, 12m wide and 4m deep, was built with vertical sides. Part of this excavated ditch, north-east of the village of Forcett, has been preserved for viewing. At the bottom of the ditch was found a well-preserved Celtic sword in a wooden scabbard and a human skull with sword-cut wounds on it.

Around AD 68 a further 240 hectares were added to the site with a great enclosure to the south, but this was never completed. The gateway on the south was commenced with overlapping rampart ends. The area of the whole site was approaching some 300 hectares, too large for an efficient defence. Around AD 74, the Roman governor Petillius Cerialis launched an attack on Venutios and his Brigantes, and Stanwick fell. We do not know what the fate of Venutios was or whether Cerialis allowed the now ageing Cartimandua, and her second husband Vellocatos, to return as ruler of the Brigantes. In all likelihood, the Brigantes were now ruled directly by the Roman governor from London.

Another interesting hill-fort stands at **Staple Howe**, Scampston (SE 898749). It stands on a flat-topped hill, a little apart from the main escarpment of the Wolds, and is dated to 500 BC. Initially there was an oval dwelling some 9m long, surrounded by a wooden palisade; two circular buildings were later added. The oval dwelling had walls of stone or chalk with a gabled roof and a clay oven and hearth. The circular buildings had stout timber walls and thatched roofs. One building contained a loom. Another construction which seems to have been a granary stood on the highest part of the hill. Considerable quantities of burnt grain have given a radio-carbon date of 400 BC through to 150 BC. Bones of livestock – cattle, goats, sheep and pigs – indicate a farming community. Remains of wild animals and fish were also found. Two bronze razors date to 500 BC.

Victoria Cave, Langcliffe (SD 838650) is worthy of note for it was not only used in palaeolithic times (finds include the bones of a hippopotamus, a woolly rhinoceros and an elephant) but was even inhabited in the Early Celtic period and during the Roman occupation. Bronze Age, Iron Age and Romano-British pottery have been discovered there. Similarly, **Windypits**, Scawton, were primarily used for Beaker burials but at **Ashberry Windypit** (SE 571849), one chamber contained Romano-British objects, including a bronze trumpet brooch, bangle, chain, armour and bone spoons.

Durham's only significant promontory fort is another **Maiden Castle** (NZ 382460). It stands overlooking the River Wear, whose original Celtic form was Visur, the water river. It enclosed 0.8 hectare with the neck of the promontory cut off by a strong bank with a ditch. The bank still stands 2m high and is 5.5m wide. The rest of the fort is protected by steep, now wooded slopes, on all sides except the west. There has been only limited excavation.

We now move north-east into Northumberland which was the tribal territory of the Votandini, who straddled Hadrian's Wall. The further north we move, the less, unfortunately, we know about the individual tribes found there. A typical fort in this area

is **Alnham Castle Hill**, Alnham (NT 980109), which is a
multivallate type enclosing 0.3 hectare. There are triple ramparts
and broad ditches containing traces of several dwellings. The
entrance is on the east and remains indicate that a settlement may
have been built beside it.

A series of three camps constitute **Dod Law Camps**, Dodington
(NU 004317), presenting an interesting complex. The western
camp is a D-shaped enclosure with double ramparts 4.5–6m wide
and up to 3m high, in which a number of huts 4–6m in diameter
were enclosed. The Middle Dod Law is much the same shape, with
single bank and ditch, but no dwellings have been found: this
might have been a stock enclosure. The East Dod Law is an oval
enclosure with a single rampart and ditch. What makes this group
interesting is that within the area some of the finest prehistoric
rock carvings in the country are contained.

Great Hetha Camp, Hethpool (NT 885274) is a small oval fort in
which several wooden huts have been traced. This site overlooks a
smaller fortress on Little Hetha, 0.5km to the north.

The most extensive settlement found in the area is situated on a
south-facing slope above the River Breamish, a Celtic name
meaning 'the roaring river' and cognate with the modern Welsh
brefu, roar. It is situated at **Greaves Ash**, Ingram (NT 965164).
Altogether there are two enclosures with the traces of some forty
dwellings, while around them are field systems and indications of
cattle enclosures. Some 30m west of this main complex is a double-
walled enclosure with a single entrance while 90m north-east of the
main enclosure is another group of about a dozen dwellings. The
evidence is of a prosperous agricultural settlement spread over 8
hectares and occupied from about the fifth century BC until the
Roman occupation.

Harehaugh Camp, Holystone (NY 969998) lies on a steep-sided
east-west ridge overlooking Coquetdale. It is protected on the east
by two ramparts and ditches and on the west by three ramparts
and ditches.

Dating from the first century BC is **Hetha Burn**, Kirknewton (NT
881275), a fort on the north-west slope of a hill. Below it (NT
878276) are two rectangular settlements which are unusual in that

encloses 0.3 hectare within three ramparts; four dwellings were Low walls of turf and stone enclosed the area and traces of huts have been found.

Overlooking the Till and Glen stands a fort on **Humbleton Hill**, Wooler (NT 967283), which has a central enclosure with an entrance to the north-east. There is a semicircular annexe on the eastern side. On the north is a larger annexe. All the enclosures show traces of dwellings. Steep slopes surrounding the fort add to the defensive system.

Lordenshaws, Hesleyhurst (NZ 054993) is another of the forts which overlook the Coquet River, lying on a moorland spur. It is protected by three ramparts, ditches and a counterscarp bank, enclosing 0.3 hectare. Inside there are traces of circular dwellings which were occupied until the period of the Roman conquest. A defence bank 60m to the south-west cuts across the spur. About 270m south-west stand two stones with cup and ring marks. There are also six cairns to the north east of the fort.

In this area, of course, a visit to the **Museum of Antiquities, University of Newcastle upon Tyne**, will be rewarding. Although the 'Iron Age' material is sparse and poor in quality, the museum does have some visually fascinating items, such as a gilt-bronze brooch from Great Chesters, made just prior to the Roman incursions in this area. Most famous among Celticists are the bronze harness mounts from South Shields, which are dated to the second century AD. One of the most intriguing items is the 'Birth of Mithras' statue from Housesteads dated to the third century AD. A local carving influenced by the Roman cult of Mithras, it contains the twelve signs of the zodiac: this provides some of the earliest evidence of astrology in Britain.

Originally a circular enclosure, **Old Bewick**, Bewick (NU 075216) was later expanded into a figure-of-eight plan. It is strongly defended, lying on the southern side of a spur above the River Breamish. With double ramparts and ditch on the edge of the escarpment, the whole is enclosed in a rampart and ditch. In the western enclosure there are traces of dwellings but quarry workings have obliterated some of them.

At Doddington lie two fortresses: **Ringses Camp** (NY 013328)

they have been dug into the hillside on a series of levelled areas. found in the centre. **Roughting Linn Fort** (NT 984367) is a rectangular promontory fort, standing by The Linn, a waterfall. The name is derived from the Celtic *lei*, to flow, cognate with the Welsh *lliant*, stream. This lies at the north-east corner of the fort, while the streams run on the north, west and south. The eastern approach is guarded by three banks and ditches with a counterscarp. The entrance is at the north-east.

At **West Hill** Kirknewton (NT 909295), stands an oval enclosure in which the foundations of eight stone dwellings have been found. A further enclosure to the north-west encloses four circular dwellings. This stands on a knoll overlooking the junction of the College Burn and the River Glen.

Wooler Fort (NT 984274) is an oval defence work divided by triple ramparts into east and west sections, connected by an entrance. No dwellings have been recognized within the fort.

Yeavering Bell, Old Yeavering (NT 928293) is an important hill-fort enclosing 5.2 hectares and two summits and the saddle of the hill. It stands 360m above sea-level. It is enclosed by a single stone rampart 4m wide with entrances midway to the north and south and with a third on the north-east. Annexes stand at the east and west. No fewer than 130 circular dwellings have been traced. The eastern end seems to have been the earliest part of the construction with a wooden palisade nearly 50m in diameter. Early excavations did not record the contents but later excavations have found some Samian ware from the Roman occupation period, coins and an additional two rectangular buildings overlying circular ones. Yeavering Bell is derived from the Celtic compound containing the word *gafr*, goat, the earliest recorded name being Adgefrin in which may be recognized the *gafr* and the word *bryn* (mutated *fryn*) meaning 'hill'. So this was the 'hill of the goats'. When the Anglo-Saxons drove the Celts from the area they established a royal town of Adgefrin at the foot of the hill.

Moving into Cumbria there is an immediate feeling of being more 'in touch' with things Celtic. This is not surprising for Celtic place-names still abound here, especially in the highlands. Cumbria is the same word as the Welsh name for Wales – Cymru, pronounced 'Cum-ree'. A language similar to Welsh, Cornish and Breton survived in Cumbria until the twelfth century AD and possibly as late as the fourteenth century in the Eden valley. The Eden is one of the two main rivers in Cumbria, taking its name from the Celtic Ituna meaning 'to gush forth'. The other main river is the Derwent, also retaining its Celtic name and meaning 'the river where oaks abound', a fairly common river name whose root word appears in Darwent, Dart and Darwent.

This area was originally part of the Brigante territory, but after the Roman conquest a new kingdom was defined here. Its capital was at Carlisle, or Caer Llywelydd, which originated from the original Celtic Luguvalos, a town named after the god Lug. The Romans called it Luguvallium and the Celtic Cumbrians later added their word for a fort, *caer*. The kingdom which emerged in Cumbria after the departure of the Romans was independent for some centuries but was later annexed to the British Celtic kingdom of Strath-Clota (Strathclyde) whose inhabitants, in medieval times, joined with their northern Gaelic cousins into the kingdom of Alba, which we now call Scotland. During this period many Anglo-Saxons had settled in Cumbria, mainly in fertile valley spots. During the wars between William Rufus of England (1087–1100) and Maol Callum (Malcolm Canmore) of Scotland (1058–1093), the English managed to annex Cumbria. It was never retaken by Scotland and more English settlers were encouraged to put down roots there, driving the Celtic inhabitants further into the hills. Eventually, the Celtic elements became absorbed by the English.

A museum of particular interest to those in search of Early Celtic Britain is the **Senhouse Roman Museum** (The Battery, Maryport, Cumbria). This museum opened in April 1990 and houses some exceptional artefacts of Celtic craftsmanship, some of which are difficult to date. Maryport has been particularly rich in Celtic finds and has produced the largest collection of Celtic 'horned god' carvings in Britain. It is the home of the Serpent Stone which is thought to be the largest free-standing Celtic sculpture in Britain; it is certainly one of the most spectacular, being a phallus standing some 1.3m high with a serpent on the front and a severed head carving on the back.

A settlement is situated at **Barnscar**, Muncaster (SD 135958), which comprises half a dozen dwellings with central hearths. East of the huts is a group of cairns numbering in the region of 360.

One of the best-preserved Brigante settlements lies on a gentle north-facing slope at **Burwens**, Crosby Ravensworth (NY 621123). Thought to date from the second or first century BC, this rectangular enclosure of 0.4 hectare contains a village street which leads through a series of circulr dwellings, some which attached courtyards. Sadly, the village has not yet been excavated. Nearby, to the north and east, are traces of a field system. It has been suggested that the village was occupied into the Roman period.

Carrock Fell, Mungrisdale (NY 343337) stands on the eastern slope of the Caldbeck Fells. It is an oval fort which is strongly defended. The name Carrock means 'rock' and there are, indeed, precipitous crags at the south-western end. Some 2 hectares are enclosed by a dry-stone wall whose facing has survived in several places. It has a western entrance and another on the southern side. At the eastern end of the fort is a cairn. Numerous other cairns lie on the northern slope.

Castle Crag, Mardale (NY 469128) is a fascinating little fortress standing 120m above the Haweswater reservoir. It encloses an area of 0.4 hectare in which traces of dwellings and hearths have been discovered. Entered only from the west, it is oval, protected to the north and north-east by the steepness of the rock climb and to the south by two rock-cut ditches and a now-crumbled stone rampart. Another **Castle Crag**, this time at Shoulthwaite (NY 300188), stands on the eastern side of Castlerigg Fell in a rocky clearing of woodland. Entered on the east, it has a rampart of earth and stone 2.2m high and there are two lines of ditch. It commands the precipitous slopes of Shoulthwaite Gill.

Another small fort, standing 395m above sea-level, is **Castle Folds**, Great Asby (NY 650094). Enclosing 0.5 hectare in a stone rampart about 2.5m thick, it is rectangular in shape. Dwellings have been discovered inside. The entrance is on the south side.

Castlehead, Grange (SD 421797) is a promontory fort with a dry-stone rampart cutting off the neck of the spur on the north side.

Castlehowe Scar, Crosby Ravensworth (NY 587155) is another small fort (these seem more numerous in Cumbria than elsewhere). Containing 0.5 hectare, it is on a narrow east-west ridge near Bassenthwaite Lake. To the north and south there is natural protection but to the west there are four banks and ditches as well as artificial scarping of the hillside. It has been suggested that the fort was occupied during the Roman occupation by Romanized Celts.

Above the River Lowther, whose ancient Celtic name means 'bath', (so the river for bathing, perhaps?) stands **Castlestead**, Yanwath (NY 510852). This is one of the smallest forts, enclosing only 0.1 hectare with three concentric banks and two ditches.

Crosby Garret (NY 719064) is the centre of a Celtic field system interspersed by ancient roads and settlements which have been clearly shown by aerial photography. The largest settlement is on the south-east slope of Begin Hill, with hut enclosures and field boundries radiating from it. A small settlement stands 640m to the north-east and 270m further on, above Crag Wood, is another settlement.

Dunmallet, Dacre (NY 468246) is a small univallate hill-fort with counterscarp. The name of the nearby River Dacre, from *dakru*, means simply 'a trickling stream'.

Ewe Close and **Ewe Lock**, Crosby, Ravensworth (NY 609135) are two enclosed settlements. Ewe Close has two separate groups of dwellings and 'garden' areas. At the centre of the western group is a large circular dwelling with a paved floor. All the huts have fairly thick – 1.8m – stone walls. Ewe Lock, 640m south, has a hut group and paddock area. It was constructed before the Roman conquest, and several Romano-British objects have been discovered here.

At the southern end of The Helm above Saint Sunday's Beck, stands the small oval hill-fort of **Helm Hill**, Nathand and Stainton (SD 531887), enclosed behind two ramparts and an intervening bank. The ramparts are unnecessary on the eastern side due to the precipitous slope.

Traces of a series of enclosures for animal husbandry can be seen at **Holborn Hill**, Great Asby (NY 682123), where there is an oval enclosure of 135m diameter, used no doubt as a cattle pen.

A settlement at **Holme Bank**, Urswick (SD 276734) has produced traces of two huts, one 7.5m in diameter and the other 4.5m in diameter, with another dwelling and attached paddock 22m to the north-west. Other settlements can be traced at **Howarcles**, Crosby Ravensworth (NY 627132), on a slope above Woodfoot, at **Hugill** (NY 437010) and at **Langthwaite Green** (NY 161209). Two more settlements stand on the moorland above Scandal Beck at **Smardale Demense**, Waithby (NY 730072). The larger contains dwellings and adjoining animal pens while the smaller, 450m to the north-east, consists of a dwelling in a simple oval enclosure.

A large enclosure stands on the northern slope of the moorland at **Threlkeld Knott**, St John's in the Vale (NY 329241). This is rectangular, about 120m by 90m, with four or five dwellings and a similar number of animal pens. The centre dwelling has been excavated and seen to be 6m in diameter with walls 1.5m thick. Traces of Celtic field systems can be seen nearby, as well as some thirty cairns. These are all fairly large, being 6–7.5m in diameter, and some contained traces of charcoal, suggesting that they were the base of pyres for funeral cremations.

Traces of a settlement at **Urswick Stone Walles** (SD 260741) have been nearly destroyed by quarrying. However, an oval enclosure surrounded by a stone wall about 3m wide enclosing three dwellings and paddocks has been excavated and is thought to have been occupied into the Roman period.

There is a rectangular earthwork at **Waitby** (NY 755074), containing three circular dwellings, and another at **Yanwath Wood**, Yanwath (NY 519260), which is a D-shaped spur above the River Lowther. It encloses 0.4 hectare and is entered on the north-west and south-west.

Chapter 8

Wales (Cymru)

Ynys Mon (Anglesey), Gwynedd, Clwyd,
Dyfed, Glamorgan, Gwent and Powys

Wales, the land of the *weahlas* or 'foreigners', according to the
Anglo-Saxons' viewpoint, but called Cymru in the Welsh
language, has remained a Celtic country until modern times. The
Celtic population here remained undisturbed by the invasion of
the ancestors of the English which eradicated their fellow Celts in
that part of Britain which was to become England. The inhabitants
of this western area were able to secure a border between
themselves and the invaders and within this border developed
independent Celtic kingdoms which eventually united under
Rhodri the Great (AD 844–77). However, it could be argued that
Hywel Dda (AD 916–50) was the more unifying monarch: he is said
to have organized the first codification of Welsh Celtic law and
summoned a parliament at Whitland, Carmarthen.

Wales remained independent, a prosperous medieval kingdom,
producing a great wealth of literature in its Celtic language, until
the thirteenth century. England had never lost its early ambition to
conquer the entire island of Britain and several times had tried to
invade this Celtic territory. On 11 December 1282, Llywelyn ap
Gruffydd, the Welsh ruler, was slain by an Englishman, Stephen
Franton, at Cilmeri. His brother, Dafydd ap Gruffydd, succeeded
him and continued to fight against the English invasion but was
captured and beheaded. For the next century, the Welsh rose
periodically against the English conquest. Finally Owain Glyndwr,
a descendant of the Welsh ruling family, managed to secure Welsh
independence again in 1400. He summoned a parliament at
Machynlleth. The English began the slow process of reconquest
and the tide began to turn for Glyndwr in 1409. By 1415 Wales
was again under English control. Through the Acts of Annexation
(later called Union) in 1536 and 1542, Wales became part of

England and the Welsh language was to be 'utterly extirp'd'. In spite of this, the Celtic language of Wales has survived, though pushed into a minority position by the various and often vicious attempts to eradicate it. It now has a degree of official status but only 18.9 per cent of the population (503,549) speak Welsh, according to the 1981 Census. However, a mood of independence still permeates Wales, although in legislative and political terms it is still part of England, and remains a Celtic country, proud of its Celtic heritage.

According to Roman sources, such as Tacitus, the small island of Mona (Ynys Mon, Anglesey) was a centre of resistance against the Roman conquest of Britain and the headquarters of the druids, the religious leaders, philosophers and keepers of the law, history and oral literature of Celtic civilization. Caesar had previously said that a druidic 'university' was sited in Britain and the Celts of Gaul sent their offspring to study, sometimes for twenty years, in Britain. The island of Mona seems to be named after the Celtic ocean god, Manawyddan, son of Llyr (known in Irish tradition as Manannán Mac Lir). The Isle of Man (Ellan Vannin) is also thought to have been so named.

In AD 59 C. Suetonius Paulinus was appointed governor of Britain and soon after commenced a campaign in the area of which is now North Wales, in the country of the Deceangli. In AD 60/61 he reached the Menai Straits and prepared to take the island of Mona. Tacitus, whose father-in-law, Agricola, was serving as a young tribune with Paulinus, tells us that he was opposed not only by Celtic warriors who gathered on the shore but by druids in ceremonial dress, men and women, bearing lighted torches. When the Romans gained a bridgehead they set about a massacre of everyone, flinging the druids into ceremonial fires. News of the Iceni uprising prevented Suetonius continuing the subjugation of Mona.

In AD 74 Julius Frontinus was appointed governor and conducted several campaigns against the Silures of South Wales and the Ordovices of Central and North Wales. But it was left to Agricola, appointed governor in AD 78, to return to Mona. In a campaign in the late summer of AD 78, Agricola massacred the

Ordovices and then marched north to take Mona itself.

Bwrdd Arthur (AN 585815) is a hill-fort enclosing 7 hectares within ramparts which are faced with large limestone slabs and, although pre-Roman, it was occupied during the Roman period. Nearby is an extensive system of Celtic terraced fields and round huts.

At **Caer y Twr**, Holyhead (SH 218830), on the rocky summit of Holyhead Mountain, a hill-fort encloses 7 hectares, defended by ramparts of dry-stone walling. The wall exists on the north and west sides, standing to 3m high and to a width of 4m. Nearby is a man-made breach where the wall seems to have been deliberately thrown down, perhaps by the Romans. The site is unexcavated at the present time. Also on Holyhead Mountain stand two groups of huts, fourteen in one and six in the other: **Ty Mawr** (SH 212820). These are thought by some to have been constructed during the Roman occupation. One of them was clearly used by metal-workers. Copper was extensively mined on the island and, when the Romans took over, they continued to develop this mining. At the Ty Mawr hut group finds of querns, mortars, spindle whorls, pottery and coins reinforce the proposition that the site was occupied in the Roman period.

A point of interest is that on Holy Island one of the most fascinating 'hoards', representing the period of 200 years before the Roman conquest, was discovered at **Llyn Cerrig Bach**. These finds are now in the **National Museum of Wales**. Some 138 bronze, iron and wooden objects were found, evidence of a wealthy artistic culture; these were sufficient remains to allow the reconstruction of a Celtic chariot. The consensus is that Mona was a focus of wealth in the hands of the priestly caste of druids, thereby supporting the Roman claim that the island was a druidic centre.

Castel Bryn-Gwyn, Llanidan (SH 464671) was begun in neolithic times but refashioned as a defence work early in the first century AD when the Romans threatened the island. It is an area 54m in diameter, enclosed by a bank 3.6m high and 12m wide. The

Ty Mawr hut circles, Holyhead Mountain, Anglesey. Known as *Cytiau'r Gwyddelod* in Welsh (huts of the Irish)

A reconstruction of a pre-Roman chariot, part of the Llyn Cerrig Bach hoard

interior ground-level is actually 3m higher than that outside.

A promontory fort is situated on a rocky headland on the north coast protected by 60m-high sea-cliffs on three sides. This is **Dinas Gynfor**, Llanbadrig (SH 391951). To the south the slope is steep and there is a marsh at the foot. Two walls of limestone blocks protect this side of the fort with two gates.

Enclosing 7 hectares in an oval hill-fort, with dry-stone walling of massive limestone blocks, **Din Sylwy**, Llanfihangel-Din-Sylwy (SH 586815) has two entrances, south and west. The ground steeply slopes away on all sides. The fort wall is about 2.4m thick but there are no ditches.

The **Pant-y-saer Hut Group** (AN 514825) is an oval enclosure with circular dwellings. Pottery and a fine sixth-century AD silver brooch have been discovered here.

Crossing back to mainland Gwynedd, **Caer Euni**, Llandderfel (SJ 000413) is a narrow oval fort. It is on a high ridge enclosed by a stone rampart and ditch with pronounced counterscarp. There are traces of fused stonework which may be the result of an attack on

A wrought iron firedog from Capel Garmon, Denbighshire and gang-chain from Llyn Cerrig Bach, Anglesey

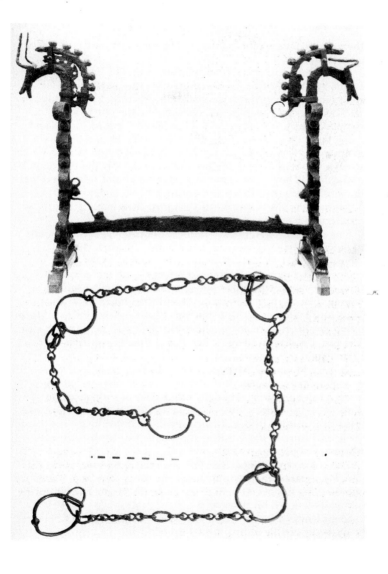

the fort and an attempt to burn it. The ramparts protected a dozen circular huts.

One of the most spectacular hill-forts is that of **Carn Fadrun**, Llaniestyn (SH 280352), which dominates the Lleyn peninsula. It is a triangular-shaped fort originally of 5 hectares but extended to 10.5 hectares by a rectangular enclosure on the north. Stone ramparts which still stand 2m high enclosed the fort. Round and rectangular dwellings were built inside. In the twelfth century a Norman castle was built on the west. A Bronze Age stone cyst stood near the centre of the fort and was probably the first feature of the area. The fort has not been excavated but it is believed that the northern extension was built during the Roman period. Numerous dwellings surrounded the fort, especially to the northern side.

One remnant of Agricola's ruthless campaign against the Celts of the area, the Ordovices, is the remains of **Castell Odo**, Aberdaron (SH 187284). Circular, with double banks and enclosing less than one hectare, this fort was no more than a protected village which numbered nine or ten circular timber houses. The original site was burnt and abandoned for a while. Then new buildings and fortifications of stone were erected. More round dwellings were constructed. The gate was on the north-east. The fort was destroyed about AD 78, the time of Agricola's campaign in this area.

Conway Mountain, Mynydd y Dref, Conway (SH 760778) is a rectangular stone-walled fort of 3 hectares. It is protected to its north by steep slopes and on the other sides by a single stone rampart. Excavation shows that the entrance on the southern side was by means of a bridge. It enclosed circular dwellings; a separate stone enclosure to the south-west contained six more, some of which have been excavated.

There is an oval-shaped hill-fort at **Creigiau Gwineu**, Rhiw (SH 228274). A stone rampart surrounds the rocky mass and at least one dwelling has been found in the eastern section. The hill-fort is particularly noted for its view.

Dinas Dinlie, Llanwrog (SH 43763) is a fort of some 1.5 hectares enclosed by double ramparts on a rounded hill. The entrance was on the south-east and dwellings have been discovered inside. It stands beside the sea and it has been argued that it guarded a sheltered harbour which has now been silted up.

More impressive is **Dinas Dinorwig**, Llanddeiniolen (SH 549653). The name of the fort has been interpreted as 'the fort of the Ordovices' but it is hardly big enough to have been their tribal capital. It covers only 1.2 hectares on a ridge above a tributary of the Seiont. The inner wall, 3.4m thick, is guarded by two massive banks of earth and rubble still standing between 6 and 9m high. There is a north-west gateway in the stone wall, and a second blocked gate nearby. It is thought to date from the sixth century BC.

Dinas Emrys, Bedgelert (SH 606492), although begun in the pre-Roman period, achieved some fame in the post-Roman period. Enclosing only 1 hectare with a single entrance on the south-west, the main defences seem to date from the fifth and sixth centuries AD, although the dominant feature of the site is a twelfth-century tower. The pool and artificial cistern at the south-west were constructed in the fifth or sixth century. Dinas Emrys is mentioned by the writer Nennius who associates it with Vortigern (The Overlord), the ruler of southern Britain who made the mistake of inviting a group of Jute and Anglo-Saxon mercenaries into Britain to help him in his wars. They stayed and took over the kingdom, carving England out of south-east Britain. The fort is named after Emrys (Ambrosius) who overthrew Vortigern. Certainly archaeology records that it was inhabited at the time of these events.

Dinllaen, Edern (SH 275416) is a promontory fort cutting off 5.6 hectares by two cross-dykes 60m in length. The earthworks have been badly damaged by a golf course and some quarrying. The fort would have controlled a harbour below.

A small settlement, lived in during the Roman occupation, stands at **Gaerwen**, Llanwnda (SH 501583). A quadrangular wall enclosure contained a circular dwelling 7m in diameter and two rectangular buildings, one of which was clearly a blacksmith's shop. Nearby, on the other side of the road, are the remains of four circular dwellings.

Garn Boduan, Boduan (SH 311394) is associated with the Celtic chieftain Buan (*c.* AD 600–650) although it was begun in the pre-Roman period. Enclosing 10 hectares, it was built on a rocky height and contained a number of springs. Some 168 dwellings of a circular nature have been found inside its walls, which are still 3m thick and standing 2m high. There was an entrance on the south-east and another on the north-east. The houses were built of stone but excavation of four of them failed to produce dating material. Access to the top rampart was by stone steps. The fort was still occupied in the late Roman period, which may provide some justification for its association with Buan.

Moel Goedog and Trackway, Morfa Harlech (SH 614325) is a small circular fort enclosed by double ramparts except on the north where there is an additional one. The entrance was at the south-west. Nearby are two groups of huts and field boundaries while an ancient roadway passes north and south to the west of the fort, its course marked by a series of standing stones. The area was obviously a centre for agriculture.

Another interesting, and fairly unusual, small oval fort is **Pen-y-Dinas**, Llanaber (SH 607209). With stone-faced walls 4.5m wide, the fort stands on a spur overlooking Egryn Abbey. The entrance is on the north-west, sunken and probably entered over a bridge. It is inturned with guard chambers. To the north and west are double ramparts and traces of a third. Traces of a rectangular dwelling are inside. Below, enclosed, was a settlement.

The interesting feature of **Pen-y-Gaer**, Llanbedr-y-Cennin (SH 750693) is its *chevaux-de-frise* on the west and south. The pointed stones were set close together to make approach difficult. The ramparts are of stone and are some 4.5m wide.

There is no doubt that **Tre'r Ceiri**, Llanaelhaearn (SH 373446), standing on the most easterly of the three peaks of Yr Eifli, on the Lleyn peninsular, is one of the most spectacular of all hill-forts in the country. It stands 450m above sea-level and is oval in construction, being 290m long and 100m wide. The main ramparts enclosed circular dwellings which in Roman times numbered about 150. A second rampart was added on the north-west and enclosures for stock on the south-west. The ramparts still stand to a height of 4m in places; there are sloping ramps to enter by, with two main gates at the south-west end and three smaller gates at the west. The lintel stone of one of the postern gates is still in position. Excavation showed that some of the dwellings were occupied between AD 150 and 400.

Clwyd is the territory of the Deceangli, whose name seems to have survived in Deganwy and Tegeingl. There are a number of forts in this area. Typical is **Caer Drewyn**, Corwen (SJ 08744), which is a circular construction enclosing 3.2 hectares with stone-built ramparts. Traces of dwellings are seen inside. Among the several forts along the west side of the River Clwyd is **Castel Cawr**, Abergele (SH 937768). This still has walls 3m high and a ditch 1m deep. However it is mainly overgrown.

Dinas Bran, Llangollen (SJ 223430) is a fort of 1.7 hectares now dominated by a medieval castle, although the defence works of the Iron Age fortifications can be seen.

Sadly, one important hill-fort – Dinobren – (SH 968757) has been totally destroyed by quarrying.

An interesting hill-fort from the medieval period is at **Foel Fenlli**, Llanbedr-Dryffryn-Clwyd (SJ 163601). The chieftain, Benlli, who lived here was reported to be 'iniquitous and tyrannical'. He lived around AD 400 and opposed St German. He and his city were reported to have been consumed by a fire from heaven, but if this was his capital the archaeological evidence does not support the legend: there is no sign of any consuming fire. The hill-fort enclosed 10 hectares in an oval plan with double or treble ramparts depending on the terrain below. The entrance was at the west end. Two dozen dwellings were found at the west end and there is a spring in the centre. No excavations have confirmed a date as yet.

Llwyn Bryn Dinas, Llanrhaeadr-y-Mochnant (SJ 172247) enclosed 3 hectares, 270m above the Tanat valley. It is a contour fort with a single rampart and ditch and an entrance on the south-east.

Moel Arthur, Llandyrnog (SJ 145661) stands 455m above sea-level and dominates the Vale of Clwyd. The fort encloses 2 hectares in two ramparts with ditches and counterscarp. The entrance is on the north-east.

An important fort which is sadly being destroyed by quarrying is **Moel Hiraddug**, Dyserth (SJ 063785). It stands 264m above sea-level and dominates the area towards the sea. A large site, it encloses 8 hectares within a single rampart except to the east where two further ramparts rise with dry-stone facing. Circular and rectangular dwellings have been found inside. There is a gate at the north-west which had guard chambers. The evidence suggests that the fort was attacked by the Romans around AD 50, when the inner rampart collapsed. The debris provides proof of a battle with, among other items, fragments of a bronze shield and iron sword blade.

Moel-y-Gaer, Bodfari (SJ 095708) is the site of a small semicircular defence system with rampart, ditch and counterscarp. **Moel-y-Gaer**, Llanbedr (SJ 149618) is 4 hectares in extent and defended by double ramparts on all sides except to the north-east where there is an additional rampart. Two entrances, both inturned, lie on the west and north-east. Yet another **Moel-y-Gaer** stands at Rhosemor (SJ 211691). It is a contour fort with ramparts and ditches and was built in the fourth century BC. The site has been excavated in preparation for the construction of a storage reservoir. Refortification occurred in the third century BC and circular dwellings were built. It seems to have been deserted for a while and then around the first century BC was refortified again. Little pottery was found in the area excavated but items connected with sling warfare were found.

Perhaps the largest hill-fort in the area is that of **Penycloddiau**, Nannerch (SJ 129677), which encloses 20 hectares on the summit of the Clwydian range. In spite of its size it has only a single stone rampart and a ditch. In places the ditch measures 12m from bottom to top.

A fort which may well have been destroyed by the Romans there is evidence of slighting just after the Roman invasion – is **Pen-y-Corddyn-Mawr**, Llanddulas (SJ 914765). Atop a limestone outcrop east of the River Dulas, it encloses 12 hectares within

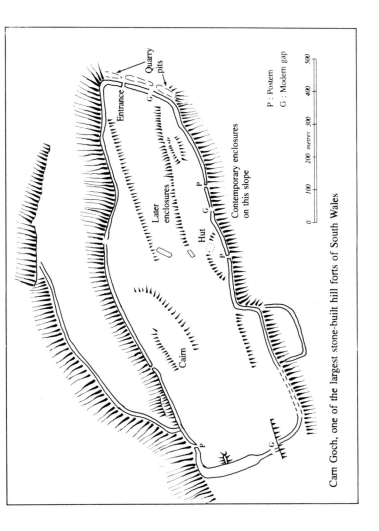

Carn Goch, one of the largest stone-built hill forts of South Wales

P : Postern
G : Modern gap

Entrance

Quarry pits

Later enclosures

Hut

Cairn

Contemporary enclosures on this slope

0   100   200 metres 300   400   500

stone-revetted ramparts. There are three entrances into the main enclosure and a spring nearby. Traces of circular dwellings have been found inside the fort. There is also an annexe of 6 hectares.

Moving into Dyfed we are in the territory of the Ordovices except in the south-west, which is the territory of the Demetae, the least known of the tribes of Wales. There is a promontory fort enclosing 2 hectares at **Bosherton** (SR 971948): this used to lie between two estuaries, which are now silted up. It is cut off by three defence lines consisting of ramparts, banks and ditches. An excavation discovered a ring-headed pin of the early Iron Age.

A stronger fort is situated at **Carn Goch**, Llandeilo (SN 691243) which encloses 10.5 hectares in a rectangular defence system. It dominated the River Towy with large dry-stone walls some 20m wide, lined with slabs of stone. The main entrance is to the north-east and there are two small gates. There are traces of a round dwelling and two later rectangular dwellings.

A centre of livestock farming was **Clegyr Boia**, St David's (SM 737252), where a rectangular fort is situated. Its ramparts contain an area 100m in length by 25m in width. The fort is on a rocky outcrop and the sides of a dwelling, dating back to neolithic times, are cut into the rocky hillside. Another neolithic house can be traced nearby. Interestingly, axes and pottery found here seem to have Irish origins.

What makes **Craig Gwrtheyrn**, Llanfihangel (SN 433402) of interest is that this small hill-fort overlooking the River Teifi had a *chevaux-de-frise* defence system. It enclosed 1.3 hectares with stone ramparts and had an entrance on the south-west with two barbicans.

Dolaucothi (SN 6640) was where the Celts mined gold by means of open cast workings and underground galleries. As soon as the Romans pacified the area they commenced to exploit the mine and a fort was established nearby (under Pumpsaint village) to protect their interests. All the visible evidence here is from the Roman occupation.

In Pembrokeshire Coast National Park, the heartland of the

Demetae, stand three promontory forts in close proximity: **Flimston Castle**, Castlemartin (SR 930946), **Crocksydam Camp** (SR 936943) and **Buckspool Down Camp** (Sr 954934). A word of warning: all are in the area of Castlemartin firing range and access is often restricted.

A fort which appears to have been occupied from about the sixth century BC into the Roman occupation is **Foel Trigarn**, Whitechurch (SN 158336). The defences enclose 1 hectare in a semicircular pattern. There are traces of circular dwellings and beads and pottery have been discovered here.

Llanddewigaer (SN 144160) and **Caerau Gaer**, 200m west, in Llanddewi Velfry, are two hill-forts of fairly slight defences.

A fort that saw its final stage of building around the first century BC stands at **Pen Dinas**, Aberystwyth (SN 584 804). It is figure-of-eight shaped and lies on a ridge between the Rivers Yswyth and Rheidol. Two hill summits are enclosed and it seems likely that the forts were separate enclosures before being joined. The ramparts were stone-faced and outlying ditches are still 3m deep. A number of circular dwellings have been traced in spite of the interior being damaged by ploughing. It is believed that the southern section was deliberately destroyed before being remodelled in the first century BC.

Another fort of interest is that which stands at **St David's Head**, St David (SM 723279). This was excavated in the nineteenth century and pottery, spindle whorls and beads were found. It appears to be a Demetae farming settlement and the enclosures east of the fort are associated with cattle-ranching. The fort itself is on the headland, enclosing 2.5 hectares within dry-stone ramparts which seem to have been 4m high and 3m wide. Within the fort seven circular dwellings averaging 7m in diameter have been found.

Crossing southward we enter the territory of one of the most famous tribes, the Silures. It was Tacitus who noted that they were physically different from most of the other tribes of Britain, being curly-haired and swarthy-skinned. From this it has been

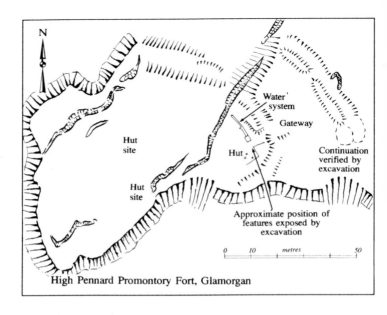

High Pennard Promontory Fort, Glamorgan

conjectured that they might have been Iberian Celts. The Severn marked their eastern boundary and they played a prominent part in trying to regain British independence from Rome. They supported Caratacos in his nine-year struggle against Roman conquest. Yet even after Caractacos' capture, Ostorius Scapula failed to quell the Silures. Indeed, for some years the Roman army could not advance beyond the east bank of the Severn. So tenacious was their opposition to the Roman conquest that the emperor was reputedly prompted to declare that he wished the Silurian tribe to be completely obliterated.

First we cross into Glamorgan, in their eastern territory. **The Bulwark** at Cheriton (SS 443927) is not a hill-fort but an agricultural settlement on the eastern tip of the Llanmadoc Hill.

Caerau, Ely, Cardiff, is a triangular fort enclosing 5 hectares in which children now play. The triple ramparts and ditches no longer rise massively as they once did. There are three entrances,

one at the western apex, one to the south and one to the east.
Some foundations for buildings have been found inside.

As might be expected, one of the best Early Celtic museums is
the **National Museum of Wales** (Amgueddfa Genedlaethol
Cymru), Cathays Park, Cardiff. Its 120-page 'Guide Catalogue of
the Early Iron Age Collections' is well worth obtaining for the
detail of its information. The pride of the museum lies in the
Abergele Hoard, the Lyn Fawr Hoard, the Tal-y-llyn Hoard and
the Llyn Cerrig Bach Hoard. It is an almost impossible task to give
a simple taste of the excellent collections of artefacts in the
museum but some especially noteworthy exhibits are: the wrought-
iron firedog from Capel Garmon, Denbigh, the bronze plaque
from Llyn Cerrig Bach, the tankard from Trawsfynydd,
Merioneth, the magnificent coin collection, the range of tools and
implements found at Llyn Cerrig Bach, the swords and spearheads
and the bronze cauldron from Llyn Fawr, Glamorgan, and the
bucket from Arthog, Merioneth. If possible, a journey in search of
the Early Celts of Wales should have its start at the National
Museum.

Another triangular fort stands on a promontory at **Castle
Ditches**, Llantwit Major (SS 960674). It is defended by three
ramparts and ditches and by the steep slopes to the north and
south.

Yet another promontory fort guards Dunraven Bay on the
Trwyn-y-Witch headland. This is **Dunraven**, St Bride's Major (SS
887728). The fort was defended by double ramparts but erosion
has destroyed much of it.

Harding's Down, Llangennith (SS 434907) consists of three
enclosures which were for stock-rearing rather than forts.
Harding's Down West is oval with traces of dwellings, one
measuring 10m in diameter. There is a rampart. Harding's Down
East seems simply a stock enclosure while to the north is a small
circular enclosure protected by a strong bank, ditch and
counterscarp.

Promontory forts are numerous in this area and **High Pennard**,
Pennard (SS 567864) is perched on cliffs which protect it to the
west and south. From landward it is defended by two lines of

rampart and ditch. The inner enclosure was for houses but outer enclosures seem to have been for stock. It was abandoned after the Roman conquest.

Another cliff fort defended by the sea is that of **The Knave**, Rhossili (SS 432864). Pottery was found in this small semi-circular fort which is protected from the landward side by double ramparts. Another promontory fort lies at **Nash Point**, Macross (SS 915684) and was reached by an old roadway.

On a rocky promontory on the western edge of the Gower peninsula, **Thurba Fort** stands in Rhossili (SS 422870). It is an oval area defended by stone ramparts which enclosed three stone dwellings, and possibly two others.

Moving into Gwent we are in the eastern border territory of the Silures. It was here that the Romans built one of their two key sites for the control of what is now Wales: the fortress of **Caerleon**(ST 3490), which they called Isca, the place of the water. The legionary fortress was established in AD 74/5 when Frontinus moved against the Silures. Caerleon in the south and Chester in the north were the major controlling forts of this turbulent area. A visit to Caerleon and its **Roman Legionary Museum** is worth while for information on life among the Silures at the time of the Roman conquest.

Caerwent (ST 4690) was, according to the Romans, the tribal capital of the Silures. They called it Venta Siluram. For the student of the Roman occupation it is considered one of the most impressive sites in the whole of Roman Britain. The **Newport Museum**, John Frost Square, Newport, has an excellent exhibition of archaeological finds from Venta Siluram.

Gwent has over thirty known hill-fort sites but most of them are obscure. The best examples are the following.

Near Caerwent, at **Llanmelin** (ST 460925), is a fort enclosing 1.2 hectares in a double rampart, ditch and counterscarp. There is also an annexe. The fort was originally built in the second century BC. The entrance was refortified around AD 50, a date coinciding with the Roman incursions into the area. By the mid-70s the hill-fort had fallen into disuse. It has been suggested that this was the Silurian capital before the Romans enforced a move to Caerwent. However, it does seem small for the principal fort of a people as strong and well organized as the Silures.

Caerau (Ponthir) is of interest for the fact that, after a short salvage dig by the Glamorgan/Gwent Archaeological Trust in 1986, traces of a circular dwelling were discovered outside the boundaries of the fort.

Coed-y-Bwynydd (Bettws Newydd) is a third-century BC fort situated above the River Usk with substantial defences enclosing 1.4 hectares.

Sudbrook Camp, Portskewett (ST 505873) was a triangular fort captured from the Silures by the Romans because of its dominant position at the constriction of the Severn estuary. Sea-cliffs protect it on the south while three ramparts and ditches defended it on the north-west and north-east side. It was built during the first century BC and numerous coins have been found dating from as early as AD 40. Roman soldiers defended it from about AD 60 until the defeat of the Silures in AD 74. The site became the western terminal of the Severn estuary ferry-crossing until the end of the Roman occupation and the latest coins found there date from AD 376.

Twyn-y-Gaer, Cwmyoy (SO 294219) is an oval fort standing 426m above sea-level and enclosing 1.8 hectares. It was first built in the fifth century BC, and over the years was refortified and expanded. The circular western section appears to have been the last area of the fort which was occupied while the other sections were abandoned.

We move north again into Powys, an area where the territories of the Silures, the Ordovices and possibly the southern Cornovii met. There are several interesting hill-forts here. At **Beacon Ring**, Trelystan (SJ 265058) stands an oval fort of 2 hectares some 408m above sea-level on the highest part of Long Mountain. It is defended by a single bank and ditch with its entrance on the south side.

Brecon Gaer (SO 0029) was, incidentally, one of the largest and

most important Roman military forts in this area and was built
during or soon after the campaign of AD 74. It was permanently
garrisoned until the end of the second century. The Romans would
appear to have utilized a Celtic roadway to **Castell Collen** (SO
0562), overlooking the river Ithon, where, again in AD 74/5, they
built another fort for an infantry garrison 1000 strong. Another
camp, this time a marching camp, at **Y Pigwn** (SN 8231) seems to
have been erected at about the same time.

The Breiddin, Bausley (SJ 292144) is of particular interest. Its
original construction was begun in the eighth century BC. It stands
overlooking the Severn some 365m above sea-level. The entrance
is from the east and it is defended by two stone ramparts with a
third to the north which is protected by a ditch. It was occupied
until the Roman conquest, being refortified several times. Many
rectangular buildings can be traced within the fort. Outside it are
signs of a Celtic field system and an enclosure for cattle. Probably
during Frontinus' attack on the Silures in AD 74, the interior of the
fort was destroyed by fire together with its entrance. The fort was
deserted for many years but was reoccupied towards the end of the
second century AD. It appears to have been lived in until the fifth
century.

Another fort which looks interesting but which has not been
excavated is that of **Burfa Camp**, Burfa (SO 290613). On a hill
above Hindwell Brook, it encloses 8 hectares within multiple
stone-revetted ramparts. There is an entrance at the north-west
protected by a second line of defences, and a second entrance on
the north-east. Forest grows over it, making excavation difficult.

Castell Dinas, Talgarth (SO 178302) controls a pass which runs
from Talgarth to Crickhowell. It has double ramparts of
considerable strength with an entrance on the north. The Normans
constructed a motte within the fort.

Standing 335m above sea-level is a circular fort with double
ramparts enclosing 8 hectares. This is **Castle Ring**, Evenjobb (SO
266636), which has its entrance at the north-west.

Cefn Carnedd, Llandinam (SO 016900) encloses 6 hectares in an
oval plan 277m above sea-level. Three ramparts protect the north
side while the steep inclines to the south-east provide natural

fortification with a single rampart. The gate is at the south-west. It seems to be a cattle-ranching centre with dykes marking off boundaries close by.

Middleton Hill carries a rather exposed contour fort on its summit. This is **Cefyn y Castell**, Middletown (SJ 306134), which encloses 0.8 hectare in an oval plan. It has two entrances, one to the north-east and the other to the south-west. On the lower north-east end of the ridge is **Bausley Hill Camp**, with multiple ramparts and a simple entrance.

Craig Rhiwarth, Llanrhaiadr (SJ 0527270) clings to a precipitous cliff which protects its southern ramparts; there is a stone wall to the north. It encloses some 16 hectares and has two entrances, one central and another to the west. Inside, there are traces of numerous circular dwellings.

Another fort crowns Table Mountain at 451m above sea-level, although it is dominated by Pen Cerrig-calch to the west. Ths is **Crug Hywell**, Llanbedr (SO 225206). It is defended by a stone rampart and ditch with counterscarp bank.

Ffridd Faldwyn, Montgomery (SO 216970) was inhabited in neolithic times but in the third century the Celts started the construction of this oval hill-fort. It continued to be refortified with timber lacing, a bridged gateway and an outline of defence. It was burnt and then rebuilt during the first century BC, being expanded to enclose 4 hectares with stone-revetted ramparts and a ditch. Parts of the original fort remained and, like the gateway, were enclosed in the new structure. Sometime during the Roman attack on this area, c. AD 74, hurried repairs seem to have been made, but the fort was abandoned. The exploratory excavation did not reveal signs of a Roman attack.

A rectangular fort stands at **Gaer Fawr**, Guilsfield Without (SJ 223130). The lines are much obscured by woodland but the fort was enclosed by three ramparts to the west and two to the east. There were two entrances, south and north-east. A statuette of a tiny bronze boar was found here dating from the period of Roman occupation.

Gaer Fawr is also the site of two circular forts at Llanelwedd (SO 058531). Both are on south-facing spurs of Carneddau, Gaer

Fawr to the west and Caer Einon to the east. Each encloses 1 hectare with Gaer Fawr being more complicated in defences.

Llanymynech Hill, Llanymynech (SJ 265220) has been claimed as Caratacos' headquarters during his nine-year fight against the Roman invasion. The reason for this is simply that it is the largest hill-fort in Wales, enclosing 57 hectares. Its steep sides provide a natural defence but on the north and east double-sided banks and ditches exist. On the west there is a single rampart, later cannibalized to construct Offa's famous dyke. Offa was the King of Mercia in the eighth century who, after a series of wars with his fellow Anglo-Saxon monarchs, dominated the English kingdom and turned his attention to the Welsh. He defeated the King of Powys, whose capital was at Pengwern. Offa pressed the men of Powys westward and Pengwern was renamed Shrewsbury. Offa then built a fortification, a dyke, stretching 130km from the Severn to the Dee (from Chepstow to a few miles south of Prestatyn), as a border between the English and the Welsh. Of course, the Welsh were pressed even further west at a later date and hence the Welsh/English border today does not follow the line of Offa's Dyke. Llanymynech Hill is badly preserved and no dwelling houses within the interior have been recognized: there is therefore no evidence to support the view (put forward by A H A Hogg, *(Hill-forts of Britain)*) that Caratacos ran his campaign against the Romans from this site. However, it is a romantic theory.

At Fennifact, **Pen-y-Crug** (SO 029303) is the name of a hill-fort north-west of Brecon. It is surrounded by three, sometimes four, banks and ditches and counterscarp, with an entrance on the south-east side.

Rhos-Maen, Glascm (SO 143579) is a circular fort 24m in diameter. The area has, unfortunately, been greatly disturbed by ploughing and there is evidence that many of the stones in the area have been moved in recent times. Local lore has it that the ramparts were fortified by several dozen large stones, but only a few remain today.

At **Welshpool** you will find the Powysland Museum, affiliated to the National Museum of Wales, which houses the collection of one of the oldest antiquarian societies in Wales – the Powysland Club (founded in 1867). As there is no full-time curator, hours of opening are variable, but the museum has some fascinating exhibits from the period, including fragments of shields and decorated plaques from Moel Hiraddug.

Chapter 9

Scotland (Alba)

There is little doubt that some of the best-preserved and most spectacular remains of the Early Celtic period are to be found in Scotland. Here the Celts built structures that have outlasted the ravages of man and time: great stone buildings whose average wall thickness is over 3m. While stone-robbing over the centuries is much in evidence, as new generations used the old materials for their own buildings, a lot of the early Celtic structures remain in relatively excellent condition. Forts dating from the eighth century BC, in varying designs and sizes, are still to be found with, interestingly, high-density concentrations in the southern Scottish counties especially within the vicinity of Hadrian's Wall. Many of these were obviously built or refortified to keep out the Romans. But Scotland has other remains not found in profusion elsewhere in Britain.

The broch is peculiar to Scotland and its islands. Indeed, as discussed in the Introduction, only a dozen of the 500-600 brochs noted have been found outside northern and western Scotland and the northern isles. Some of them still stand to a height of 12-15m, being 9-12m in internal diameter with walls 3m thick.

Another feature here are duns, not to be confused with a fort (also called *dun*, the Celtic word for a fort) but meaning fortified homesteads.

Then there are crannogs, lake dwellings, circular timber-framed houses protected by the water, some of them 15m in diameter. They are assigned to the first century BC or first century AD and many are found in southern Scotland. The reason for these striking remains of the early Celtic period is obvious; Scotland was not occupied by the Romans to any great extent. Its fortresses and settlements were not destroyed to the same degree as those in the south. Similarly, Scotland missed the destruction wreaked on Celtic Britain by the incoming Anglo-Saxons.

Scotland, like Wales, remains, in part anyway, a Celtic country conscious of its Celtic heritage. By the early eighth century AD, the Brythonic and Goidelic Celtic kingdoms which had emerged in Scotland were united under the High Kingship of Aonghus Mac Fearghus of the Tuath Cruithin (the Picts). The country was consolidated under Coinneach Mac Alpin (822–860) and by the eleventh century, the Brythonic Celtic language of the southern areas of Scotland had given way to the Goidelic (or Gaelic) language. But Scotland as a united Goidelic-speaking country did not last long, for the Anglicization process started early, English being adopted by the Scottish monarchy by the thirteenth century. Although Robert Bruce is on record as holding the last all-Gaelic-speaking parliament at Ardchattan in 1308, and James IV (1488–1513) is recorded as the last Scottish monarch to speak Gaelic, English replaced Gaelic as the language of the royal court and this practice permeated through all strata of Scottish society.

Scotland remained a totally independent kingdom until 1603 when the Anglicized James VI was invited to ascend the throne of England as James I and the 'Union of Crowns' took place. Scotland continued to be self-governing until 1707 when the kingdoms of Scotland and England united into the United Kingdom of Great Britain. The uprisings which manifested themselves in the century following the Union led to the vigorous repression of the Scottish Gaelic language and its culture, especially in the wake of the 1745 uprising. Indeed, the Celtic language of Scotland, with its attendant culture, became one of the worst oppressed languages in Europe and every effort was made to eradicate it.

However, internal pressures within Scotland were intent on destroying Scotland's Celtic character long before the Union – pressures which received impetus from the Reformation which, from a Gaelic viewpoint, was a great engine for cultural genocide in the country. Gaelic was driven back towards western Scotland and today (according to the 1981 Census) only 1.6 per cent of the Scottish population (79,309), mostly in the western islands, still speak the Celtic language.

But the Romans had little success in subduing the Celts of Scotland, which the Romans called Caledonia. In the spring or summer of AD 79, the year after his devastation of the Ordovices of North Wales, the Roman governor Agricola turned north, pushing through the territory of the Brigantes up to the Tyne-Solway line. It was here, probably at Corbridge (Corstoptium), that he went into winter quarters before commencing his attempted conquest of the northern region. His campaigns lasted five years but were not conclusive. His son-in-law Tacitus tells us that in about AD 82, Agricola welcomed an Irish chieftain to his headquarters, a chieftain who had been driven from Ireland by 'rebellion'. Agricola decided to keep the Irishman as a 'hostage', 'nominally a friend, he might be used as a pawn in the game,' comments Tacitus cynically. Agricola was to tell his son-in-law that Ireland could have been reduced with one legion. However, even the many legions he had at his disposal had not been able to control Scotland.

With the new campaign against the Caledonian tribes, Agricola advanced with two armies and these converged at the Forth estuary. Marching camps have been found near Birrens, at Torwood Muir (near Lockerbie), Castledykes and Loudoun Hill, where pottery of Agricola's time has dated the Roman forts. Time was running short for Agricola, if he wanted to achieve a reputation as the general who brought Caledonia under the *pax Romana*. He had completed his four-year term of office as governor and the new emperor, Domitian (who had succeeded his brother Titus Vespassian who died in AD 81), wanted detachments of the IX Hispana and II Adiutrix to be sent to Germany. Agricola could not spare the troops and a lot of prevarication went on. Clinging determinedly to the task, in AD 83 he began a sixth campaign, and it is only now that we learn the name of the Celtic leader against whom he was fighting. The man was Calgacos, the swordsman, who had welded the Caledonian tribes into a formidable fighting force. During this campaign of AD 83 the Celts exerted heavy pressure against the Romans, attacking their marching forts and supply lines. It seems that Calgacos was trying to cut off the Romans from their bases. Agricola split his army into three, so as to avoid encirclement, according to his son-in-law. The Celtic chieftain merely picked the weakest of the columns, the one containing the IX Hispana, and attacked it just before dawn. Only the timely arrival of Agricola himself, with another of his columns, saved the day.

Agricola withdrew south. But, still determined to conquer the north, he decided on another campaign in AD 84. The XX were in winter quarters at Inchtuhill, in Perthshire. The IX Hispana and II Adiutrix were ordered from their quarters at York and Chester and moved north again. Agricola sent a fleet up the coast to 'spread uncertainty and terror' about a landing. Unlike previous campaigns, Calgacos now decided to face the Romans in a set battle. The site of this battle has never been identified successfully: it was called Mons Graupius, the Graupian Hill, by the Romans. Agricola estimated the Celts to number 30,000 against his 20,000 Romans. The Romans, in their accounts, always liked to increase the odds against them. Tacitus puts an interesting speech into the mouth of Calgacos, a speech which even Shakespeare might have envied. It contains many famous lines, but one especially 'They create a desert and call it peace!' was a cry which many a colonial people were to echo. The battle was long and bloody and Tacitus says that 10,000 Celts fell that day compared with 367 Romans. One must forgive Tacitus a slight exaggeration.

Agricola was now firmly called back to Rome. The Romans, however, did not follow up their success and make an effort to pacify the Caledonian tribes. In fact, Roman garrison troops in the new province of Britain were reduced to only three legions in AD 86. By AD 105 any pretence that Roman rule was established in Caledonia was given up and the frontier was fixed from coast to coast from Carlisle to South Shields. Indeed, around AD 118 the Brigantes with the Novantae and Selgovae of southern Scotland rose up. In AD 122, when the uprising had been crushed, the emperor Hadrian visited Britain and, as a consequence of his visit, a wall was constructed to mark the northern border of Roman-occupied Britain with independent Caledonia. It stretched for 117 km.

In AD 138, however, a new emperor, Antoninus Pius, determined to extend the northern boundary and sent the governor Lollius Urbicus into Caledonia. He pushed as far north

as the Forth-Clyde isthmus and there constructed a second
wall the Antonine Wall, a continuous rampart stretching from sea
to sea with a series of forts and a road on its southern side. It
differed from Hadrian's Wall chiefly in having a more simple
design and less elaborate structure. It was only 60 km miles long,
from Bridgeness to Old Kilpatrick.

Britain was not an easy province to hold. There was always
unrest and insurrection. In AD 154, the Brigantes were again in
revolt and were not subdued until the following year. In AD 180
the Celts of Caledonia swept across the Antonine Wall and pushed
back the Romans to Hadrian's Wall, already damaged by the
attack of the Brigantes on the south. Ulpius Marcellus was sent to
deal with the uprising and managed to regain the Antonine Wall
and refortify it, but soon after this, the Antonine Wall was
abandoned. There was no peace in northern Britain: either in
Caledonia or in the land of the Brigantes, uprisings against the
Romans continued through the third century AD. It was not until
213 that the Romans made a complete withdrawal from Caledonia.
However, as late as 367/8 Theodosius led the last invasion
attempted by the Romans into Caledonia.

Before considering the remains we should address ourselves to
the myth of the Picts, for ever since the Caledonians were called
Picti ('the painted ones') by those Roman soldiers serving in the
garrisons of Hadrian's Wall, this people has been the subject of
countless myths and misconceptions. Indeed, many people still
think of them as a people separate from the Celts. The term 'Pict'
was first recorded in a Latin poem of AD 297 and it was simply a
nickname given to some of the Celtic warriors who, in order to
give themselves a more fearsome appearance in war, painted or
tattooed their bodies: *Picti* is the past participle of the Latin
pingere, to paint.

The Picts were not a new element among the Celtic tribes of
Scotland. It would be as if someone started an argument 2000
years from now that there lived in England a different group of
people to the English called 'Limeys'. From Roman references it
appears that a process of tribal confederation was taking place,
perhaps as a direct result of their attempted invasions. Smaller

tribes, seeking protection from the Roman incursions, united in political unions with larger tribes. The Caledonii and the Maecatae became the centre of such unions and both these tribal confederations had, by the end of the third century AD, been labelled as Picti by the Romans. They appeared to call themselves Priteni, which in Gaelic became Cruthin, if one remembers the famous substitute of 'qc' for the 'p' sound.

Professor Kenneth Jackson points out that there are no texts extant in a 'Pictish language' and that both the king-lists in Latin and the place-names are unquestionably Celtic moreover, they are P-Celtic (i.e. Brythonic). However, within a few centuries after the Roman period, a switch had been made by the Picts to Goidelic (Gaelic) Celtic; certainly by the time the historical record of the Pictish kings begins in the eighth century, they were absorbed into a Gaelic culture. There is an intriguing reference to Pictish literacy in the eighth century, but if any distinctive Pictish illustrated manuscripts or annals were produced they must have fallen foul of the destructive zeal of the Reformation.

The remarkable group of incised and carved boulders and stones which are classified as 'Pictish Symbol Stones' are now attributed to a late period the seventh to ninth centuries AD and so, for the purposes of this guide, do not concern us. However, the symbolic designs and animals used on the stones are very Celtic. The stylistic links with Irish illuminated manuscripts are obvious while the designs of animals are comparable to some of the animal statuettes found in other parts of the Celtic world.

It was because, then, of Caledonia's different history, compared with that of Roman-occupied southern Britain, and the fact that it grew into an independent Celtic kingdom which lasted until modern times, with a Celtic language still being spoken in north-western areas and the islands, that Celtic sites here remained in a better state of preservation than those in southern Britain. The spread of great urban areas and a high-density population has not contributed to the same degree of destruction as in the south.

Because of the wealth of remains in Scotland, I have decided to divide this chapter into six parts. I have found it more convenient to keep to the old Scottish county system for itineraries and have divided the area of Central Scotland between the North-west and North-east sections.

a. Southern Scotland

Berwick, East Lothian, Midlothian, West Lothian, Peebles Selkirk, Roxburgh, Dumfries, Lanark, Renfrew, Ayr, Kirkcudbright and Wigtown

In Berwick we are in the territory of the Votadini, whose lands stretched through Northumbria along the east coast into Berwick and the Lothians and also into the neighbouring counties of Peebles, Selkirk and Roxburgh. At **Edinshall**, Berwick (NT 772603), lying on the north-east flank of Cockburn Law, is a hill-fort enclosed in two ramparts, 135m by 73m with an entrance to the south-west. The fort dates from the first century BC. However, inside the fort, in the early second century AD, a broch was built, 16m in diameter with walls 5m thick, containing three sets of chambers. About this time a settlement was also constructed, as we can see from the circular stone foundations to the north-west area of the court.

A fort and settlement lie at **Marygold Hill Plantation**, Berwick (NT 806605). The fort is oval in shape and was built around the first or second century BC, according to pottery finds. With its double ramparts, it seems to have been used as an open settlement at a later time.

Codingham Loch, Berwick (NT 899688) also has a fort and settlement. There are traces of several circular stone houses and it seems that the settlement sprang up in the second century AD.

On the summit of Tun Law, standing at over 150m, is **Earn's Heugh** (NT 892691). Built in about the first century BC, the fort contains several circular stone foundations; in the settlement materials date from AD 150–400.

A promontory fort near Cockburnspath, **Dean Castle** (NT 808702), is guarded by two ramparts and ditches and precipitous slopes on three sides. Another fort stands at **Habchester** (NT

944588), oval in shape, but much obliterated by ploughing. Also oval in shape is **Addinston**, Carfraemill (NT 523536) which stands prominently on the skyline above Addinston Farmhouse and is enclosed by two strong ramparts. Several circular stone foundations lie within the fort; one measures 11m in diameter.

Nearby is a fort defended by two heavy ramparts which stands at **Longcroft**, Carfraemill (NT 532543). Inside, the circular stone house foundations indicate that the fort was still in occupation in the second and third centuries AD.

Double ramparts with external ditches enclose an area 132m in diameter at **Blackchester** (NT 508504) near Lauder. There is also a settlement here with several stone houses.

Finally, near Cambridge, is **Haerfaulds** (NT 574500), a fort and settlement. The fort stands on open moorland and is still impressive, dominating the Blythe Water. It is oval in shape, measuring 116m by 73m; one wall is still 4.5m thick. The attached settlement has a number of stone circular foundations, about 1m thick. It was occupied in the second century AD.

To the north we enter the Lothians, East, Mid – and West Lothian. The Lothian counties must not be confused with the old kingdom of 'Lothian'. In the sixth century AD groups of Angles and Flemings began to settle around the mouth of the River Tweed and to impose their rule on the Brythonic Celts in this area. The kingdom they established was called Bernica but the Celts called it Leudduniawn or Lothian. With its ruling class of Angles and its peasant class of Celts, the southern part of Bernica disappeared into the kingdom of Northumbria while the northern part, that area north of the Tweed, became Berwick. The evidence is that this kingdom of Bernica did not stretch much beyond the Lammermuir Hills. The modern-day Lothian counties therefore merely echo the name of Leudduniawn and do not occupy the same area.

On the border of Berwick and East Lothian we encounter **North Berwick Law** (NT 555842), a fort which occupies one of the most dramatic sites in the country. It stands at an elevation of 152m and encloses an area of 152m by 91.5m. Unfortunately, in spite of the views, its remains are scanty. Three ramparts can be detected and the traces of numerous circular foundations. On the south toe of the hill, now obliterated by a quarry, stood an enclosure, possibly for cattle. Several Iron Age artefacts were found here.

Kaeheughs, just north of Haddington (NT 518763), is a fort standing at the east end of the Garleton Hills. The eastern part is no longer in existence, sheered off by quarrying. The remainder is sizeable enough, measuring 140m by 70m within three ramparts. Traces of timber-framed houses have been discovered here.

The point of interest about **The Chesters**, standing 1.6km south of Drem (NT 507782), is that it is overlooked from an outcrop 15m above it from which the most simple bowman or stone-slinger could direct missiles into the interior of the fort. Yet the interior fortifications enclose 116m by 45.75m, defended by a series of complicated ramparts and ditches. The overall defences cover an area 274.5m by 152.5m. Circular stone foundations of houses of varying sizes have been discovered inside. It was still occupied in the second century AD.

3.2km south-east of East Linton stands **Traprain Law** (NT 581746), built in the fifth century BC and occupied until the Angles began to establish themelves in this area. Rising 152.5m above the plain north of the Lammermuir massif and enclosing 16 hectares, this is thought to have been the capital of the Votadini. Archaeologists have recovered a great wealth of Celtic material and a spectacular hoard of Roman silver from the fort. It is thought that it underwent several major reconstructions over a lengthy period in which several sets of defensive works were erected.

When the Romans arrived, the Votadini city, for such it was, had reached its final form and covered 16 hectares. Its inhabitants were variously employed in agriculture, stock-breeding, trading and metal-working. The fact that the main rampart was rebuilt in the first century AD indicates that it was probably refortified as news of Agricola's invasion reached the inhabitants. Some archaeologists have suggested that it was reconstructed twice more, coinciding with the attacks on the Romans in AD 197 and 297.

If, as some writers claim, the Votadini of Traprain Law

Part of the Traprian Treasure: a vast hoard of silverware found at Traprian Law, an East Lothian hillfort, in 1919. It dates to the late fourth century

concluded a treaty with the Romans and as a result were left to their own devices, under Roman supervision, the fort would have had a unique position in the Roman province.

There are traces that the defences were reorganized once more, late in the Roman period, to enclose only 12 hectares, and that this was the area held when the Angles began their invasions of the district.

Blackcastle Hill (NT 712718), south-west of Innerwick, is a fort which was constructed to protect a number of circular stone houses in the sixth or fifth centuries BC. The area, enclosed by stone ramparts, covers 51m by 45m.

Gifford is the centre of numerous interesting forts. Indeed, few other areas have such a concentration of forts and the question inevitably arises as to why this is so. This was a high-density population centre for its time and, of course, the most northern territory of the Votadini. Only further excavation could answer the question. **Kidlaw** (NT 512642) to the south-west is an excellent circular fort some 113m in diameter, enclosed in three ramparts with external ditches. Homesteads have been found in the interior and dated to the first century AD. Nearby is a promontory fort called **Stobshiel** (NT 497638), which is isolated on the east and north by Birns Water and on the south-west by a steep gully. Ramparts protect the north-west and the north-east, where there are also an outer rampart and external ditch. At one point the rampart is 9m thick and 4.5m high. In the same area is **Witches Knowe** (NT 519635), a hill-fort surrounded by three ramparts, the innermost being 3.5m thick. There is an external ditch and the area enclosed is 103m by 42m. To the south of Gifford is another fort called **The Castles, Dumbadam Burn** (NT 531642). This is a multivallate promontory fort set in an angle of the Dumbadan. It is oval, measuring 91.5m by 45.75m. Much of its stonework is missing. The interior has been ploughed and no remains have been discovered here.

To the east of Gifford stands **Harelaw** (NT 546632), a substantial fort on a rocky summit on a north-east spur of the Lammermuir Hills. It is at an elevation of 381m and permits an extensive view over the East Lothian plains. The timber-laced stone walls are still about 3.5m thick, although there is much evidence of stone-robbing. It is now hard to estimate the original enclosure but it would probably have been 61m by 30.5m. Traces of other ramparts and ditches can be seen and the only entrance is from a narrow pathway to the west.

South-east of Gifford is **Park Burn** (NT 571652), a fort that has been greatly damaged by ploughing. It would seem to have measured 57m by 49m with the inner rampart being 6m wide, protected by two outer ramparts and ditches. Close by is **Black Castle** (NT 580662), a circular fort about 116m by 107m, enclosed within two ramparts and a median ditch. As with Park Burn, the inner rampart is 6m thick. There are entrances on the west and south marked by causeways across the ditch. **Green Castle** (NT 582657) is also south-east of Gifford. It is a triangular fort on the right bank of Newlands Burn, measuring 68m with a base of 58m within double ramparts. The entrance is at the west apex. The interior is almost featureless.

The final fort in this vicinity is **Friar's Nose** (NT 664632), some 14km east-south-east of Gifford. This is another promontory fort lying between the Whiteadder Water and Killmade Burn, which forms the boundary between East Lothian and Berwick. Four ramparts survive on the west while at the north-west the lines of the ramparts have been confused over the years and may be the result of two differing periods of construction. Two stone foundations of houses stand in the north-west; it is thought that these dwellings were built at a later date than the rest of the fort, perhaps after the Roman invasion.

At a distance of 3.2km south-east of Garvald stands **White Castle** (NT 613686), another promontory fort easily approachable from the south. The fort measures 70m by 54m with three lines of ramparts, still rising in one place to 2.5m in height. To the south of Garvald is **Garvald Mains** (NT 583698) which is situated on a plateau on the right bank of the Papana Water. It is protected to the south and west by steep inclines. The fort is circular in plan within a strong single rampart. There are no signs of remains here.

To the south-east of Garvald stands **The Hopes** (NT 570636), a defence work which is both large and complex. Ramparts and external ditches form an arc to the north-west, 30.5m in length, reaching the ends of a steep ridge which is bordered by a bank and ditch. Other ramparts and ditches proliferate in complicated patterns. There has been little excavation here although it is thought that the fort – if fort it is, and not merely a fortified settlement – was built in two phases.

A few kilometers east of Stenton is **The Chesters** (NT 660739), a large circular bivallate fort which has been robbed of much of its stonework over the years. The interior has been destroyed by ploughing. Yet this was surely an impressive fortress, being 106m in diameter within what was once two strong ramparts with external ditches. The inner rampart once spread to a width of 18m and is still 2m high, while the outer rampart was 14m wide and 1.5m high. The entrance is in the east-south-east, and the western entrance may also be original.

Moving west into Midlothian, the principal place to make for is **Edinburgh**, the capital of Scotland, where the fourth-largest defended settlement in Scotland is situated. This is **Arthur's Seat** (NT 275728), strictly speaking the name of the highest peak of the hill which occupies most of The King's Park. However, Crow Hill, a subsidiary peak, is also part of the fort, which enclosed some 8 hectares. The only easy approach to this fort is from the east, now blocked by the ruins of two formidable stone walls. Because the interior has been ploughed, no traces of dwellings have been uncovered. Also in The King's Park is **Dunsapie** (NT 282731), a fort on the summit of a rocky hill on the east side of Dunsapie Loch. The ramparts have been robbed of much stone but the fort seems to have enclosed an area of 106m by 61m and several platforms indicate the presence of timber-framed houses dating to the early Iron Age.

Another strategic site in the city is, of course, **Castle Hill**, around which the modern city has grown. Edinburgh became Scotland's capital by a decree of David I in 1124. Up to this date, Scone (Sgàin) had been the capital. The castle which was built on the hill has obliterated any earlier Celtic fort but we know that in the sixth century AD Dinas Eidyn (Eidyn's fort) stood here and was the capital of a Celtic tribe called Y Gododdin, perhaps a sept or development of the Votadini. When the area became part of Alba, and Goidelic Celtic replaced the Brythonic Celtic form as the language, it was Gaelicized as Dùn Eadainn, which was eventually Anglicized to Edinburgh. It was Symeon of Durham who created a popular myth by miswriting it as Edwinesburgh, causing people to think that the city had been founded by the Angles under a king named Edwine.

From Dinas Eidyn, the court of Mynyddawg Mwynvawr, ruler

of the Gododdin, some 300 warriors went on a raid in an attempt to drive the Angles out of Caertraeth (Catterick, in Yorkshire). The attack failed and the warriors were slain. We have a record of this event in *Llyr Aneurin* (The Book of Aneurin), the writings of a sixth-century poet who lived at Dinas Eidyn. '*Y Gododdin*' is one of the most famous 'Welsh' poems (i.e. written in Brythonic Celtic) and contains the first reference anywhere to Arthur. It is perhaps confusing to some, with little knowledge of the history of Britain at this time, that the first poetry in what is now regarded as Welsh was actually written in this area of Scotland. Taliesin and also Llywarch Hen (to whom some poems have been ascribed because they are about him) were born and brought up in lowland Scotland when Brythonic Celtic was still the language there.

Edinburgh is, of course, the centre for the **National Museums of Scotland**; the *Royal Museum of Scotland*, Queen Street, contains one of the most extensive and remarkable collections of Early Celtic artefacts. Perhaps the most famous items are the Deskford Carnyx, the Torrs Chemfrein, the massive snake armlets, the famous collar from Stitchhill, a gold torque terminal from Netherurd plus the selection of dragonesque brooches. There are also some excellent mirrors and ornaments from Galloway.

16km south-south-west of Edinburgh are the remains of a settlement at **Braidwood** (NT 193596), situated on a low hill forming part of the Pentland massif. The earliest buildings were all timber constructions within enclosures, some of the enclosures plainly being used for stock. The original palisade was later strengthened and a ditch was also built. New buildings were erected: a dozen or so timber-framed houses. It is estimated that the settlement was occupied from the first century BC to the first or second century AD.

Castle Law stands 5km south-west of Fairmilehead (NT 229638). It was refortified immediately before the arrival of the Romans in AD 80. The interesting feature of this fort is a well-preserved souterrain (fogou in Cornish). Traces of occupation until the third century AD have been discovered. Nearby, just 6.5km south-west of Fairmilehead, is **Lawhead** (NT 216622) which seems to have been built in the sixth or fifth century BC. It is only 3.2km from

Braidwood settlement and whether there is a connection is a matter of speculation. Traces of two timber-framed houses have been found in the interior but it is thought that several more could be discovered.

Just west of Balerno, **Dalmahoy Hill** (NT 135669) and **Kaimes Hill** (NT 130665) stand on twin summits. Both forts are thought to date from the first century AD and to have been occupied during the Roman period. However, the defence works of both mark them as of earlier construction. Dalmahoy Hill encloses an area of 366m by 122m, with an inner enclosure of 42m by 26m. A gold cup was found here with several fragments of moulds. Kaimes Hill encloses an area of 168m by 67m within a stone wall 3m thick. Outworks increase the defended area to a size of 305m by 122m. Kaimes seems to have been occupied well after the Roman period.

There are two more forts south of Pathhead. **Longfaugh** (NT 404617) is a circular fort with concentric ramparts of earth, faced with stone and timber. The fort stands on the main Roman supply route to Inveresk. There seems to have a Roman post here as there are some building stones with Roman carving on them which are built into an adjacent souterrain of obviously post-Roman date. The other fort, a little to the south of this one, is **Crichton** (NT 384618), which is dated to the seventh or eighth century BC. It is at the west end of the village of Crichton and has a single rampart standing 1m above the interior.

Four forts and a settlement form a group to the north of Stow. **Middle Hill** (NT 444519) is 6.4km north and has been designated a settlement although there are no traces of dwellings here. However, the circular plan, 26m in diameter, with shadow ramparts and a median ditch, recalls the palisade settlements in other locations. A digression here to a point 3.2km south of Stow leads to a broch which stands at **Bow** (NT 461416), also known as Bow Castle. It is one of the ten Tay-Tweed brochs, situated 3.2km north of its fellow at Torwoodlee (q.v.). Originally the broch's internal diameter was 10m with walls 5m thick. Pottery, including some Roman pieces, was found here together with a Celtic bronze brooch of a cock.

Of the four forts, the **Hodge Cairn** (NT 409514) stands further to the north-west than the settlement. It is the southernmost of a group which lay in the angle between the Heriot and Gala Waters. Oval in plan, it has two concentric ramparts some 12m apart with a median ditch. It measures 122m by 76m. The inner rampart still stands 3m higher than the ditch. The next in this cluster is **Halltree Rings** (NT 400519), crowning a summit 335m above sea-level between the Heriot and Gala Waters. This fort is circular and 79m in diameter. The entrance is at the west and the rampart rises 3m above the ditch level. The interior has been ploughed so that no traces of interior buildings can be discerned. **Corsehope Rings** (NT 392519), while designated a fort, actually covers a considerable area and may well have been a fortified settlement. The interior of the defence system has been ploughed but it is still possible to distinguish a score or so of circular house sites. The final fort in this area is an oval one at **Heriot Station** (NT 406547) which, unfortuantely, has been levelled by the plough and robbed of its stones. Originally it measured about 76m by 61m within two ramparts with a meridian ditch. It is thought that the forts in this area were of the Selgovae, bordering the country of the Votadini.

West Lothian has three forts of interest. **Craigie Hill**, just west of Cramond Bridge (NT 153757) is on a ridge. It measures 222m by 55m its east side marked only by the precipitous face of the hill. The other three perimeters are defended by three ramparts. The most interesting point about this fort is the interior foundations of several circular stone dwellings, measuring from 6m to 8.5m in diameter. There is another oval enclosure to the north of the fort. **Cockleroy** (NS 989745) is south of Linlithgow and occupies a very conspicuous position on a hill; it encloses an area of 125m by 61m. The entrance is in the south-east. It is similar to the structure on **Bowden Hill** (NS 977745) 1.5km to the west. Unfortunately, Bowden Hill has lost many of its stones but parts of its walls remain impressive.

Moving south to Peebles we are in another area which was very densely populated in the Early Celtic period. This is the central territory of the Selgovae. Within Peebles the remains of eighteen forts, three settlements and four homesteads are worthy of note.

To the north of Eddleston is **Northshield Rings** (NT 257493), enclosed in three ramparts and ditches and measuring 73m by 64m. It is fairly well preserved and lies on a ridge which dominates the valley of Eddleston Water.

There are two forts known as **Cademuir Hill** (NT 220375 and NT 224370). The first is on the south-west ridge of Cademuir Hill dominating the valley of the River Tweed and of Manor Water. It encloses 3 hectares within a single stone rampart with entrances at the north-east and south-west. Traces of between thirty and forty dwellings of the timber-framed variety have been found. The fort seems to date from the early Iron Age but to have been abandoned with the coming of the Romans. The second fort, a smaller stone-built one, stands on a minor summit of the same ridge, about 0.8km from its larger neighbour. This one encloses an area 70m by 46m, and it has some substantial fortifications including a stone *chevaux de frise*. Traces of several timber-framed houses have been found here. It is dated to the early Iron Age.

To the north-west of Peebles itself is the **White Meldon** (NT 219427). This was once an impressive fort on the summit of the hill, rising 427m above sea-level. The main enclosure measures 213m by 152m within two ramparts. Sadly, it has been almost obliterated in places. Traces of timber-framed houses can be discerned in the interior. Nearby is **Harehope** (NT 203448), the remains of a palisaded settlement within a rectangular earthwork. Remains of timber-framed houses were found here and it was thought that the earliest house was built in the Late Bronze Age. The settlement was occupied from that time through to the coming of the Romans. Overlooking the settlement is **Harehope Rings** (NT 196445) at an elevation of 396m above sea-level. This is a circular fort, 58m in diameter, with two ramparts and a median ditch. There are two entrances. Surface traces of a dozen timber-framed houses can be discerned. Also in the vicinity is **Green Knowe** (NT 212434), an unenclosed platform settlement on the east face of Green Knowe at an elevation of 274.5m. There are nine platforms: the fourth from the north, when excavated, showed a circular timber-framed house 8m in diameter. Some fifty pieces of pottery were found, from which was recreated a tall vessel datable to the fourth century BC.

Romannobridge has two forts to the south. **Henderland Hill** (NT 149459) lies south-west. It is an oval fort measuring 67m by 42m enclosed in two ramparts with external ditches. The inner rampart rises to 3.5m above the ditch and the outer to 2.7m. It has been possible to detect a few timber-framed houses within the fort and date it to the seventh or sixth century BC. However, much has been destroyed by ploughing and by the use of the fort for public and private celebrations. The second fort is **Whiteside Hill** (NT 168461) to the south-east of Romannobridge. This is a circular fort measuring 73m in diameter and it is thought to be one of the best preserved and most impressive forts in southern Scotland. It is situated on an eastern spur of the hill over the valley of the Lyne Water and dominates the area. Excavations show that it was built in four phases and that timber-framed houses stood in the interior.

Ladyurd Rings (NT 152424) stands 3.2km south-east of Blyth Bridge on high ground commanding the confluence of the Tarth Water and Lyne Water. Two strong ramparts (still standing to a height of 2m) enclose an area about 55m in diameter. Ploughing and the removal of stones have made it rather featureless.

Broughton is a centre for four forts and several settlements, probably because of its strategic position dominating the Broughton valley which was a main route through to the north. To the north-west is **Langlaw Hill** (NT 100382). Standing 152.5m above the valley of Broughton Burn and dominating the view in all directions, incuding the whole of the Biggar Gap, this fort crowns the hill with rampart and ditch. At Broughton itself **Helm End** (NT 110353) is both fort and settlement, occupying a ridge dividing the Biggar and Holms Waters and commanding the eastern end of Biggar Gap and the route through the valley. Two ramparts form the oval fort, 104m by 82m. The settlement lies within the defence works of the fort and at least five stone-walled circular dwellings have been found.

South-west of Broughton is **Chester Rig** (NT 099320), another fort and settlement. It is situated on a protrusion from Blakehope Head commanding the south side of the Holms Water. Two ramparts with a median ditch contain an area 55m in diameter. Within this circular fort some eight stone-built houses, three of

which have been well preserved, have been found. Nearby is
Glenachan Rig (NT 106328) which is a palisade settlement in which
three timber-framed houses were found. One of these, which is
6.5m in diameter, was excavated and dated to the early Iron Age
period.

To the south-east of Broughton is the last fort in this complex.
This is **Dreva Craig** (NT 126353). It overlooks the bend of the
River Tweed at Drumelzier above its confluence with the Biggar
Burn. It commands the eastern end of the Biggar Gap. Two stone
ramparts enclose an area of 58m by 43m. The fort has a *chevaux
de frise* to the south-west of the outer wall formed by stones.
Traces of settlements can be found on the north-west face of the
hill below the fort and several circular stone dwelling foundations
have been discerned here but not excavated.

West-south-west of Broughton is **Parkgatstone Hill** (NT 083353),
which is a small settlement between Biggar Water and Kilbucho
Burn. The remains of four timber-framed houses can be traced in
a circular enclosure 49m in diameter. This has been severely
damaged by ploughing.

Just north-east of Drumelzier is **Henry's Brae** (NT 139339), a
fort enclosing at least thirty timber-framed houses, but ploughing
in part of the fort seems to have ruined any prospect of finding
more. A rampart runs for 244m but the single stone wall has been
robbed of most of its stones. Nearby stands **Tinnis Castle** (NT
141344) which occupies a ridge on the lower slope of Venlaw and
contains the ruins of a medieval castle which has destroyed the
interior; the oval outer ramparts of 61m by 26m can be seen and
recognized as a timber-laced stone wall. Outside this, two more
ramparts and some minor defence works are discernible. Here also
is **Drumelzier Ford** (NT 123327), near an old ford across the
Tweed where three timber-framed houses were found in a circular
stone enclosure.

Kerr's Knowe (NT 182384), north of Stobo, sits on the summit
of an isolated hill and has the distinction of being enclosed in no
fewer than six ramparts. The interior measures 91.5m by 53m with
an entrance at the west. The entrance is inturned and this is one of
the most well defended structures in the country.

Biggar forms a centre for visits to three fortifications. To the south-east stands **White Fort** (NT 055338). It is 396.5m above sea-level and is a contour fort. The earliest enclosure was entirely of wood, with two ditches. They were replaced as new ramparts were started but these were never completed. The fort encloses roughly 122m by 73m. Nearby stands **Mitchelhill Rings** (NT 062341) which is a circular fort some 52m in diameter. This is on the north-east extremity of White Hill. It has been robbed of much of its stone but traces of its ramparts are evident. The last fort in this series is **Muirburn Castle** (NT 090412) 8km north-east of Biggar. Two concentric ramparts enclose a circular area 76m in diameter.

An interesting settlement is that of **Caerlee Hill** (NT 324367), which is just west of Innerleithen. While the settlement has been almost destroyed by quarrying, its boundaries can be seen around a small inner enclosure of 61m by 45m with traces of timber-framed houses, of which only six survive the quarrying. Excavations produced penannular bracelets with expanded terminals. These have been dated to the Late Bronze Age.

Selkirk has only two forts of interest. The one at **Torwoodlee**, Galashiels (NT 475381) has suffered from mutilation by quarrying. The fort, which encloses an area 140m by 107m, seems to have been occupied by the Selgovae until AD 80 when Agricola overran the area. The fort was sacked and its defences were destroyed. A lot of material, left by the Romans during their brief occupation, has been found. However, in about AD 100, before Hadrian's Wall was constructed, the Celts returned to build a broch, one of the ten brochs known to be situated in the area, on the ruins of the inner ramparts of the fort. In AD 140, when the Romans returned, they knocked down the broch and scattered its stones.

The second interesting fort is also in the neighbourhood of Galashiels. **The Rink** (NT 480327) is an oval fort some 152.5m by 91.5m within a single rampart. It lies on a ridge and traces of several rectangular buildings have been found there.

Crossing south into Roxburghshire we find that the closer we are to the Roman wall the more numerous the defence systems become. The reason for this is obvious and quite logical. A fortress of the Selgovae can be found at **Eildon Hill North**, south-

Traprian fluted bowl. Much of the silverwork from Traprian Law had been hammered down, probably by pirates, ready for the melting pot

east of Melrose (NT 555328): this appears to have been abandoned during the first Roman invasion of the area under Agricola in AD 80. Three different periods of construction have been discerned, with signs of timber-framed houses. The two main ramparts enclose up to 16 hectares. The Romans must have pushed out the occupants and built a signal station within the ramparts, doubtless contented with a fort and supply base they had built at the foot of the hill.

At **Little Trowpenny**, near Ancrum (NT 631256) is a promontory fort which is almost circular with a diameter of about 60m. The remains of a stone wall rampart can be seen: this was about 4m thick with an eastern entrance. Three additional ramparts protect it. Nearby are the substantial remains of **Castle**

Hill (NT 624249), whose oval central enclosure measures 61m by 50m within a rampart measuring 3m thick.

South-west of Kelso, **Ringleyhall** (NT 667312) is situated on the right bank of the River Tweed. Only a rampart remains, indicating a site measuring 58m in diameter. There is some evidence of two more ramparts.

An interesting minor fort is **Hownam Law** (NT 796220), protected by a single rampart some 3m thick. It contains traces of at least 155 timber-framed houses and covers 9 hectares. **Hownam Rings** (NT 790194) nearby is one of the most important forts in Britain because of an excavation carried out in 1948 which revealed a series of occupations and reconstructions, and painted a clear picture of the development of the fort. It is contained in three ramparts, with external ditches, some 3m thick. After the fort was abandoned, an open settlement within a circular stone wall was formed with houses similar to the types in Northumberland. The result of the excavations here was a breakthrough in the understanding of the sequence of structural techniques over 500 years.

Within the same area is **Hayhoe Knowe** (NT 860176), a settlement consisting of an oval enclosure containing fourteen timber-framed houses. Also nearby is **Loddan Hill** (NT 755111), an example of a circular fort which contained traces of timber-framed houses. Within the ramparts the remains of at least five houses have been uncovered.

Burnt Humbleton (NT 852280) is an oval enclosure crowning a hill. It seems to have been built in the first century AD, and the remains of the ramparts are still impressive. **Steer Rig** (NT 859254) shows the remains of a farming settlement with traces of at least five timber-framed houses.

Jedburgh provides a centre for three interesting forts. **Peniel Heugh** (NT 654263), to the north, stands on a hill and was built with an oval plan and two ramparts, the remains of which are not prominent. To the south-east **Shaw Craigs** (NT 673095) and its small neighbour **Hophills Nob** (NT 707094) are of interest in that they were constructed in three phases. Further to the south-east is **Woden Law** (NT 7681250), a fort of similar construction where there are signs of Roman siege works. Whether this fortress was reduced by the Romans is uncertain: it has been argued by some archaeologists that the siege works were merely training exercises for the Romans stationed at Pennymuir, nearby, before they moved against the northern Caledonii.

There are three homestead sites within reach of Morebattle. **Shoulder Hill** (NT 825233) stands 3.2km to the east, and the remains of three timber-framed houses within a palisade have been found here. **Mowhaugh** (NT 816208), to the south-east, is an enclosure surrounding a timber-framed house, while **Greenbrough Hill** (NT 813169), also south-east, contains an all-timber homestead, with traces of two further timber structures.

Kaim Law (TNT 512131), south-east of Hawick, is a fortress which held at least five timber-framed houses of circular type measuring 7.5m in diameter. The fort measures 109m by 27m. East of Hawick is **Bonchester Hill** (NT 595117) where the fort has revealed a La Tène brooch and a ring-headed pin. However, some of the circular stone-wall houses have been dated only to the second century AD. Again to the east of Hawick is a spectacular peak on which **Rubers Law** (NT 580155) stands. The early fortification, an enclosure measuring 274.5m by 183m, appears to have been abandoned. Then a new enclosure was formed and this time the ramparts consist of reused Roman stones (marked by a diamond broaching), implying that when the Romans were driven south of Hadrian's Wall, the Celts re-established a fort here.

East-south-east of Hawick is **Southdean Law** (NT635094), originally constructed in the eighth or seventh century BC. Abandoned in the first century AD, it was succeeded by an open settlement of stone-walled houses. Still further to the south-east is **Tamshiel Rig** (NT 643062), another fort of the early Iron Age which was developed into an open settlement in the first century AD, when several circular stone-wall houses were built.

To the south of Hawick, another settlement is situated at **White Knowe** (NT 494079). It contains eleven timber-framed houses within the remains of two slight banks and a median ditch. Again to the south is **Penchrise Pen** (NT 400062), a small fortification in which traces of at least four timber-framed houses have been identified. Moving south-south-west, **Gray Coat** (NT 471049 and NT 471052) is the site of a settlement and homestead. Eight timber-framed houses have been traced here with the ruin of a wall, while 275m to the north is a large homestead within traces of a twin palisade.

Moving west of Hawick, **Highchesters** (NT 450135) is a fort measuring 67m by 49m on a ridge of Teviotdale. It is enclosed within three ramparts. To the west-north-west is **Kemp's Castle** (NT 438165), a settlement where four houses stood within a palisaded enclosure.

Finally in Roxburgh is **Carby Castle** (NY 490844), some 3km south of Newcastleton. The six circular stone houses have been thought to date from no earlier than the second century AD but it is argued that the oval fort might have been built at an earlier date with timber-framed houses of which no surface trace remains. The stone rampart enclosed an area of 87m by 68.5m.

Moving south-west into Dumfries we are in the border territory of the Selgovae. This area was the centre of a particular school of Celtic art in the second and first enturies BC. There are many hill-forts here. **Ward Law** (NY 024667), south-east of Dumfries town, overlooks the River Nith and the Lochar Moss. Enclosed by two ramparts, measuring 64m by 55m, it commands the Solway Firth and is now ploughed almost to obliteration. A Roman fort was erected nearby when the fort was abandoned by the Selgovae. To the north-east of Dumfries is **Kirkmichael Fell** (NY 014893) which is a characteristic type of local fort on the south flank of Kirkmichael Fell, enclosing within a single rampart an area of 68.5m in diameter. The entrance is in the south-west.

Briershaw Hill (NY 370917), a few kilometres north of Langholm, is a circular fort with two ramparts and a median ditch. The ditch is 9m wide and 2m deep. To the north-west of Langholm is **Bailiehill** (NY 256905), again within two ramparts and a median ditch.

Although almost covered by forest, **Castle O'er** (NY 242928), also north-west of Langholm, is worth a visit for its intricate ramparts. The overall measurements are 152.5m by 106m. Further on is the site of **Over Cassock** (NT 231044), a fort on a low promontory on the left bank of Barr Burn, 1.6km north of Eskdalemuir Observatory. It encloses an area 35m by 24m.

Woody Castle (NY 073837), north-west of Lochmaben, is circular, a type of fort which often goes by the name of 'birren'. It measures 61m in diameter and is set on low ground giving strength to the argument that it was more of a settlement than a defence work.

Corncockle Plantation (NY 090861), north of Lochmaben, is formed from massive stony ramparts with a broad external ditch. The interior is oval, measuring 49m by 39m.

At **Burnswark** (NY 185785), a few kilometres south-east of Lockerbie, is a fortress which is dated back to the seventh or sixth century BC and which, it is argued, might have been the principal fort of the Novantae. In this area there was a tribal boundary between the Novantae and the Selgovae. Hardly anything is known of this tribe except that they were a border tribe living along the shadows of the Roman wall. This fort dominates most of Annandale and is visible for many kilometres. It grew from an oval enclosure of 27m by 198m to an irregularly shaped area 503m in length and 7 hectares in extent. The Romans built camps to the north-west and south-east flanks and in the south-east corner of the encampment raised a small fortress. The Roman remains have been dated to the period AD 140–155 when the Caledonian tribes rose up and the nearby Roman fort at Birrens was destroyed.

Broomhill Bank Hill (NY 131911), 9.6km north of Lockerbie, and **Broom Hill** (NY 154916) just to its east, are two forts typical of the area. The first is oval, the second circular, defended by ramparts and a ditch.

Range Castle (NY 086764), south-west of Hightae, is on the west side of Annandale. It is a circular defence system some 91.5m in diameter.

Barrs Hill (NY 015834), 1.6km north-east of Amisfield Town, commands an extensive view over Nithsdale and Annandale. It is an oval fort with ramparts fallen into decay but with a broad external ditch outside which two more ramparts and a median ditch can be seen.

Friars Carse (NX 918852), north-west of Holywood, crowns a knoll on the right bank of the River Nith. The stone circle in the interior was erected in 1827.

Tynron Doon (FX 820939) stands on a height 289m above a bend in the Shinnel Water, 4.8km west of its confluence with the River Nith. The ramparts are in ruin but the outline of the fort, an enclosure measuring 46m by 39.5m, can still be seen.

Shancastle Doon (FX 815908) is east of Moniaive. Although decayed, it is magnificently sited between the Shinnel and Cairn Waters where a road joins two valleys. It was an all-stone structure, which included some large blocks, but it has not been excavated. To the north-west of Moniaive is another fort at **Dalwhat** (NX 728940), where the remains of three ramparts and external ditches enclosed an area some 76m by 49m. It dominates the valley of Dalwhat Water.

Mullach (NX 929870) stands 1.6km north-west of Dalswinton dominating central Nithsdale from a height of 244m. Oval in shape, it has two concentric ramparts and quantities of vitrification proclaim they were of timber-laced construction. A Roman fort lies not far to the south.

Morton Mains Hill (NS 892006) is a settlement just over 3km north-east of Carronbridge, thought to have been built in two phases. No signs of habitation have been discovered.

Kemp's Castle (NS 770089), 1.6km south-west of Sanquhar, occupied a promontory at the confluence of Euchan Water and Barr Burn. Traces of a wall have been found running all round the promontory.

Beattock Hill (NT 065021) has a stone fort on its summit measuring 64m by 30.5m. The rampart is now in a state of decay although an entrance to the south can be seen.

Another fort is situated at **White Hill** (NT 075117) 6.5km north of Moffat. A pair of ramparts and a median ditch enclose an area 70m by 55m with an entrance in the east. There is an inner work measuring 52m by 38m with an entrance in the east-south-east. Nearby is another fort, **Tail Burn** (NT 186146), which is on the left bank of the burn. More than half its defences and interior have been swept away by the action of the water where it runs to join Moffat Water via a waterfall known as the Grey Mare's Tail. It would seem that the fort was originally built as a D-shape with stone ramparts and an external quarry ditch.

Crossing north into Lanark we move into another border area between the Damnonii in the west and the Selgovae to the east. **Candybank** (NT 06411) is a few kilometres north-east of Biggar. It is an oval fort measuring 85m by 58m enclosed in the remains of three ramparts. Inside are traces of timber-framed houses, five of which can be discerned clearly. 5km west of Biggar is **Quothquan Law** (NS 987384), whose original measurements were 122m by 76m, atop a hill dominating a bend in the River Clyde (the Clota). The defences on the hill are visible for many kilometres. Traces of fourteen timber-framed houses can be seen here.

Park Knowe, south of Thankerton (NS 970367), is an oval fort, some 61m by 52m, enclosed in two ramparts, on an isolated hill north of Tinto. The interior is featureless. To the north-west of Thankerton, however, is **Chester Hill** (NS 952396), which overlooks the area from a height of 61m. It is circular, enclosing an area 85m in diameter. It commands a large bend of the River Clyde between Thankerton and Hyndford Bridge.

There are two settlements at **Cow Castle** (NT 042331) which are of interest. The early settlement is enclosed in a D-shaped single rampart and external ditch. The smaller, secondary settlement is also D-shaped. Traces of timber-framed houses are discernible in both areas. A crannog was found in a marsh just to the north but destroyed in drainage operations during the nineteenth century.

Just south-east of Culter stands **Nisbet** (NT 035321), which straddles a ridge dividing the Culter Water and Nesbit Burn. There are two defence works, indicating, according to some opinions, two distinct stages of construction. The inner area measures 61m by 35m while the outer is 77m by 50m.

South-west of Lamington stands **Devonshaw Hill** (NS 953284), a promontory fort with an almost sheer drop of 100m to the west to the plain of the River Clyde. However, the approaches are from the other sides. The fort is oval, measuring 61m by 46m within a single rampart. There are traces of six timber-framed houses in the interior.

Arbory Hill (NS 944238), 1.6km east-north-east of Abington, is one of the more well-known and well-preserved sites. It crowns a promontory overlooking the Clyde valley at the point where the Romans utilized the older Celtic roadways to construct their military routes down Clydesdale. The interior contains traces of timber-framed houses, a rectangular foundation and a pile of stones of uncertain purpose. It is enclosed within triple ramparts with an external ditch. West of Abington is **Black Hill** (NS 908239). This fort is on the south-east extremity of the hill and overlooks Duneaton Water. The circular fort is 36.5m in diameter within a single rampart and external ditch. A secondary rampart enlarges the earthwork to an area 61m in diameter.

There is a settlement at **Crawford** (NS 944215) enclosing timber-framed houses in an area 85m long by 42.5m wide on the lower slopes of a massif known as Castle Hill, bordered to the south and west by the River Clyde. Enclosures would indicate cattle pens. Nearby, about 800m to the west, is Crawford Fort at (NS 952219) which occupies a knoll separated from Castle Hill by a channel. It is oval, measuring 110m by 40m, but has been robbed of much of its stone. The rampart was protected by an external ditch.

Finally, the uppermost fort in the Clydesdale area is **Bodsberry Hill** (NS 963169), standing 122m above the valley and controlling the approaches to Dalveen Pass to the west. Stone ramparts enclosed an area 100m by 85m with four entrances of an inturned nature. Extra defences have been built on the north-west and south-east entrances. Traces of a few timber-framed houses can be seen.

Moving north-west again we cross into Renfrew, still in the territory of the Damnonii. **Craigmarloch Wood** (NS 344718), north-west of Kilmacolm, stands in open woodland on a hill separating East and West Kilbride. It is oval in plan and excavation has traced a palisade dating back to the eighth century BC. The measurements are 49m by 24m, within the border of a stone rampart which was once 3m thick.

Walls Hill (NS 411588), south-east of Howwood, crowns a steep rocky hill with a flat top; it measures 488m by 213.5m, enclosing 7 hectares. Excavation has revealed only two early Iron Age occupations with circular timber-framed houses. It has been argued that this must have been a principal if not *the* principal township of the Damnonii.

Just south of Glasgow's reaching tentacles stands **Duncarnock** (NS 500559). It is still possible to appreciate the extensive view from the summit where the fort contains an area 192m in length by 100m. Early Celtic pottery has been discovered here.

Finally, **Dunwan** (NS 5474489), south-east of Eaglesham, stands on an isolated hill looking out over marshland. It is triangular in plan, measuring 79m by 49m with a single rampart, originally at least 3.5m thick. The interior contains traces of two circular timber-framed houses. There are the remains of an outer line of defence round the lowest slopes of the hill.

South into Ayr we are in the heartland of the Damnonii. This area switched from its Brythonic Celtic language to the Goidelic form (Gaelic) in the closing centuries of the first millennium AD. During Macbeth's time a certain degree of bilingualism was evident: the local chieftain of Strathclyde was called Owain Mac Dhòmhnuill, a Brythonic first name and Goidelic patronymic. Gaelic was spoken in this part of south-west Scotland until the eighteenth century. It was known as the area of the Gall-Ghàidheal (Galloway), the foreign Gaels. Robert Burns was one year old when Margaret MacMurray of Culzean, near Maybole, died. She was accredited with being the last native Gaelic speaker of Carrick. Burns was born 'on the Carrick border' at Alloway in 1756.

There is a dun, or fortified house, at **Duniewick** (NX 116851), 4km north-east of Ballantrae on the summit of a craggy hill. It measures 30.5m by 26m. Near Minishant, another dun called **Monkwood** (NS 337139) stands on the left bank of the Water of Doon. Circular, it is 15m in diameter and has walls 4.5m thick.

Portencross, 3.2km west-north-west of West Kilbride (NS 171491), is the site of both a fort and a dun. They occupy a ridge named Auld Hill, and both are in a bad state. The dun measures 13.5m by 8m, while the fort to the north is nearly rectangular in shape and covers an area 30m by 15m.

A site which has been much looted is **Dow Hill** (NX 192962), south-east of Girvan. It is a circular fort some 15m in diameter with additional enclosures and evidence of five decayed ramparts.

Hollowshean (NS 244063) is 1.6km south of Kirkoswald A fort measuring 73m by 46m, it has three outer ramparts crossing the neck of a ridge but little else is discernible.

Kildoon (NS 298074) is south of Maybole, where Gaelic was last spoken in this region. Double ramparts enclose an area 45m by 30m. North-east of Maybole stands **Dunree** (NS 347125), a dun commanding the River Doon on a hill at an elevation of 61m. The main wall seems to have been 3m or 3.5m thick. The enclosed area measures 36.5m by 30m.

Overlooking Largs Bay from a height of 217m is **the Knock** (NS 202268). The summit is surrounded by a rampart enclosing an area of 50m by 29m. There is evidence of vitrification, suggesting a timber-laced wall.

Knockjargon (NS 235473) is the site of a fort and cairn just 5km north of Ardrossan. It overlooks the Firth of Clyde and commands a view to Arran and beyond from an elevation of 231m. The area enclosed is 45m by 30m.

Although in an extremely wasted condition, **Carwinning** (NS 286528), north-west of Dalry, is still recognizable as a circular fortress dominating the valley of Picton Burn. It is 91.5m in diameter with a small stony mound which might represent the remains of a dun.

Hadyard Hill (NX 259989) to the south-west of Dalry commands a view over the valley of Girvan Water towards the Firth of Clyde. The fort is oval, measuring 82m by 70m within two ramparts which in some areas extend to 7m in width and over 1m in height.

South-west of Dundonald stands **Harpercroft** (NS 360325), which crowns a summit of the Dundonald range. It is a circular fort some 91m in diameter, with two ramparts. Nearby is **Wardlaw** (NS 359327), which stands on the highest summit of the range and is oval in shape, measuring 103m by 61m. The stony rampart still stands to a height of 1.5m and is 6m in width. It is less than 400m from Harpercroft.

Another dun is situated 1.6km south-west of Dundonald. This is **Kemp Law** (NS 335336), which is circular and measures 11m in diameter. The walls are over 4m thick and the dun has been burnt, robbed and ruined.

Crossing south into Kirkcudbright we find quite a heavy concentration of early Celtic forts, settlements, duns and crannogs. We are, of course, in the heartland of the Novantae.

There are three duns of interest. The first is **Castle Haven** (NX 594483), which is just over 3km west of Borgue. Relics found here show occupation through the Iron Age into Roman times. It measures 18m by 10.5m and has a large outer court. **Lochangower** (NX 692661), north-east of Laurieston, has walls 30.5m in length and 3.5m thick. **Auchencairn** (NX 804508) is similar in construction with walls 33.5m long by 24.5m wide and 3.5m thick.

At **The Moyle** (NX 848575), south-east of Dalbeattie, there is a large fort of triangular shape enclosing an area axially 283.5m by 152.5m with a rampart some 3m thick. This is the largest structure in the area. The inner enclosure of 36.5m by 27.5m has, unfortunately, been robbed of its stones and therefore it is difficult to ascertain its outline, its purpose or whether it was built separately from the main enclosure. Incidentally, this has the distinction of being the only Celtic hill-fort on the telephone – within it stands a forestry watch-tower! Several kilometres to the south-east of Dalbeattie stands **Barean Loch** (NX 8655) in which a crannog was found when the water-level sank in 1865. A timber structure, it was occupied in the second century AD; one of the artefacts found was a cooking pot, now in the National Museum.

Just to the north-west of Rockcliffe stands **Mark Moat** (NX 845540), which has been destroyed by stone-robbers and others. Standing overlooking Rough Firth, it measures 82m in length and from 17m to 32m in width at various points. The timber-laced stone wall has been fired and is vitrified: this might have happened in Roman times. An excavation discovered various items here which suggested occupation through the Roman period, as well as articles dating to the early medieval period. South-east of Rockcliffe a second fort, **Barcloy** (NX 854524), stands on a promontory on the east of the Urr Water. This is an oval fort of 43m by 29m within ramparts which are 3m thick and faced with square block stone. Some pottery was found here, now in Dumfries Museum, but this has been dated to the medieval period.

Spoons, a ladle and strainer from the Traprian Treasure. This most likely represents loot carried north by Celtic raiders from some southern villa or town, perhaps even from as far afield as Gaul

There are two crannog sites in this area. On the north-west shore of **Loch Arthur** (NX 902690), 800m east of Beeswing, oak piles and horizontal beams were found in 1874, together with a dug-out canoe nearly 14m long and 1.5m wide at the stem. This is now in the national collection. The second crannog was found at **Lochrutton** (NX 898730) where a 24.5m diameter foundation built of logs was found on an island. The wooden floor of the structure stood on this. The construction was dated to the eighth or seventh century BC but the artefacts found here were all from the medieval period. Another two crannogs were found in **Milton Loch** (NX 839718), 14km west of Dumfries. These appeared when the water-level was lowered in 1953. Objects recovered here included an early Celtic plough stilt and head, part of a rotary quern and an enamelled bronze loop dated to the second century AD. The two crannogs stood 800m apart, one to the south-east of the loch, the other to the north-west, but only the latter was excavated. It was set on a stone-covered island some 10.5m in diameter. Strong timbers supported the roof and the interior was radially divided into rooms. A causeway led from the shore to the door. Behind the house were the remains of a quayside or dock.

Yet more crannogs were discovered in **Carlingwark Loch** (NX 765615), immediately south of Douglas. When the waters of the loch were lowered, four crannogs, two dams and a causeway were discovered. A number of interesting finds, including dug-out canoes, a bronze sword, a cauldron, numerous tools, implements and weapons, and a tankard (dated to the second century AD) came from this area.

Within striking distance of Castle Douglas are two forts. To the south-east is **Castlegower** (NX 792589) which stands 24.5m above the countryside on a rocky hill. Oval, it measures 38m by 15m and its ramparts show heavy vitrification. To the south-east again, at **Dunguile** (NX 773572), stands a hill-fort which measures 180m by 155.5m and is enclosed in three ramparts. The interior has been under cultivation and the fort is greatly denuded but traces of timber-framed houses can be seen in the interior.

A settlement, with earthworks, is situated at **Little Merkland** (NX 689738), 3.2km north of Parton. However, apart from the earthworks, no traces of habitation are visible and, until excavation, little is known about the site.

Drummore (NX 687456), situated 5.6km south of Kirkcudbright itself, occupies a hill overlooking Kirkcudbright Bay on the eastern side. Oval, it encloses 64m by 49m within three ramparts and a median ditch. To the north-east of Kirkcudbright, at a distance of 8km, **Dungarry** (NX 757536) is enclosed in two stone ramparts on the summit of a rocky hill. Its measurements are 64m by 38m. The inner wall is 3.5m thick and the outer one is nearly 2m thick. The entrance is to the east. There is a small annexe to the north-east. 3km to the south-east stands **Suie Hill** (NX 765508) which is very similar in size and design.

Kirkcarswell (NX 752497), nearly 2km north of Dundrennan, is defended by two concentric ramparts with a median ditch. It is 67m by 24.5m with an entrance to the west.

Just south-west of Twynholm stands **Twynholm** fort (NX 658539), also called Campbeltown Mote. It is a small structure of 27.5m by over 15m with a wall and some outworks. A similar structure is that of **Edgarton** (NX 673630), standing almost 2km south-west of Laurieston. This is 23m by 14m but its single rampart has been much mutilated and some traces of vitrification have been found.

Barstobric Hill (NX 687607), also known as Queen's Hill, stands 10km north of Kirkcudbright. It is a large fort some 259m by 114m and enclosed by a much denuded rampart that once stood 3m thick. Today a 11m high pyramid dominates the fort, a memorial to James Beaumont Neilson, inventor of the hot-blast furnace.

Barnheugh (NX 599475) stands looking over Wigtown Bay from the east and is 3.2km west-south-west of Borgue. Oval in shape, it is 36.5m by 23m and three circular stone house foundations have been found here. Nearby is **Borness Batteries** (NX 619446), a fairly typical promontory fort guarded by cliffs on the seaward side and by three ramparts with ditches on the landward side.

Another small fort is **Trusty's Hill** (NX 588561), just to the west of Gatehouse of Fleet. Measuring 27.5m by 18m within a rampart, with further outworks, this fort is noteworthy for the discovery of some Pictish artwork carved at the entrance, including the famous double disc and Z-rod motif, the lacustrine monster.

Within a few kilometres of Kirkpatrick Durham there are two forts. **Glengappock** (NX 750704), to the west, is a fairly typical small fort, much robbed of its features, about 30.5m by 18m. To the north-west stands **Margley** (NX 770733), a circular fort 30.5m in diameter.

Occupying a position dominating the passes running by the Water of Ken and the Stroanfeggan Burn stands **Stroanfeggan Fort** (NX 637921), 10km north-by-east of St John's Town of Dalry. The ruins of its ramparts extend to a thickness of 8m, and the main enclosure measures 43m by 38m. The fort has been much denuded.

West into Wigtown, we find another high concentration of forts. Most of them are comparatively small, such as the **Doon of May** (NX 295515), which is 14km west-by-south of Wigtown. It is only

43m by 30.5m and is now overgrown by trees. The Doon of May is another Anglicized form of Maiden (Mai's dun). A fort of similar size is **North Balfern** (NX 436509), a few kilometres north of Sorbie. This is oval in plan, enclosed within two dry-stone wall ramparts. 3.2km west of Sorbie is **Dowalton Loch** (NX 4074), where numerous crannogs were excavated in 1863–64. Evidence of timber structures and foundations dating from the early Iron Age were found, together with artefacts from the Roman period. In fact, when the lochs in the area were drained, several crannogs were reported.

The coast of Wigtown has several promontory forts as might be expected from its position, dominating the eastern side of the North Channel. The three forts situated on **Burrow Head** (NX 454341) are the best examples of such defence works and are to be found 3km south-west of Isle of Whithorn. The remains of the series of ramparts and ditches are extensive. Another promontory fort is that of **Barsalloch Point** (NX 347413), just to the south-east of Port William. Two ramparts and a median ditch guard the landward side.

There are two duns in the area. **Chang** (NX 299481), to the north-west of Port William, is 33.5m in length by 21m wide. Relics show occupation from the eighth or seventh century into the Roman period. **Chippermore** (NX 297483) seems to have been 27.5m by 24.5m with walls 2.75m thick, but it has been used as a stone dump and sheep-fold and its remains have been obscured.

Also within a few kilometres of Port William, to the east-south-east, is the **Fell of Barhullion** (NX 374418), a fort standing 122m above sea-level and dominating the Whithorn peninsula. Oval in shape and measuring 43m by 18m, the fort is enclosed in two ramparts, the inner one of which was 2.5m thick. There has been little excavation here.

Bennan of Garvilland (NX 215627) stands on a rocky hill some 5km north-east of Glenluce. It measures 91.5m by 61m with two ramparts which appear originally to have been 3.5m thick. To the east-south-east of Glenluce there is another fort, **Knock Fell** (NX 255557), which is also large in size, 174m by 91.5m with walls up to 4m thick on the outer rampart and 2.5m thick on the inner.

Another fort in the Glenluce area is **Laigh Sinniness** (NX 216522), about 5km south-by-east of Glenluce. This is a promontory fort defended on the landward side by a sturdy dry-stone rampart originally 4.5m thick. Nearby is **Stairhaven** (NX 208534), a broch which is much denuded. There is some argument about identification; however, its structure can still be roughly discerned. The fourth and last fort in the area, some 5km north-by-west of Glenluce, is **Cruise Back Fell** (NX 179623), which is a small oval enclosure on a rocky plateau surrounded by a heavy stone wall. Internal measurements are about 12m by 15m.

The most dominant position in this countryside is occupied by **Cairn Pat** (NX 044564), standing 5km south-south-west of Stranraer. Two ramparts and external ditches enclose an area of 137m by 125m. Just 5km east of Stranraer is **Black Loch** (NX 114612) where a crannog was situated on an island. The original structure, whose wooden floor was over 15m in diameter, was dated to the early Iron Age and relics included material dated to as late as the first and second centuries AD. There is a broch 5km north-east of Stranraer, **Teroy** (NX 099641), standing on a promontory. The interior diameter is nearly 9m with walls measuring 4m thick.

Stranraer has two duns worth visiting in its vicinity. **Craignoch** (NX 012668) is perched on a rocky knoll on the left bank of the Craigoch Burn, some 8km north-west of Stranraer. It is circular, measuring 8m and the wall is over 2m thick in places. At **Jamieson's Point** (NX 033710) 10km north-west of Stranraer, is the second dun, also circular and nearly 17m in diameter with a wall 3m thick in places.

Caspin (NX 005733), 5km north-north-west of Kirkcolm, is another promontory fort near Milleur Point at the mouth of Loch Ryan. It is defended by cliffs and is cut off from the mainland by a natural gully although this is bordered by a dry-stone wall rampart some 2.5m thick.

The largest promontory fort in the area is **Kemp's Walk** (NW 974598), just over 6km north-north-west of Portpatrick. It is situated on a promontory overlooking Larbrax Bay. It is nearly 52m at its greatest width and defended by several ramparts with an

entrance on the east end of the promontory. Also near Portpatrick
is **Kirklauchlane** (NX 035506), another promontory fort which is
defended by three ramparts on the landward side with external
ditches. The inner rampart still rises as much as 2.5m above the
bottom of the ditch. The area enclosed now measures 55m in
length by 26m in width.

South of Drummore are two forts. Nearly 5km south stands the
circular fort of **Portankill** (NX 142323) which is 12m in diameter
and sits on the tip of a promontory. To the landward side are three
ditches. Then 5km to the south-west is **Dunman** (NX 096335),
dated to the eighth or seventh century BC and defended by natural
gullies with ramparts that originally measured 2.5m to 3.5m in
thickness. Just over 5km west-by-south-west of Drummore is the
site of another broch which was demolished to make way for a
lighthouse. This is **Crammag Head** (NX 088340), whose walls were
said to have been 2.7m thick and to have surrounded an area 18m
in diameter. Only a sector of the south-western arc still survives.

b. North-West Scotland

Argyll, Inverness, Ross and Cromarty
Sutherland and Caithness

Argyll, Airer-Ghàidheal, the seaboard of the Gael, was said by the
Romans to contain two tribes. The Epidii occupied the Mull of
Kintyre, while to the north were the Caledonii, a powerful tribe
whose territory extended into Inverness. The Caledonii later
became a confederation of tribes whom the Romans nicknamed
Picts and from whom they named the entire territory of Scotland
'Caledonia'.

There are several hill-forts of interest in the area, as well as
many fortified homesteads. First we will deal with the hill-forts and
settlements. The fort of **Casteal na Sith** (Cowal) is near Kames
(NR 962691) and occupies the summit of a rocky ridge; it
measures 79m in length by 36.5m wide and is defended by a dry-
stone wall rampart.

Perhaps the most famous fortification is **Dunadd**, Lochgilphead, Mid-Argyll (NR 837936), which was built around 600 BC. It stands on an isolated hill over the flood plain of the River Add and measures 30.5m by 14m. Outside the fort are some Pictish carvings, including the likeness of a boar. These are from a later date. According to the *Annals of Ulster*, Dunadd was occupied by the Gaels of Dàl Riada and besieged by the Picts in AD 683 and 736. There is an Ogham inscription here, which it has not been possible to transcribe because of weathering.

Early Iron Age remains have been discovered at **Duntroon**, near Lochgilphead (NR 803959) in a fort situated a short distance from the north-west shore of Loch Crinan. It is an oval enclosure of nearly 43m by 27.5m. The timber-laced walls are about 3m thick. This fort shows signs of being burnt. Among the items excavated are thirty-six saddle querns. Another fort is **Slockavullin**, Kilmarton (NR 815980) which is a simple oval defence work measuring nearly 35m by 15m with walls some 3.5m thick.

A 3.5m thick dry-stone rampart encloses **Dun a Chogaidh**, Tayvallich, Knapdale (NR 745876) which is 46m long by 23m wide. It overlooks Loch Sween and the Sound of Jura.

Dun Skeig, on Kintyre, near Tarbert (NR 757571) stands at a height of 143m overlooking the mouth of West Loch Tarbert. It is oval in plan, measuring 27.5m by 20m. There are signs that the fort was burnt as there is evidence of vitrification. Just north-east is a fortified dwelling measuring nearly 14m in diameter with walls 4m thick. The entrance is on the east.

Another fort which shows signs of being burnt is that at **Carradale**, Kintyre (NR 815364). This is an oval fort on the central part of Carradale Point, a narrow peninsula which is isolated at high tide. It measures 58m by 23m. This was perhaps burnt in the Roman campaigns while **Benderloch**, near Oban (NM 903382) was not only burnt by the Romans but appears from the remains found to have been occupied by them afterwards. The fort itself acquired the Latinized name of Berigonium. It stands on a rocky ridge at the head of Ardmucknish Bay, its timber-laced walls surrounding an area measuring 213.5m by 30.5m. It is also known as Dùn Mac Sniochan.

Loch nan Gobhar near Corran (NM 970633) is another fort which seems to have been burnt. It measures 76m by over 9m. Access to the fort is gained on the east of the ridge.

Moving from Kintyre northward we will visit the most interesting duns. We have already mentioned Dun Skeig (q.v.). A dun stands at **Kildonan Bay** (NR 780277) 10km north-east of Campbeltown; it is comparatively well preserved and dates from the eighth or seventh century BC. The interior measures 21m by 12m with walls varying from 1.5m to 4m thick. Finds indicate an occupation lasting nearly 1000 years. Another dun in the Kintyre area is at **Ugadale Point** (NR 784285). This is on a promontory at the north end of Kildonan Bay and measures nearly 17m by 10.5m with walls some 2.5m thick. Excavation rescued items dating from the seventh century BC through to the sixteenth century AD.

In the Knapdale area of Argyll are three duns of note. **Druim an Duin** (NR 781913) stands at the end of Loch Scotnish in Knapdale Forest. The walls, still rising in places to a height of 2.75m, are nearly 5m thick, and the structure measures 15m by 9m. **Dun Mhuirich** (NR 722845) is 4 km west of Tayvich; this interesting oval dun measures 13.5m by 12m with a wall 2m thick. It stands guarding the rock and shore of Linne Mhuirich. The third dun in this area is **Dun a' Choin Dhuibh**, early 8km west of Tarbert (NR 804641), in Achaglachgach Forest. It is circular, 12m in diameter and with walls 3m thick.

Mid-Argyll also has three duns worth visiting: **Torbhlaran** (NR 866943) is 6.5km north of Lochgilphead. This is a circular dun measuring 15m in diameter, enclosed in a square fortification. To the north-west, 11km from Lochgilphead, is **Ardifuar** (NR 789969). This has been excavated and dated to the early Iron Age by the various objects found. The dun itself is circular, measuring 20m in diameter within a wall 3m thick and still standing 3m high. The final dun in this area is **Dun Mhuilig** (NM 776019) which is 6.4km west-north-west of Kilmartin. It stands on a promontory of Loch Craignish and its galleried wall survives, being 3.5m thick; the lintels of the gallery also remain in position.

As well as the dun at Benderloch (q.v.) there is another dun in Lorn that is worthy of a visit – **Suidhe Chennaidh** (NN 029243),

1.6km north-north-west of Kilchrenan. This is circular, some 12m in diameter, with 4m thick walls which, some years ago, still stood as high as 6m.

One final dun worthy of note is in north Argyll: **Rahoy** (NM 633564), some 13km north-north-west of Lochaline, stands on the north-east shore of Loch Teacuis. This is circular, measuring 12m in internal diameter. During excavations in 1936–7 dynamite was used! The walls were found to be vitrified and, in spite of the sledge-hammer tactics, some artefacts were found including a bronze Celtic brooch of La Tène I style and a looped-socket Iron Age axe together with saddle querns and scrapers. These dated the dun to the period of the eighth and seventh centuries BC.

Inverness covers the territory occupied by the Creones in the west, the Caledonii in the centre and the Vacomagi in the north-east. There are numerous fortifications here. To begin with there are five duns worth noting. **Craig Phitiulais** (NH 930140) stands just over 3km north-east of Aviemore on a small hummock looking towards Strathspey. It measures 9m by 6m within the ruin of a substantial wall. **Onich** (NN 029619) is nearly 3km west-by-north-west of North Ballachulish, and is a small oblong dun on a rocky knoll. It measures 14m by 9m within the ruins of a wall and appears to have been burnt at some time. Then **Auchteraw**, 4km south-west of Fort Augustus (NH 349070) is also a victim of burning. This fortification overlooked the passage between Loch Ness and Loch Oich from an elevation of 61m. It measures 15m by 6m. The other two duns stand near Glenelg (q.v.).

At **Craig Phadrig**, just west of Inverness (NH 640453), we have a famous fort whose ramparts date from 500 BC. It crowns an afforested hill overlooking the end of Beauly Firth. The inner wall are heavily vitrified, and enclose an area measuring 75m by 23m. The walls are 9m thick in places. The outer walls are also heavily vitrified. How the fort was burnt, or when, is difficult to assess. Its fame rests in the artefacts found here, including a hanging bowl of the seventh century AD.

Cabrich, also just west of Inverness (NH 534428), dominates the north-east flank of Phoineas Hill. However, the fort is covered by conifers and the remains of the stone fortifications are difficult to see. To the south-west of Inverness is **Ashie Moor** (NH 600316), which is oval in plan measuring 38m by 33.5m within a ruined stone wall. There is an outer wall. Both have entrances in the south-west. While keeping to the west of Inverness, 13km to be precise, we find **Castle Spynie** (NH 542421), a broch which has an interior diameter of 11m and walls 4m thick. It is variously dated to between the first century BC and the second century AD and is defended by outworks.

Loch Bruicheach (NH 455368), 11km south-west of Beauly, is the site of a crannog which lies close to the north shore. No evidence of the date of construction has been discovered but the remains, a stone and timber dwelling, were found to have been burnt.

Strone Point, near Drumnadrochit (NH 530286) was originally erected in the Iron Age but is now occupied by the medieval Urquhart Castle. The best preserved ruins are to the south.

Dun Scriben, Drumnadrochit (NH 491235) stands nearby. It is a small fortification on the brink of a hillside overlooking Loch Ness. It is square, measuring almost 18m in either direction.

Invergarigaig, near Dores (NH 526238) occupies one of the most spectacular positions in the countryside. It stands on the summit of a rock which protrudes above the mouth of the River Farigaig like a tooth and commands the waters of Loch Ness. The fort has to be approached through Dirichurachan. The ramparts of walls some 4.5m thick, encloses an area 24.5m by 13m. There seems to be a well at the western apex. There are traces of vitrification.

Glen Nevis, near Fort William (NN 126702) shows massive signs of vitrification. This fort, known as **Dun Deardail**, stands on the steep west side of Glen Nevis, some 344m above sea-level, 4km west of the summit of Ben Nevis. It measures 46m by 27.5m. The entrance is at the north-east. Massive burning has taken place here.

Yet another vitrified fort is at **Arisaig** (NM 693839) which is on a promontory on the north side of Loch nan Uamh. The landward side is protected by stone ramparts. The fort has, at times, been called Arka Unsekel, Ard Ghaunsgoik and Ard Ghamhgail.

Eilean nan Gobhar, near Arisaig (NM 694794) is perched on a high rocky island in the mouth of Loch Ailort. Its walls show considerable vitrification.

Am Baghan Burblach, near Glenelg (NG 832199) forms an area measuring 52m by 30.5m and containing a circular enclosure 12m in diameter. Signs of a more recent croft and other foundations can be seen. There are two brochs in the vicinity of Glenelg, both to the south-west within 400m of one another. The first is **Dun Telve** (NG 829173) which, like Mousa, is one of the best preserved with an interior diameter of 10m and walls 4m thick. The walls still stand to 10m. Many relics were recovered here which are now in the National Museum. The second broch is **Dun Troddan** (NG 834073) which has an interior diameter of 8.5m and walls of 4m, rising in places to 7.5m. Nearby is **Am Baghan Galldair** (NG 822207), a circular dun standing at an elevation of 145m overlooking Glenelg Bay and measuring 21m in diameter. Another dun of note is **Dun Grugaig** (NG 852159) which is 5km south-east of Glenelg. Its walls still stand to 2.5m in height in places and are 4m thick. The D-shaped enclosure was 14m in length. Chambers and entrances with door checks are still to be discerned.

Dun Chliabhainn, neary Beauly (NH 476460) is a small fort with walls measuring 3.5m thick, enclosing an area some 23.5m by 14.5m. Not far is **Tighnaleac** (NH 457452) which is of similar construction with walls between 4.5m and 5.5m thick.

Avielochan, near Aviemore (NH 905171) is a promontory fort overlooking Strathspey above Loch Vaa. The walls are formed by stones but the interior is an impenetrable jungle of junipers. It measures 67m in length by 24.5m wide.

Laggan, near Dahwhinnie (NN 582930) has a superbly strategic location. It is on the nose of a long promontory ridge which divides Strathspey from Strathmashie. The fort is of a contour plan, measuring 140m by 79m within a wall that varies in width from 4m to 7m. The remains still rise as high as 3m in places.

Two tribes, the Carnonacae to the east and the Decantae to the west, occupied the area which is now known as Ross and Cromarty. Hardly anything is known about these two tribes except their names. 3.2km north of Inverness, but in Ross and Cromarty,

Dun Telve, Inverness, is one of the finest and best-preserved examples of a broch. The walls stand to over 10 m high. Many interesting items were discovered here and are now in the National Museum of Scotland

stands **Kessock** (NH 663491). On the Ord of Kessock, 193m above sea-level, stands a fort measuring 274.5m by 70m and still surrounded by a stone wall. The hill is now planted by forest, which makes the fort difficult to see. However, an entrance can be discerned in the south.

Knock Farril, near Strathpeffer (NH 505585) is a fairly

conventional hill-fort of some 129.5m by 38m. However, little is known about it. There is evidence that at some time it was burnt causing the vitrification of its walls.

Unfinished ramparts are a feature of **Cnoc an Duin**, near Evanton (NH 696769). The main walls are about 222.5m in length and 76m wide but only half of them appear to have been completed. The interior is flat and barren and has no traces of occupation.

At **Gairloch** (NG 802753) stands a little fort on a promontory called **An Dun** (the fort). The entrance to the south has a lot of vitrified matter showing that the entrance was burnt at some time.

Creagan Fhamhair, Gairloch (NG 823726) stands nearby on a rocky hill above the River Kerry. The west and north are protected by 15m high cliffs, the east and south by ramparts enclosing an area 30.5m square. The wall was at least 2m thick in recent times and stood as high but some enterprising builders have removed the stones.

Dun Lagaidh, near Ullapool (NH 143914) has both a fort, on the south-west shore of Loch Broom, and a broch. The fort measures 91.5m by 36.5m; the rampart is still 3.5m thick in places. It was built in about the seventh century BC. There is evidence of the fort being burnt, perhaps by one of the Roman incursions? The emperor Severus campaigned in the north of Scotland in AD 208–9 and his son Caracalla continued until the Roman withdrawal from Scotland in AD 211.

Standing on the shore looking to the Summer Isles, about 1.5km north of the mouth of the River Kanaird, is **Dun Canna**, near Ullapool (NC 112008), enclosing an area of 43m by 12m. The western end of the fort has been subjected to vitrification, indicating that it was another victim of burning. A few kilometres south of Ullapool is **Rhiroy** (NH 149901); this broch stands only 1.6km distant from Dun Lagaidh (q.v.). Although much dilapidated, its walls can be traced as being 4m thick. The best-preserved section still stands to a height of nearly 3m while the internal diameter was 11.5m.

There are three duns worthy of inspection in Ross and Cromarty. **Culbokie** (NH 603587) which is 8km north-east of

Cononbridge, has been much reduced by stone-robbing but one can see its three circular ramparts, the innermost of which is nearly 17m in diameter with walls 2.5m thick. **Kintail**, 8km south-east of Dornie (NG 939207), is oval and measures 17m by 7.5m. The walls are ruined and the rubble spread over an area 4.5m wide. Lastly, there is **Strathanaird** (NC 166019), which is 1.6km east of Strathanaird, occupying a small hill at the confluence of two small streams. It measures 10m by nearly 10m, is D-shaped, and its walls are over 4m thick.

With Sutherland and Caithness we are moving into an area where no fewer than four tribes are said to have had territories: in the west the Caereni and Smertae, and in the east the Cornovii (bearing a similar name to the Cornovii of Shropshire and of western Cornwall) and the Lugi. Again, apart from their names, we know little of these tribes.

There are five interesting hill-forts in Sutherland and eight brochs worthy of a visit. **Dun Creich**, Bonar Bridge (NH 651882) stands 113m above the estuary waters which link Dornock Firth with the Kyle of Sutherland. The fort, unfortunately, is not clearly definable due to afforestation. However, the rampart encloses an area some 79m by 67m.

Dunrobin (NC 870013), a few kilometres east of Golspie, is a broch with an interior diameter of 9m and an entrance passage 5.5m long, with stair lobby and chambers.

Duchary Rock, Brora (NC 850050) dominates Loch Brora and is a strong fortification, protected on all sides except the north-west. There are stretches of inner and outer ramparts up to 3.5m thick. The interior measures 238m by 55m. Near Brora there are also two brochs. **Cinn Trolla** (NC 929081), 5km to the north (the name translates as 'Troll's Head'), has an interior diameter of 9.5m. The passage was 5.5m long, 2m high and nearly 1m wide. Chambers and stair lobby can also be discerned. To the north-west, about 14km from Brora, is **Castle Cole** (NC 795133), a smaller broch which has an interior diameter of 6.5m and walls 4m thick. This has some very well-preserved details such as double door checks and wall recesses.

The highest hill-fort in Scotland stands on **Ben Griam Beg** (NC

831412), at 580m above sea-level. Stone walls, 2m thick, enclose an area of 152.5m by 61m. The fort was probably built around the seventh or sixth century BC. There are traces of enclosures, perhaps for cattle, nearby.

Kilphedir (NC 995187) is 5km north-west of Helmsdale. It is a broch which stands in its own enclosure with a commanding view. The interior diameter is nearly 10m with a wall 4.5m thick.

Nearly 10km south of Bettyhill stands **Dun Viden** broch (NC 726518). This is also in a commanding position, on a hill 23m high overlooking the River Naver. The internal diameter is 9m with walls 4.5m thick. There are outward defences, including the remains of a stone rampart standing 3.5m high.

Dun na Maigh (NC 552531) is 6.4km south-west of Tongue, standing on a rocky hill overlooking the Kyle of Tongue. It is a small broch, 8.5m in internal diameter, with 3.5m thick walls standing to a height of 4.5m.

14km north-west of Altnaharra is the broch of **Dundornadilla** (NH 455449), with an interior diameter of over 8m and walls 4m thick. The wall, in places, stands to a height of 6m.

Portskerra (866661) stands just west of Holborn Head (q.v.) between the headlands of Rubha na Cloihe and Rubha Brha on a promontory. It is 30.5m wide by 76m long and can only be approached by a narrow ridge from the land. The sides rise 24.5m above sea-level. Often the strip of land leading into the fort is less than 1m wide.

At **Culkein**, near Lochinver (NC 041340), a high rocky headland known as Rubh 'an Dunain protrudes north-east from the shore-line between the Bay of Culkein and the Point of Stoer. On it stands a promontory fort, protected by a wall 12m long and over 2m thick, enclosing 30m of land from the tip of the headland. Access is only by a bridge of natural rock. 8km north-west of Lochinver is **Stoer** (NC 036278), a broch standing by the sea, defended by outworks. The interior diameter is 10m within walls 4m thick which stand in places to a height of 2m. Some 10km north-west of Lochinver stands a promontory dun at **Clashnessie** (NC 055315) which overlooks the west side of Clashnessie Bay and measures 10.5m by 7.5m.

Sutherland has one other dun of interest: the circular dun of **Loch Ardvair** (NC 168332) which is 13km north-west of Inchnadamph. It is interesting as it stands on a rock at the south end of the loch. The 3.4m thick walls enclose a structure over 7m in diameter.

Five interesting forts stand in Caithness. **St John's Point**, Mey (ND 310752) is the most northerly promontory fort on the island of Britain and is protected by a stone rampart, still 3m high, across the landward end of the headland. The entrance is from the western extremity. **Holborn Head**, Thurso (ND 108715) is a particularly awe-inspiring fort formed on a precipitous headland with fissures and chasms in the ground.

Once known as Cnoc na Ratha, **Sherrery**, near Reay (ND 052577) has ramparts of stone slabs about 3m thick surrounding an area measuring 91.5m by 70m. There are two enclosures, one of which might be a house structure 9m in diameter. This fortress stands 1.6km away from **Ben Freiceadain** (ND 059558) which is the northernmost hill-fort of any size on the island of Britain. Built in the early Iron Age, the fort measures 274.5m in length and 143m in width within a single rampart about 3.5m thick. The entrance is to the west-north-west. It stands on the summit with an extensive view over Caithness to the Orkney islands and across the broad panorama of Sutherland to the west. The fort, in local tradition, is called Oscar's Town (Buaile Oscar), Oscar being the hero son of Ossian, the son of Fingal (in Irish, Fionn Mac Cumhail).

In addition to the forts there are two homestead sites that are of interest, dating from the third or second century BC. They are situated at **Langwell** (ND 102218), 1.6km west of Berriedale, and at **Forse** (ND 204352), 1.6km north-east of Latheron. The Langwell homestead is circular with 2m thick walls, and is 8m in internal diameter. There are two entrances, one of which gives access to a galleried structure measuring 14.5m by 4m within a wall of similar construction to the house. The doorway was 1m wide through a passage whose stone slab roof was 2m high. Some saddle and rotary querns were found here, and a piece of corroded iron, but no pottery. The Forse homestead is 14m in diameter within a stone wall over 1m thick. There are ruins of other buildings nearby and the whole is within an oval enclosure. Small finds of the early Celtic period have been discovered.

Caithness also has its share of brochs. In fact, well over 100 brochs are discernible here but the vast majority are little more than mere traces. There are five which are worthy of note.

Westerdale (ND 133510), 8km south of Halkirk, is on the right bank of the Thurso River. It is 8.5m in diameter within walls 3.5m thick. **Ousdale** (ND 072188) is 6.4km south-west of Berriedale, on the right bank of the Ousdale Burn. It is about 8.5m in diameter in the interior with a 4m thick wall. **Bruan** (ND 310394), 12km south-west of Wick, is one of a great number of brochs that were built on this fertile valley between Wick and the Ord of Caithness. The stones of the majority have been used to build farmsteads over the centuries. Bruan is typical of the remains of such brochs. **Keiss** (ND 353611) is a broch which shows evidence of reconstruction and later use. It is 10.5m in diameter in the interior within 3.5m thick walls. The fifth broch worthy of a visit is at Skirza (ND 394684) some 5km south of Duncansby, where it stands on precipitous cliffs. The interior is nearly 7m in diameter and the walls are over 4m thick. The entrance is to the east.

There is one dun of note 800m east of Auckingill. This is **Sgarbach** (ND 373637), which stands on a cliff-head promontory cut off by a wall 19m long and nearly 4m thick. Many interesting features remain, such as the entrance passage and one room measuring nearly 6m.

c. North-East Scotland

Dunbarton, Stirling, Clackmannan
Kinross, Fife, Perth, Angus, Kincardine
Aberdeen, Banff, Moray and Nairn

In Dunbarton we are in the border territory of the Scottish Damnonii, who are not to be confused with the Dumnonii of the south-west of Britain. There are two particularly interesting sites in this area. The principal one is Dumbarton Rock, on the southern outskirts of **Dumbarton** (NS 400745), which means 'fortress of the Britons', a name given to it (Dùn Breatann) by the Gaelic-speaking Celts. It is from this that the town and the county derive their name. It is considered to be the site of Alcluyd, the capital of the kingdom of Strath-Clóta (Strathclyde), which came under the rule of the kingdom of Alba (Scotland) during the reign of Constantine MacBeth (AD 900–42. It is speculated that the original Damnonii fort may have been built on the summit of the rock on the north shore of the Clyde estuary, but there is no evidence of any Early Celtic remains.

At a distance of 1.6km east of Dumbarton is the site of a dun at **Dunbuie Hill** (NS 421752), on top of a hill overlooking the Clyde estuary. It is circular, with an internal diameter of 9m and walls nearly 4m thick. Excavations found querns and other items dated to the early Iron Age.

The remains of a fort are clearly visible on **Sheep Hill**, near Bowling (NS 435744). Built on a rocky hilltop overlooking the Firth of Clyde near its junction with the river proper, the fort encloses an area 91.5m by nearly 46m. The wall was originally a timber-laced structure. The remains here are vitrified.

Crossing into Stirling, **Dumyat**, originally called Dun Myat, stands just over 4km east of the Bridge of Allen (NS 832973). The fort stands on the western shoulder of the hill. The descent is precipitous to the Carse of Forth 305m below. Two stone walls defend the exposed area to the north and west but the south and east are defended by an almost sheer drop. The interior enclosure, also protected by ramparts, which are 3.5m thick, seems to have been built after the original fortifications.

There is little left of **Abbey Craig** fort, which stands 1.5km north-east of Stirling (NS 809956). The construction of a tower and outbuildings in the nineteenth century has destroyed the heavy stone walls in many places. It was originally a timber-laced structure measuring about 53m by 38m. There are signs of vitrification.

There are two interesting homesteads in the vicinity of Stirling. **West Plean** (NS 810876), 5km south-east of Stirling, has been revealed as one of the most important early Celtic sites in Britain.

A circular house 27.5m in diameter bounded by a ditch, it was a wooden structure, and excavation shows two successive timber-framed houses. The house also had a porch. Finds showing occupation from the Late Bronze Age through to the first century AD were made. The excavation, in 1955, increased our understanding of the construction of timber-framed circular houses and enabled several 'living history groups' to build replicas. The second structure is at **Keir Hill of Gargunnock** (NS 706942), 8km west of Stirling. This is a timber-framed house but disturbance of the soil has destroyed the outlines. Small finds suggest occupation into the first century AD. Though nothing can be seen of the house, the site is worth a visit. It should be remembered that Keir is an Anglicized form of the Brythonic Celtic *caer*, a fort.

South-west of Stirling, 5km to be precise, is **Castlehill Wood** (NS 750909), the site of a dun which stands on a protruding point of Touch Hill. An oval fortification, it is 23m by 15m with walls nearly 5m thick. This dun is of interest in that it has an external stairway. Some finds were made here, including Roman glass and an early Celtic saddle quern. It is thought that the dun was inhabited into the Roman period.

Turning to the south-west of Stirling, at a distance of nearly 5km stands **Suachie Craig** (NS 763893). This fort stands on a rise, overlooking Bannock Burn, the famous battlefield where, on 24 June 1314, Robert Bruce of Scotland decisively defeated Edward II of England and secured Scotland's independence from the English imperial designs of the time. The fort is oval with ruins of stone ramparts enclosing 65.5m by 33.5m.

At a distance of 4km north-west of Balmaha is **Strathcashell Point** (NS 395930) on Loch Lomond. This is the site of a crannog which measured over 21m in diameter. It stands 30m from the shore and just breaks the surface when the water-level is normal. Great timbers form the foundation of this island dwelling.

Craigton dun (NS 628872) is about 1.5km from Fintry to the north-east, standing 14.5m by nearly 13m with walls 3m thick.

A typical fort of southern Scotland is that at **Braes**, near Dunipace (NS 797847), a small oval affair with evidence of vitrification. Such fortresses are numerous in the territory of the

Damnonii. A Danish observatory now stands on top of the isolated hill.

Nearly 5km north-west of Larbert stands **Langlands** (NS 822854), occupying a ridge in an otherwise flat landscape. It can only just be recognized as a circular enclosure. The stone wall here was once 3.5m thick and much of it was probably taken by enthusiastic builders over the years. Near here, 3.2km north-west of Larbert, is **Tor Wood** (NS 8333849), the site of a broch which stands on the brink of a cliff. It has an internal diameter of 10.5m, its double walls are 6m thick and it stands to a height, in some places, of 2.5m. It has been excavated and the finds are in the Falkirk Burgh Museum.

Myot Hill fort (NS 781825), near Denny, is a small fort confined within a single rampart on an isolated hill, with the north, west and south flanks being so precipitous that no defences exist there save natural ones.

The last fort of note in this area is **Meikle Reive** (NS 639789), just north-east of Lennoxtown and occupying a small promontory at the foot of the Kilsyth Hills. The ramparts were originally 3.5m thick and the enclosure measures 44m by 36.5m.

North into Clackmannan we find **Castle Craig** on the northern outskirts of Tillycoultry (NS 911976). It is a fort on a promontory on the southern face of the Ochil range and overlooking the upper part of the Firth of Forth. Although a quarry has started to destroy its defences, the original outline of the fort can still be clearly seen, enclosing an area of some 16,000m². Inside is another circular enclosure but it is thought that this was added later during the second or third century AD.

Once into Kinross we are in the territory of the Venicones, whose northern border appeared to be the line of the River Tay (which the Romans recorded as Tavae). Kinross has three forts of interest. There is **Benarty**, some 5km south-east of Kinross town (NT 154979), which is on a hill rising to 305m, and overlooking Loch Leven, whose island monastic buildings were endowed by Macbeth and his wife, Gruoch. Contrary to the Shakespearian depiction, Macbeth was one of the best kings Scotland ever had, ruling from AD 1040 to 1057 when, after three years of war

between Scotland and England, he was slain. Lulach became High
King for less than a year until he, too, was slain in the conflict with
England and Malcolm Canmore, who had been raised at the
English court since he was a child, was set on the throne. The fort
here is like a distorted letter 'D', enclosing nearly 2 hectares. Its
remains are rather scanty but there are a few stretches of
interesting rampart stone-work, including several boulders which
are 3m in length.

South-west of Cleish is **Dummiefarline** (NT 088968), a fort
occupying a rocky prominence of the Cleish Hills. The ramparts
were of stone and 3m thick, but are no longer traceable. There are
interior buildings and the remains show signs of vitrification.

Some 91.5m below this fort and just over 1km further on is
Dumglow (NO 076965), a promontory fort at the apex of the
Cleish Hills. The defences are of four low stone ramparts placed
only 3.5m apart and pierced by an entrance at each end.

The name Fife is a survival of one of the ancient provincial
kingdoms which later became known as An Mhaorine, the
stewardry. This designation survived in the Anglicized form of
Mearns (Angus and Mearns). Each stewardry was governed by a
mòr-mhaor (mormaer) under the High King. According to
Andrew, Bishop of Caithness (d. AD 1184): 'Seven of Cruithne's
children divided Alba [Scotland] into seven divisions: the portion
of Cat, of Cè, of Cìrech; the portions of Fiobh, of Moireabh and
of Fòtla and of Fortiu. And it is the name of each man of them
that is his own land.' We find Cat surviving in Caithness, Moireabh
surviving in Moray and Fiobh surviving in Fife.

Fife has several interesting forts. North-west of Dunfermline
stands **Craigluscar** (NT 060910), which is enclosed in three
ramparts, the innermost of which is 3.5m thick. The fort itself
measures 53m by 33.5m. On the summit of **Dunearn Hill**, north-
west of Burntisland (NT 211872), is a fort commanding broad
views south over the Forth and Edinburgh. There are two periods
of building, the first producing an inner fort of 122m by 39.5m and
the second an outer fort enclosing the whole in a circular wall
about 3.5m thick.

East Lomond, south-west of Falkland (NO 244062), is situated

411.5m above sea-level on the summit of a hill commanding views to the Firth of Forth to the south and the Tay estuary to the north. It seems to have been constructed in the seventh or sixth century BC and contained evidence that it was also occupied in the sixth or seventh century AD. As well as hollow glass beads, and a mould for casting ingots, a slab with Pictish stone carving was found here.

To the south-west of Cupar is **Scotstarvit** (NO 361109), an oval enclosure, 30.5m by 27.5m, excavated in 1944–67. Three timber-framed houses were found to have stood in succession on this site, all belonging to a period prior to the first century AD.

North-north-west of Cupar stands **Greencraig** (NO 323215), a fort formed by two stone ramparts enclosing an irregular oval shape. There is a secondary structure within enclosing the summit of the hill. At the foot of the hill stands a homestead (NO 324215) which was excavated in 1947. The boundaries are rectangular in plan, measuring 20m by nearly 17m and within them stands a circular house nearly 10m in diameter. No finds were discovered but evidence suggested that it dates to at least the first century BC. Greencraig fort bears a superficial resemblance to its neighbour at **Norman's Law** (NO 305203), which stands on the highest summit of the Ochil range, dominating the territory to the Firth of Tay and the Howe of Fife. The main structure here is about 213.5m by 76m. There are several additional enclosures and ramparts which lead one to believe that to the original fort were added other buildings forming an open settlement in the first century AD.

Near St Andrews, to the west, is **Denork** (NO 455137), a stone fort by Denork House and within 1.5km of the broch at Drumcarrow. It consists of a stone wall about 3.5m thick enclosing an area on the precipitous flanks of a knoll some 137m by nearly 46m. It was once considered to be a post-Roman structure but this theory is now proved inaccurate. South-west, by some 5km, are the remains of what is now recognized to be **Drumcarrow** (NO 459133). It has been destroyed to such an extent that, initially, it was thought to be a large cairn.

Commanding a pass through the Ochils to the Tay estuary, **Clatchard Craig** (NO 244178), by Newburgh, stands 91.5m up the Ormiston Hill. The fort is a large one and well defended with four ramparts in places. The inner rampart was timber-laced: charred wood has been discovered, suggesting that the fort was once fired. Some of it has been destroyed by quarrying. However, excavations have been carried out recently and revealed relics dating to the early Christian period.

Black Cairn Hill, also near Newburgh (NO 234172), was built in the seventh or sixth century BC, but a lot of its structure has been taken away. Nevertheless it is discernible as an oval fort with ramparts originally 3m thick. It commands a view in all directions.

The south-east of the county of Perth, south of the Tay, formed part of the territory of the Venicones but most of this region belonged to the Caledonii. It is in Perth that the most western of the Tay-Tweed brochs is to be found. This is at **Coldoch** (NS 697982), 12km west of Stirling. Its interior diameter is 8.5m and the wall is about 5.5m thick. This wall now reaches only just over 1m in height but the rooms and stair lobby are still visible.

There are several duns which claim attention. **Tom Orain** (NN 867368) stands 3.2km west of Amulree and originally measured 19m by nearly 16m with walls 3.5m thick. 8km west of Pitlochry stands **Queen's View** (NN 8636020), which is one of the better preserved duns in the area. It is circular with a 17m internal diameter and walls 3m thick.

Two duns stand within striking distance of Fortingall. **Balnacraig** (NN 748476) overlooks the River Lyon and measures nearly 20m by 17.5m with a wall varying from 2.5m up to nearly 4m. The second is a little further on, 11km, at **Roromore** (NN 626468), a circular fortification 15m in diameter with a wall 4m thick in places.

Ceann na Coille, the head of the wood, is the site of another dun nearly 5km east of Tummel Bridge (NN 807586). It is fairly well preserved, is circular and measures nearly 17m in diameter.

Braes of Foss (NN 753560) is 9.5m east of Kinloch Rannoch and has the distinction of being the highest-sited dun in Perth. It stands 320m above sea-level and measures 26m by 23m. Much has been destroyed by ploughing.

The last dun worth visiting in the Perth area is **Strathgarry** (NN 890632), which is oval in shape within a wall 3m thick. The measurements are roughly 15m by 18m. A lot of detail has been obscured by forestry.

There are several hill-forts which command our attention here. **Moncrieffe Hill** (NO 136200), just south-south-east of Perth itself, dominates the central summit on a ridge which divides the lower reaches of the Tay and Earn. It is thought that its ramparts, of an oval plan, were built before a smaller oval structure in the interior. It has been suggested that the larger fort was abandoned and, when the Romans started their incursions into the area, the inner fort was established. Foundations of circular stone houses have been discovered.

Forgandenny (NO 100155), a few kilometres south-west of the Bridge of Earn, occupies a prominence on the north-east flank of Culteuchar Hill. This is of interest as, during an excavation in 1891, the sockets of beams were found preserved entire. Two ramparts enclose 55m by 24.5m. Not far, this time a little to the east-south-east of the Bridge of Earn, stands **Abernethy** (NO 183153), a hill-fort overlooking the confluence of the Rivers Earn and Ray. 3.2km south-west of it stands the Roman fort at Carpow. The hill-fort was of strategic importance and was built sometime after the fifth century BC. The main enclosure measures 41.5m by 15.5m and the outer ramparts are 5.5m thick in places. The inner wall varies in thickness from 5.5m to 7.5m and is still standing to a height of over 2m. A rock-cut well stands in the interior. Excavations have found La Tène style brooches. The walls were timber-laced.

Dun Mor (NN 906304), north-north-east of Crieff, stands at 457.5m overlooking the Sma' Glen and Lower Strathalmond. Nearby is a Roman fort at Fendoch. This fort of 46m by 27.5m has timber-laced walls but structural detail has vanished and it has been argued that the fort may never have been completed. It is thought that the stones were merely piled up in preparation for building.

Of particular interest is **Dundurn**, nearly 6km west of Comrie (NN 707233). It is a famous fort mentioned in the *Annals of Ulster*, compiled by Cathal Mac Magnus, Archdeacon of Clogher, in 1498 from earlier sources. The fort was besieged in AD 683 by the Dál Riadans, it being a principal Pictish stronghold. It was thought to have been built around the second century BC, and stands on a rocky knoll overlooking the River Earn about a kilometre from Loch Earn. It now consists of a series of ruined ramparts which form defended compound and courtyards all over the flanks of the knoll.

Rossie Law (NN 997124), just to the south-west of Dunning, is the largest of the forts which occupy peaks on the north face of the Ochil range overlooking Lower Strathearn from the south. It has a single rampart some 4m thick in places which encloses an area of 183m by 152.5m. There are traces of timber-framed buildings in the interior unusual, as most buildings in Scotland have stone foundations.

At **Machany** (NN 902158), north-west of Auchterarder, stands an oval hill-fort whose walls, now only rocky boundaries, were once 4.5m thick. Signs of vitrification have been discovered.

A very strongly fortified structure is that of **Evelick** (NO 199257), one of the forts on the south-west extremity of the Sidlaw Hills near Balbeggie. Oval in plan, enclosing an area of 76m by 61m, it has up to five ramparts and ditches, all pierced by an entrance causeway.

More famous in myth than in reality, is **Dunsinane** (Dunsinnan), also near Balbeggie. The fort stands on the summit of Dunsinane Hill, 19km east-south-east of the equally famous Birnam Wood. The entire enclosure measures 55m by 30.5m, within a ruined rampart which could have been a timber-laced wall. There are also the remains of three lesser ramparts. A small bi-lobbed souterrain is to be found inside the fort. Those tourists who come looking for Macbeth's castle, where the witches of Shakespeare's imagination prophesied that he would be killed 'when Birnam Wood do come to Dunsinane', will be disappointed. The battle between Macbeth's men and the English, led by Siward of Northumbria (trying to put the young Malcolm on the throne of Scotland), took place near Dundee on 27 July 1054. William of Malmesbury (c.1090–c.1143) is the earliest chronicler to mention the site of the battle and he names Dundee. Even so, Macbeth and the Scots drove out the invaders and fought for three more years before

Macbeth is recorded as being killed, most probably in an ambush. Lulach succeeded Macbeth as High King in August 1057, and was slain 'by stratagem' at Essy, in Strathbogie, Aberdeen, by Malcolm. Dunsinane is merely part of the later mythology established around Macbeth, Scotland's last great Gaelic king.

Similarly associated with the myth is **Duncan's Camp**, just to the south-south-east of Birnam (NP 046394). The fort commands the high ground over Stormont, Strathspey and Strathmore. It stands on a natural plateau and once enclosed an area 61m by 27.5m in which the shapes of two ramparts and ditches now survive. Only legend connects this with Duncan Mac Crinan (1034–40), an aggressive and unpopular king who was also an incompetent military leader. Duncan was not the elderly 'gracious king' of Shakespeare; he was only thirty-nine years old when he was overthrown after leading Scotland into several unpopular military campaigns against England and the Norsemen of the Orkneys. He had been defeated in all his battles and, according to the Celtic legal system under which he had been elected king, any king who did not maintain the commonweal of his people could be thrown out. Duncan fought back but was killed in battle and Macbeth, his cousin, Mormaer of the province of Moray, was elected High King.

Not far from here, 13km north-north-west of Blairgowrie, stands **Dalrulzion** (NO 1257), which was a sizeable settlement in which several homesteads have been identified. Some of these houses measured 8.5m in diameter with 1m thick walls. Saddle querns, pottery and other items found here date from the Early Celtic period.

Barry Hill (NO 262504) north-east of Alyth, has been almost totally destroyed. Tumbled stones mark the walls, showing that it once had massive defences and several ramparts.

Inchtuthill (NO 115393), near Caputh, is of interest in that this promontory fort, surrounded by the curve of the River Tay, provided evidence for the existence of all-timber defences in Scotland. However, the surviving works seem to have been built

An enamalled bronze dragonesque brooch dated to the first century AD

by the Romans, who appear to have captured the original Celtic fortress and occupied it. Part of the paved floor of a circular stone house was discovered in the interior.

Dominating a bend in the River Tay at Grandtully stands **Castle Dow** (NN 929513). There is little to be seen except the remains of walls which once formed ramparts of some 91.5m by 65.6m. Another fort, of almost identical measurements, is **Dun Mac Tual** (NN 778474) which is now obscured by conifers on Drummond Hill, near Kenmore. A central enclosure is protected by two outer walls. In spite of the overgrowth, it is considered one of the best-preserved fortresses of this kind.

Standing in woodland on a steeply sloped eminence about 800m from Loch Tay is **Bareyra** (NN 608333), a contour fort whose ramparts are still some 4.5m thick.

Bochastle (NN 601075) is near Callander, over a kilometre away from a Roman fort that stood on the right bank of the River Teith. Protected on the east by a steep incline and in other directions by four impressive ramparts, whose silhouette can be seen from a distance, the fort encloses an area 55m by nearly 46m.

Crossing into Angus we are in the territory of the Vacogmagi. At **Craighill**, 5km north-east of Dundee (NO 43235), are the remains of a multivallate fort with a broch nearby measuring 10.5m in diameter.

Laws Hill, Drumsturdy, (NO 493349) is another example of a hill-fort and broch. The interior of the broch is 10.5m in diameter and it has walls nearly 5m thick. The walls of the fort were made of carefully laid blocks of stone. Another broch stands at **Hurley Hawkin** (NO 333328) 6.4km west-north-west of Dundee. It has an interior diameter of 12m and walls 5m thick. A souterrain was found here. A brief excavation has found rotary querns, whorls, loom-weights and sherds.

Denoon Law (NO 355444), just to the south-west of Glamis, is a trapezoid-style fort whose ramparts are much overgrown, although one still stands to a height of 4m. Three additional ramparts protect the interior rampart and it is thought the buildings were of timber lacing.

Commanding extensive views over Strathmore is **Turin Hill** (NO

514534), where there is not only a fort, crowning a summit ridge, whose twin ramparts enclosed an area 274.5m by 122m, but also a dun, erected after the fort was abandoned and circular in shape with 3.5m thick walls and a diameter of 27m. This was built on the north sector; a second similar structure is situated to the west and a third to the east.

Floor timbers have dated **Finavon** (NO 506556) to between the eighth and sixth centuries BC. Lying to the north-east of Forfar, this fort was of a timber-laced type, measuring 152.5m by 36.5m with some of its ramparts being about 3.5m thick. There are signs that vitrification has taken place.

Perhaps most famous among Scottish hill-forts are the Caterthuns, north-west of Brechin. The **White Caterthun** (NO 548660) and its neighbour. 1.6km to the north-east, the **Brown Caterthun** (NO 555668) are very conspicuous. The White Caterthun stands only 10.5m higher than its neighbour. It is almost oval and its rampart has been described as the most imposing ruined wall in Britain. The original was 12m thick with another wall 6m thick. The combined tumble from the two walls spreads to a width of 30.5m. The walls were originally timber-laced and although they are in a ruinous condition, the site has been remarkably untouched by stone-robbers.

While its neighbour is not so impressive, nevertheless no fewer than six lines of defence corrugate the hillside. A very reduced stone wall protects the summit with a single entrance to the north. Other ramparts spread around the hill with a ditch.

Moving north-east into Kincardine there is only one small fort of note, at **Cairnton**, south-west of Fettercairn (NO 633723), overlooking the plain of the river North Esk and Strathmore. It is vitrified. North into Aberdeen we are in the borderlands of the Vacomagi and a tribe called the Taexali. **Knockargetty Hill** (NJ 455030), north of Dinnet, seems to be an unfinished oval fort, lying on a ridge above open woodland. Its lines, marked by earthworks, had not gone far when the project was apparently abandoned.

At a distance of 3.2km north of Aboyne is **Mortlich** (NJ 535017), a fort dominating Strathdee and standing 244m above the

river at Aboyne. A ruined enclosing wall has been greatly reduced
by stone-robbers for the purpose of making a modern cairn which
occupies the summit of the hill within the fort. Lying here is a slab
to the memory of the 10th Marquis of Huntly (d. 18 September
1863).

Barra Hill (NJ 803257), near Old Meldrum, is enclosed in
double ramparts and a ditch, but the site is generally featureless.

Barmekin of Echt (NJ 725070), near Echt, is a multi-rampart
defence work: indeed, it has an unusual number of ramparts,
which are pierced by five entrances with passageways within
flanking walls. One can still see the incredible complications of the
defence system.

Traces of circular stone house foundations are seen in the
interior of **Mither Tap of Bennachie**, south-south-east of Oyne (NJ
683224), a fort which stands on the highest and most easterly
summit of the Bennachie heights. It is difficult, because of the
rocky summit, to pick out the exact plan of the fort. Nearby stands
Pittodrie (NJ 694244) on the north-east extremity of Bennachie.
This is surrounded by double defences.

The hill of Dunnideer rises only 267m above sea-level but there
is no higher ground between it and the coast at Newburgh so that
it dominates the view. On the summit of **Dunnideer** (NJ 613281)
stands a large vitrified hill-fort, slightly ruined by the construction
of a medieval tower built from stones taken from the fort. Within
a few kilometres of this stands **Barmyn of North Keig** (NJ 599200),
where a stone fort crowns the summit of an isolated hill
overlooking the Howe of Alford from the north. The enclosure is
circular within two ramparts. There are the remains of a cairn in
the interior, some 7.5m in diameter.

Overlooking the plain between Insch and Rhynie, on a spur
proytruding from the Corren Hills, is a stone fort called **Cairnmore**
(NJ 503248). Enclosed in double ramparts around a domed
interior, the fort measures some 52m by nearly 46m. Near here is
Tap o' North (NJ 485293) which is visible for 50km to the east.
The fort crowns a superb site and is the second-highest fort in
Scotland (at over 564m above sea-level); the single rampart may
have been over 6m thick or more and is now heavily vitrified.

There seems to have been a well in the interior and traces of timber-framed houses have been noticed.

Westward into Banff there is only one fort which commands attention: **Little Conval** (NJ 295393), which is a few kilometres west of Duffton, at a height of 549m between Strathspey and Glenrinnes. Work on this fort seems to have been abandoned before completion but some of the plans, marked out by stones, are clearly visible.

Moray once formed part of the province of Moireabh, which stretched from the east coast of Aberdeen to the west coast of Ross and Cromarty, and from whose Mormaers the High Kings of Scotland were chosen before the coming of Malcolm Canmore from England. Perhaps the most famous Mormaer of Moray was Macbeth. Moray contains one of the most interesting fortifications in Scotland. **Burghead** (NJ 109691) appears to have been a great centre of the Caledonii, later to form a tribal confederation with some of their neighbours and to be nicknamed 'Picts' by the Romans. Certainly, Burghead was regarded as the capital of the Picts in later Roman times and has been claimed as the place where, in the sixth century AD, St Colmcille from Iona came to visit the Pictish king Brude and converted him to Christianity. Burghead was a promontory fort standing on a headland and cut off by three sets of ramparts from the landward side. These ramparts stretched for 244m, enclosing an area some 305m in length by 183m in width. An entrance ran through the ramparts. Precipitous cliffs protected the other sides. The ramparts were 7m at their base and stood as high as 6m. In 1890 an excavation showed them to be still 5m in height. Slabs of stone about 1m thick were presented to the outside. The walls were timber-laced with horizontal oak planks 50–75mm thick and 250-300mm wide. Iron bolts secured these timbers, some of them 200mm long and 25mm thick.

A large well of unusual proportions is situated in the enclosure within a rectangular chamber about 5m square and 3.5m high.

Several carved Pictish stones were discovered here dating to the eighth or ninth century AD. Certainly this was an important site in the period from the fifth to the ninth century AD. But the fort has been dated to an earlier period. It has been argued that the Romans may even have reached this Celtic fortress and attacked it. Burghead is a place of much speculation and a site of prime importance for those looking for Early Celtic remains, being encroached on by the sea on the one hand and the creeping environs of modern towns on the other.

Two more fortresses are of interest in Moray. The **Doune of Relugas** (NJ 003495), which stands in private grounds, dominates the confluence of the Rivers Findhorn and Divie, 10km south-west of Forres. A ditch and rampart enclose the fortress and in several places, particularly at its eastern entrance, masses of vitrified stones can be seen showing that it was burnt at one period.

The other fort is that of the **Knock of Alves**, just west of Elgin, rising from the plain between Forres and Elgin (NJ 163629). There are fragmentary remains of its double ramparts, which were some 5.5m apart. A mausoleum called York Tower was later built in the centre of the fortress and this, with the encroachment of trees and quarrying, has defaced this very interesting defence work.

Moving west again into Nairn, there are three forts of interest. **Dun Evan,** south-west of Cawdor (NH 827475), is also called the Doune of Cawdor. It occupies an isolated crag commanding the whole of lower Strathnairn. A wall encloses an oval fort of 59.5m by 26m in which the only feature of interest is the mark of a well. Vitrification has been recorded here and the ruins suggest timber-lacing was used in the construction.

Castle Finlay (NH 888514), a few kilometres south of Nairn, sits on the north-west flank of the Hill of Urchany, enclosing an area of 36.5m by 18m. Little is discernible here and the site seems badly chosen as a defensive centre.

Dunearn, 16km south-east of Nairn (NH 933406), stands on a wooded hill called Doune on the right bank of the River Findhorn. The fort is enclosed in two ramparts, each now merely a line of rubble. Signs of vitrification have been found here. The interior was under plough until 1906 and so there is little left to see.

d. Scotland: Inner Isles

Bute, Arran, Islay, Colonsay, Mull, Iona,
Tiree, Coll, Muck, Eigg, Canna, Skye, Raasay

To facilitate a tour of the islands, I have decided to deal with the
inner islands first, then the outer islands and finally the northern
islands. Our start will be at Bute, at the entrance of the Clyde,
then we shall head south to Arran before working northwards to
Raasay. Unfortunately, it is not known whether the islands were
extensions of mainland tribal areas of whether they were
populated by distinct tribes who were confined to island territory.
There are very few forts on the islands, some brochs but numerous
duns, or fortified homesteads. Small duns are found in great
numbers in the Hebrides; these are virtually unexplored and it has
been argued that some of them only date from the medieval
period.

There are two interesting forts on Bute. **Barone Hill** (NS
069630) is an oval structure but its two ramparts have been
destroyed with stones being taken away for building. The other
fortress lies at **Dunagoil** (NS 085530), occupying a narrow ridge
rising 30.5m above the shore near Garroch Head. Partly defended
by the steep flanks of the ridge and partly by its ramparts, the fort
has been the source of some interesting finds including evidence of
the industrial use of iron and bronze in the area, together with
lignite and steatite artefacts, some pottery and a La Tène brooch.

Bute also has three duns of note. **Dun Burgisdale** (NS 063660),
3km north-west of Rothesay, at the head of St Colmac Burn,
measures 20m in diameter with walls varying from 3m to 4m in
thickness. 8km south-west of Rothesay is **Dun Scalpsie** (NS
044580), situated above the Sound of Bute. It is now almost
ruinous but the walls measure 27.5m by 24.5m, varying between
2.75m and 4.5m in width. The last dun is that of **Eilean Buidhe**,
Kyle of Bute (NS 018754), which occupies the southern end of the
northernmost of the Burnt Islands off the tip of Bute to the north-
east. Measuring 17m in diameter, this shows signs of having been
set afire.

There are no traces of forts on Arran, which is unusual for an island of its size and proximity to the mainland, nor on Islay.

A fort does stand on Colonsay. **Dun Cholla**, 3.2km south-west of Scalascaig (NR 377914), has ramparts which are still 3m thick. Its most interesting feature is a circular stone foundation 7.6m in diameter which crosses the north-west wall and contains a ring of six post-holes. This seems to have been built after the fort was abandoned sometime in the early first or second century AD. **Dunan na Nighean** is situated 4km north-east of Scalascaig. This small dun has been greatly denuded of stone and it is impossible to estimate its dimensions except for one wall which stretches 9m.

Iona has a small dun at **Dun Cul Bhuirg** (NM 265246), a few kilometres west of St Mary's Abbey on the steep-sided western shore of the island. It measured 23m by 15m and excavations revealed the remains of a simple house with a considerable amount of pottery and other finds which date its occupation to the closing centuries of the first millennium BC.

At a distance of 14km south-west of Tobermory on the Isle of Mull stands **Dun nan Gall** (NM 433231), the fortress of the foreigners. This is a broch situated on a low headland on the north-east of Loh Tuath. It measures 10.5m in diameter with walls 3m thick. The entrance is on the eastern side. **An Sean Dun**, the old fort (NM 431563), stands 7 km west-by-north of Tobermory. This circular house, 10m in diameter, still has galleries.

Tiree is noted for a broch standing 5km north of Scarinish called **Dun Mor Vaul** (NM 046493). This is situated west of Vaul Bay and is 10.5m in diameter within a wall 4m thick. Galleries and rooms are apparent. Excavations in 1962–4 put the date of this broch at about the sixth century BC. Remains of several other such constructions have been noticed on Tiree but not absolutely identified.

On Coll two duns remain. **Loch nan Cinneachan** (NM 188568) and **Dun an Achaidh** (NM 183546) are both west of Arinagour. These are the best examples among the dozen or so sites identified on the island as dwellings of the Early Celtic farmers and fishermen of the island.

The next island in this group with the remains of a hill-fort is

Muck, where 800m south of Port Mor pier stands **Caisteal an Duin Bhain** (NM 422786). The fort measures 39.5m by 29m with a rampart 2.75m thick. Foundations of some rectangular building can be distinguished within the fort but have not been dated.

Next to Muck is Eigg, on which stands **An Sgurr** (NM 462846), occupying the summit of a sheer-sided hill rising 122m above sea-level. Only from the west is there an approach up a steep and rocky ascent. But here the rampart checks the attackers with defences 3m thick and 76m long connecting the north and south precipices and enclosing an area of 3.6 hectares.

Canna has a dun, **Dun Channa** (NG 205047), which stands on Garrisadale Point. Its dry-stone walling is 2m thick and its entrance can only be reached by a ladder or by those with a knowledge of rock-climbing techniques.

One has to go to Skye before encountering further forts in this island chain. There are three here. **Dun Gerashader**, just north of Portree (NG 489453), stands on a ridge overlooking the River Chracraig. Oval in plan, it measures 52m by 30.5m with ramparts up to 4m thick in the south. The entrance is to the east and the approaches are well fortified.

Dun Cruinn (NG 412516) is further to the north-west and this fort occupies a flat-topped rocky hill. Dry-stone walls, now very decayed, surround the plateau, and there are signs of an earthern rampart with a ditch. The entrance is in the south-west. The ruin of what may be a small fortified dwelling, a dun, stands within the fort: this measures 12m by 9m.

Finally, **Dun Skudiburgh** (NG 374647), near Uig, occupies a very prominent ridge overlooking Uig Bay. It is oval in plan with ramparts 3m thick. There are signs of other ramparts and in the interior is a dun measuring 10m by 7m. The wall of this dun varies from 2.75m to 3.5m in thickness.

Skye has the remains of several brochs. **Dun Ard an t'-Sabhail** (NG 318333), 3.2km north-by-west of Talisker, overlooks Fiskavaig from the south-west. It is 10.5m in diameter with a wall 3.5m thick. The entrance passage has what appears to be a guard chamber. Then there is **Dun Fiadhairt**, 4km west of Dunvegan (NG 230506), which has an interior diameter of 9.5m within a wall up to 3.5m thick. The entrance is on the west and fitted with two communicating rooms. Another room is in the north-west section with a stair lobby in the north and a gallery in the east and south sections.

Also near Dunvegan, 8km north-west, is **Boreraig** (NG 195531), measuring 10.5m in diameter with a wall 4m thick. The entrance is on the west. A gallery can be seen around most of the wall, which still stands as high as 2.75m.

North-by-west of Lusta stands **Dun Hallin** (NG 257593), a broch which is 11m in diameter within a wall 3m thick and still standing up to 3.5m high. The entrance is in the south-east with two rooms and a stair lobby. It is enclosed by a wall 2m thick and measuring 45.75m by 39.5m.

Just over 1.5km west of Bracadale stands a broch at **Struanmore** (NG 339386) which is one of the best preserved in the island. Some 11m in diameter, with walls 4m thick, it has an entrance to the east. The walls still stand to a height of 3.5m. Nearby is a dun (NG 340390) covering some 53m by 43m within a wall varying between 2.5m and 4m in thickness. Returning to the Portree area, some 13km north-west of the town is **Dun Suledale** (NG 374526) a broch which is 13m in diameter within a wall up to 3.5m thick. The entrance is on the west. Galleries and rooms can still be seen and the broch lies in an enclosure some 43m by 30.5m with walls about 2m thick.

Skye also contains some other interesting duns. **Dun Totaig** (NG 235484), nearly 2km from Dunvegan, is an oblong dun measuring 14.5m by 7m. **Rudh an Dunain** (NG 396160), 5km south-south-west of Glenbrittle House, is more impressive, measuring 24.5m by 11m with walls 3.5m thick and still standing to 2.75m.

e. Scotland: Outer Islands

Lewis, Harris, Berneray (Harris), North Uist
Benbecula, South Uist, Barra, Sandray,
Pabray and Berneray

Beginning in the north at Lewis and working south, we start with **Rudha na Berie** (NB 235474) which stands 24km north-west of Stornoway. It is a promontory fort occupying a rocky peninsula and is protected on the landward side by a rampart up to 7m thick which stretched from the north to 3.5m from the south, where the entrance is. A ditch and low bank give extra protection. Near here is **Bragor** (NB 286474), a comparatively well-preserved broch, on the north-east shore of Loch an Duna. The interior diameter is 9m; the walls are 3.5m thick and still stand to a height of 4m. **Dun Carloway**, another broch (NB 189412), is situated 25km west-north-west of Stornoway, but this has suffered much from stone-robbers. Even so, part of the wall still reaches as high as 9m. It is 3m thick and the interior measures 7.5m in diameter. Chambers, galleries and staircases are still visible.

There are three interesting duns of Lewis. **Lower Bayable** (NB 516305), 9.5km east of Stornoway, stands on a small island connected by a man-made causeway. It is a circular dun measuring 15m in diameter. Nearly 13km to the west of Stornoway is **Dun Cromore** (NB 400206), on the west shore of Loch Cromore, with an interior of 16m by 13.5m. The third dun, **Dun Baravat** (NB 156356), is nearly 27km west of Stornoway, close to Loch Baravat. Its walls still stand 3m high and 2.5m thick. Internally the dun measures 12m by 9m.

There is an interesting dun on Harris: **Bovemore** (NG 033940), some 11km north of Rodal. The remains are on a small hill with walls 4m thick and an inner courtyard 6m in diameter.

Caisteal Odair stands on North Uist (NF 731766) and is another promontory fort bordered by sheer cliffs except to the south-east where there is a wall 3m thick and 110m long. The remains of several circular stone dwellings were found here but there is some argument as to whether these were built at the time of the fort or afterwards.

North Uist has three duns. **Loch Hunder** (NF 905653), 3.2km south-west of Lochmaddy, occupies an island near the east shore of the loch. Causeways connect it to the shore and to another island, from which a third causeway also connects with the shore. The dun is 12m by 10m with walls varying in thickness from 1.5m

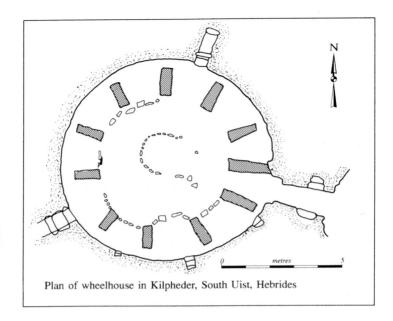

Plan of wheelhouse in Kilpheder, South Uist, Hebrides

to 3m. **Dun Torcuill** (NF 888737) is 6km north-west of Lochmaddy. This measures 11.5m in diameter with a wall varying in thickness from 2m to 4m. The walls still stand to a height of 3m in places. The third dun is at **Clettraval**, almost 17km west of Lochmaddy. This is a circular dun with an internal diameter of 8m and 2m thick walls.

On Benbecula stands **Dun Buidhe**, the yellow dun (NF 794546). This is one of several island fortifications but by far the best preserved. The fortified island measures 46m in diameter; the wall has spread to 7.5m in thickness but was probably about 3.5m thick when standing.

At **Kilpheder** (NF 735205) on South Uist stands one of the best-preserved and most easily accessible homesteads, 6km west-by-north of Lochboisdale. Finds from this house show it was occupied in the early Iron Age period. With a circular outer wall, the building was 9m in diameter. There remains a series of eleven oblong dry-stone pillars standing free of the wall. It is a stone replica of some of the circular timber-framed buildings seen elsewhere. Also on South Uist stands a dun which is worth visiting, **Dun Vulan** (NF 714297), which is typical of several on the island. The circular ruin stands on an island on Loch Ardvule, connected to the shore, and is 17m in diameter. The wall varies in thickness from 3m to 4.5m.

Dun Cuier broch stands on Barra, 5km north of Castlebay (NF 664034). The interior measures 9m in diameter with a wall 5m thick. Various objects have been recovered here including querns and materials which suggest the broch was still inhabited as late as the seventh century AD.

Sandray has a dun which takes its name from the island (NL 637914) and stands on a hillock. It measures 15m by 12m with a wall varying in thickness from 2m to 4m.

Berneray's dun (named after it) is 1.5km west of Berneray pier (NL 547802) on a promontory. A lighthouse stands close by. Some parts of the wall stand 4m thick and it is still possible to see stretches of internal gallery and door construction.

f. Scotland: Northern Islands

Orkney, Fair Isle and Shetland

There are several brochs on the Orkney islands. Four interesting ones can be seen on the mainland island. **Netlater** (HY 323173) is 11km north-north-east of Stromness. It is 10m in diameter with walls 3.5m thick. The entrance is on the east and three chambers lie in the wall at cardinal points with one to the south having an internal stair. At **Oxtro** (HY 253267), 17km north of Stromness, is another broch, a larger affair some 13.75m in interior diameter with 4m-thick walls. A considerable number of relics have been found here dating from the first century AD. Not far away, some 22km north-east of Stromness, is **Gurness** (HY 383267), where the incursion of the sea has eroded parts of the outworks. However, the broch itself is 4.5m above current high water and its interior is 10m in diameter with walls 4m thick. The interior also contains a well. The broch was used down to Viking times, when Norse settlers ousted the Celtic inhabitants. Finally, at **St Mary's** (HY 470013), another broch stands at the north end of the Loch of Ayre, at the west end of St Mary's. It measures 9m in interior diameter with walls 4m thick. The entrance is at the eastern arc.

On Rousay Island (Orkney) is **Mid Howe** (HY 371307), which is 30ft in interior diameter and surrounded by 5m-thick walls which still stand to a height of 5m. This broch contains many features such as door checks, guard rooms, galleries and staircase.

On North Ronaldsay (Orkney) stands **Burrian** (HY 762513), which is rather spectacularly placed on a cliff on the southern extremity of the island. Its 5m-thick walls enclose an area 10m in diameter. The broch itself is defended by the remains of four ramparts. A number of finds were made here in 1870 including many Pictish symbols.

The main group of forts is situated on the Shetlands and perhaps the most famous of these is **Clickhimin**, which is both a fort and a broch, on the mainland island (HU 465408). The excavations at Clickhimin were described by the archaeologist Patrick Crampton as 'a revelation'. According to Dr Crampton, the excavations carried out by J. R. C. Hamilton revealed the architectural and domestic arrangements within a Celtic fortress for the first time, showing multi-storeyed habitation. For the first time archaeologists came to understand that the Celts had buildings, in the period around the fourth to second centuries BC, in which they lived on upper levels. The chieftain's quarters overlooking the gate rose to three storeys in height.

Burland (HU 445360), 5km south-west of Lerwick, is a broch occupying a narrow headland. The cliffs fall on three sides in precipitous fashion to a rocky shore. The broch itself is 10m in diameter in its interior with walls 4.5m thick. The entrance is in the south-west.

A broch also stands at **Jarlshof** (HU 397096), just south of Sumburgh airport. With the remnants of the broch are a series of round houses and other structures which probably date to the early

Bronze Age and were certainly occupied in the Iron Age.

The **Ness of Burgi** (HU 388084) is also on the Shetland mainland island and is one of a series of forts similar to Clickhimin. Here, also, the 'blockhouse' rose to three storeys in height. The sophistication of the building work has caused historians and archaeologists to revise many of their theories regarding the abilities of the Early Celts.

Sae Breck (HU 210780), some 7km east-by-north of Hillswick, is another broch which has revealed much about life here in the first century BC and AD. The broch was about 76m in interior diameter with a wall 4.5m thick. The entrance was in the east. Two chambers survive in which over 120 sherds of pottery were recovered. The broch was surrounded by a wall 3m thick enclosing an area 36.5m by 33.5m.

Perhaps the most famous broch of all is on **Mousa Island**, Shetland (HU 457236). It stands on the west coast and measures 15m in external diameter, rising to a height of 12m. Its doorways, staircases, galleries and even secondary buildings are conceived on a grand scale and have caused it to be one of the most photographed and visited of all the broch constructions. It has been dated to the fourth century BC.

Standing on Unst Island, Shetland, is the **Hoga Ness** broch (HP 557005), which is 3.2km east of Uyeasound, near the ferry terminal. The broch is only just traceable and is not as spectacular as others that still stand although its measurements were similar. The diameter seems to have been 9m.

Another example of this type of building can be seen on Whalsay Island, Shetland: the **Loch of Huxter** (HU 558620). The 'blockhouse' here measures 12m in length by 3m wide, the same as that at Clickhimin. The circular fortress is about 21m in diameter.

On Yell Island, Shetland, another fort, that of **Burgi Geos** (HP 477034), is twice as high as that of the Ness of Burgi, with stones that are large and form a coarse *chevaux de frise*. It is a promontory fort with a 'blockhouse' some 10.5m long by 4m thick. Also on Yell Island, the broch at **Burra Ness** (HU 556956) is still fairly impressive with an interior 8m in diameter within walls 4.5m thick whose inner face still rises 3.5m above the floor.

South on Fair Isle, Shetland, stands the promontory fort of **South Haven** (HY 223723). There is an argument whether the site is Early Celtic or medieval. It measures 53m by 10m, separating South Haven from Mavers Geo, the neck protected by three ramparts and ditches.

Glossary

Ard A primitive plough which consists of a stone or hard wood as a share.

Arras culture The finds from Celtic graves at Arras, in the East Yorkshire area, the territory of the Parisi, which have revealed some spectacular chariot burials.

Atrebates A Celtic tribe of Belgic origin centred in Hampshire, Berkshire and West Sussex with capitals at Silchester, Winchester and Chichester.

Barbican An inturned entrance passage to a hill-fort, with gates at either end and guarded from a rampart above.

Belgae A Celtic people who settled in southern Britain in the second and first centuries BC, moving out of the Low Countries and northern France before the expansion of the Germanic tribes and later Roman conquest of Gaul.

Brigantes Thought to be a confederation of Celtic tribes in what is now northern England. Names of sub-tribes (Textoverdi, Carvetti, Lopocares, Garbrantouces, Setantii and Latenses) have been mentioned. However, when the Romans first encountered the Brigantes 'The High Ones', they were already a powerful political group led by a female chieftain, Cartimandua ('Sleek Pony').

Broch See Introduction.

Bronze Age Period when metallurgy was developed in Britain, divided into the early period, 2300-1700 BC. middle period, 1700–1300 BC; and late period, 1300–800 BC. Celticists and some archaeologists believe that the Celts were already established in Britain by the late period of the Bronze Age and the transition to iron was merely one of development and not a sign of an 'invasion'.

Burh/burg Fortified place of Saxon date, sometimes a reoccupied Celtic hill-fort.

Caereni A Celtic tribe in north Sutherland.

Caledones A Celtic tribe mainly in Argyll and Inverness from whose name the Roman name for Scotland, Caledonia, derived.

Cantii Also Cantiaci. Celtic tribe who gave their name to their territory of Kent.

Capstone Large stone forming the roof of a burial chamber.

Carnonacae A Celtic tribe in the north of Ross and Cromarty, bordering on Sutherland.

Cassivellauni Name given to a Celtic tribe based in the Chilterns and also referred to as Catuvellauni. The name 'lovers of Belinos' is said to have derived from their greatest leader Cassivellaunos who led British resistance against Caesar in 54 BC. Overcoming their neighbours, the Trinovantes, they transferred their capital to Colchester.

Catuvellauni See Cassivellauni.

Celt One who speaks a Celtic language. The Celts were the first Transalpine people to become known to recorded history, *c.* sixth century BC. They occupied territories from Ireland in the west to central Turkey in the east and from the Low Countries and northern France in the north to Spain and northern Italy in the south. Their civilization began its retreat before the growth of the Roman Empire from the end of the third century BC. The population of Britain was entirely Celtic at the time of the Roman invasions 55/54 BC and AD 43.

Celtic field system A recognizable form of field boundaries used by the Celts, usually delineated by banks of earth or stone hedging.

Chevaux-de-frise Sharp stones set on end in the form of ramparts to act as an added defence.

Cist A grave lined with stone slabs.

Cliff Castle See Promontory fort.

Corbelling Layers of stone overhanging each other to form the roof of a stone chamber, often found in fogou and souterrain structures.

Cordoned ware Early Celtic pottery with horizontal ribs or cordons decorating it.

Coritani A Celtic tribe in the Lincoln and Leicester area.

Cornavii A Celtic tribe on the north coast of Sutherland and Caithness.

Cornovii A Celtic tribe centred in Shropshire. A second Cornovii tribe has been listed in Cornwall.

Counterscarp A bank on the outside of a defensive ditch, often produced as a result of the ditch clearance.

Courtyard house See example at Chysauster, Cornwall.

Crannog See Introduction.

Creones A Celtic tribe in west Inverness.

Currency bars Sword-shaped bars of iron used by some Celtic tribes as a form of currency prior to the introduction of coins.

Damnonii A Celtic tribe living in the Strathclyde area of Scotland.

Decantae A Celtic tribe in Ross and Cromarty.

Deceangli A Celtic tribe in North Wales and Chester area.

Demetae A Celtic tribe in South-west Wales.

Dobunni A Celtic tribe found between the Severn and the Cotswolds.

Duck and stamp ware Celtic pottery from the West Midlands decorated with S (ducks) or V patterns.

Dumnonii A Celtic tribe living in Devon and Cornwall.

Dun A fortified dwelling. See Introduction.

Durotriges A Celtic tribe living in Dorset and Somerset.

Epidii A Celtic tribe on the Mull of Kintyre.

Fécamp defence A Belgic method of hill-fort defence consisting of a wide, flat-bottomed ditch and bank, apparently introduced into South-east Britain during the first century BC.

Fogou A stone-lined underground passage and chamber used for storage in Early Celtic Cornish dwellings. The same structure is called a souterrain in Scotland. The word comes from a Cornish word *fogo* or *fougo* which means a cave or subterranean chamber.

Halberd A dagger-like blade fixed at right angles to a wooden handle.

Hallstatt The first 'Iron Age' culture, around the eighth century BC, and named after a town in Austria.

Hill-fort See Introduction.

Hollow way A sunken roadway cut into a hillside as a protective way to a hill-fort.

Iceni A Celtic tribe in Norfolk and Suffolk.

Iron Age The period from about 750 BC to the Roman conquest when iron was the main metal for making weapons and tools. It is divided into three phases. Hallstatt (A); La Tène (B); and La Tène (C); named from particular styles of artefacts. So far as Britain was concerned, this was the Early Celtic period.

La Tène The second 'Iron Age' culture, 500–100 BC, and named after it, centre on Lake Neuchâtel, Switzerland.

Lugi A Celtic tribe in Caithness.

Menhir A standing stone, from the Celtic *maen* (stone) *hir* (long).

Multivallate A hill-fort having more than one line of rampart and ditch.

Novantae A Celtic tribe in South-west Scotland.

Oppidum Roman name (and hence archaeologists' name) for a major Celtic fortification, usually a tribal capital.

Ordovices A Celtic tribe in North-west and western Wales.

Parisi A Celtic tribe in East Yorkshire whose namesakes in Gaul gave their name to the French capital. See Arras culture.

Passage grave Stone passage leading into a roughly circular burial chamber.

Picts The name 'Pict' or rather Picti first occurs in a Latin poem of AD 297. It is thought the name originated as a nickname amongst the Roman garrisons of northern Britain for the Celtic warriors of Caledonia who used 'war paint' – the word coming from *pingere* (to paint). The Picts were not a new element in the population; they were a Brythonic Celtic-speaking people and most likely confederations of tribal groups such as the Caledones and their neighbours. By the time they emerged into recorded history they had undergone a linguistic change from Brythonic Celtic to Goidelic Celtic (doubtless influenced by the Dál Riada settlement in Argyll) and called themselves the Tuatha Cruithne.

Promontory fort See Introduction.

Quoit Cornish name for a burial chamber.

Regni The name of a branch of the Atrebates after their ruler Cogidumnos had made an alliance with Rome and become a client king.

Revetment Wall of stone, timber or turf used to hold ramparts in position.

Ring cairn A circular cairn with an open space at its centre.

Ring mark An engraved circle on a stone.

Romano-British A general, loose term for the native British Celts under Roman occupation, sometimes used more specifically for those British Celts who had adopted Roman influences.

Samian ware Glossy, red-coated pottery imported from southern Gaul.

Sarsen A form of micaceous sandstone used for the construction of stone circles and chambered tombs.

Scarping A slope that has been artificially steepened.

Selgovae A Celtic tribe in southern Scotland, on the border in the Selkirk and Roxburgh region.

Settlement A group of homesteads found outside fortified areas such as hill-forts.

Silures A Celtic tribe of South Wales who fiercely fought against the Roman conquest and were marked out by Tacitus as being 'different' from the other Celtic tribes of Britain. He maintained they were of Iberian Celtic origin.

Slighting To have been partially destroyed by attackers at some historical period.

Smertae A Celtic tribe in the Sutherland and Caithness area.

Stater A Celtic gold coin of the pre-Roman period.

Taezali A Celtic tribe in the Banff and Aberdeen area.

Terret A metal ring that formed part of a chariot or cart and through which the reins passed.

Timber lacing Horizontal cross-timbers used to tie front and back fences of a hill-fort rampart together.

Trinovantes A Celtic tribe in the Essex area who had strong trading connections with Europe.

Univallate A single line of rampart, or one bank and ditch.

Vacomagi A Celtic tribe in the Grampian area.

Venicones A Celtic tribe in the Tayside area.

Vitrification The fusing together of stone at high temperature as a result of fire, usually caused when the timber lacings of a fort were burnt. Causes of vitrification are usually put down to the burning of the fortification or building during an attack by enemies (by the Romans in many hill-fort examples). However, it is also argued that it may have happened when old buildings were fired to clear them before new constructions were made.

Votadini A Celtic tribe whose territory spread from Northumbria up to the Lothian counties.

Bibliography

(and recommended further reading)

On the Celts and their Civilization

ALLEN, D. F. (ed. D. NASH), *The Coins of the Ancient Celts*, Edinburgh, 1980.

BRUNAUX, JEAN LOUIS, *The Celtic Gauls: Gods, Rites and Sanctuaries*, Seaby, London, 1987.

CHADWICK, NORA, *The Celts*, Pelican Books, London, 1970.

CUNLIFFE, BARRY, *The Celtic World*, Maidenhead, 1979.

DILLON, MYLES, & NORA CHADWICK, *The Celtic Realms*, Weidenfeld & Nicholson, London, 1967.

ELLIS, PETER BERRESFORD, *Caesar's Invasion of Britain*, Orbis Press, London, 1978.

ELLIS, PETER BERRESFORD, *The Celtic Empire: The First Millennium of Celtic History 1000 BC–AD 51*, Constable, London, 1990.

FILIP, JAN, *Celtic Civilization and its Heritage*, Publishing House of Czechoslovak Academy of Sciences (English trs), Prague, 1960.

GREEN, MIRANDA, *The Gods of the Celts*, Alan Sutton, Gloucester, 1986.

GREEN, MIRANDA, *Symbol and Image in Celtic Religious Art*, Routledge & Kegan Paul, London, 1989.

HUBERT, HENRI, *The Rise of the Celts*, trs. Kegan Paul, 1934. With intro by Prof. Gearóid Mac Eoin, Constable, London, 1987.

HUBERT, HENRI, *The Greatness and Decline of the Celts*, trs. Kegan Paul, 1934. With intro by Prof Geraóid Mac Eoin, Constable, London, 1987.

LAING, LLOYD, *Celtic Britain*, Routledge & Kegan Paul, London, 1978.

LAING, LLOYD *Later Celtic Art in Britain and Ireland*, Shire Publications, Princes Risborough, 1987.

MAC CANA, PROINSIAS, *Celtic Mythology*, Hamlyn, London, 1970.

MACREADY, S., AND THOMPSON F. H., *Cross-Channel Trade Between Gaul and Britain in the pre-Roman Iron Age*, Society of Antiquaries, London, 1984.

MARKLE, JEAN, *Women of the Celts*, Gordon Cremonesi, London, 1975.

MEGAW, RUTH AND VINCENT, *Early Celtic Art in Britain and Ireland*, Shire Publications, Princes Risborough, 1986.

MEGAW, RUTH AND VINCENT, *Celtic Art: From its Beginnings to the Book of Kells*, Thames & Hudson, London, 1989.

NASH, DAPHNE, *Coinage in the Celtic World*, Seaby, London, 1987.

NEWARK, TIM, *Celtic Warriors 400 BC–AD 1600*, Blandford Press, Poole, 1986.

RAFTERY, JOSEPH, ed., *The Celts*, Mercier Press, Cork, 1964.

RANKIN, H. D., *Celts and the Classical World*, Croom Helm, Beckenham, Kent, 1987.

REES, ALWYN & BRINLEY, *Celtic Heritage*, Thames & Hudson, 1961.

RITCHIE, W. F. AND J. N. G., *Celtic Warriors*, Shire Publications, Princes Risborough, 1985.

ROLLESTON, T. W., *Myths and Legends of the Celtic Race*, George Harrap, London, 1911; reprint, Constable, London, 1985.

ROSS, ANNE, *Everyday Life of the Pagan Celts*, B. T. Batsford, 1970 (retitled *The Pagan Celts*, and revised, 1986).

ROSS, ANNE, *Pagan Celtic Britain*, Routledge & Kegan Paul, London, 1974.

ROSS, ANNE, & ROBINS, DON, *The Life and Death of a Druid Prince: the story of an archaeological sensation*, Rider, London, 1989.

SQUIRE, CHARLES, *Celtic Myth and Legend*, Newcastle Publishing, USA, 1975 (facsimile of 1905 edition by Gresham, London).

STEAD, I. M., *Celtic Art*, British Museum Publications, London, 1989.

General

ALLCROFT, A., *Earthworks of England*, Macmillan, London, 1908.

ATKINSON, R. J. C., & OTHERS, *Excavations at Dorchester*, Ashmolean Museum, Oxford, 1951.

BENFIELD, ERIC, *The Town of Maiden Castle*, Robert Hale, London, 1947.

BOON, G. C., AND LEWIS, J. M., eds., *Welsh Antiquity*, National Museum of Wales, Cardiff, 1974.

BRANIGAN, KEITH, *The Catuvellauni*, Alan Sutton, Gloucester, 1987.

CLARKE, HELEN, AND WADE-MARTIN, PETER, *The Iceni*, Gerald Duckworth & Co., London, 1976.

CLIFFORD, E. N., *Bagendon, a Belgic Oppidum: excavations of 1954–6*, Heffer, Cambridge, 1961.

COTTRELL, LEONARD, *The Great Invasion*, Evans Brothers, London, 1958.

CRAMPTON, PATRICK, *Stonehenge of the Kings*, John Baker, London, 1967.

CUNLIFFE, BARRY, *Hengistbury Head*, Elek, London, 1978.

CUNLIFFE, BARRY, *Iron Age Communities in Britain*, Routledge & Kegan Paul, 1978.

CUNLIFFE, BARRY, AND ROWLEY, T., ed., *Oppida, the Beginnings of Urban Civilization in Barbarian Europe*, British Archaeological Reports, Oxford, 1976.

CUNLIFFE, BARRY, *The Regni*, Gerald Duckworth & Co., London, 1974.

CUNLIFFE, BARRY, *Danebury: Anatomy of an Iron Age Hill-Fort*, B. T. Batsford, London, 1983.

CURWEN, E.C., *The Archaeology of Sussex*, Methuen, London, 1st ed., 1937, 2nd ed. 1954.

DETSICAS, ALEC, *The Cantiaci*, Gerald Duckworth & Co., London, 1976.

DOBSON, D. P., *Archaeology of Somerset*, Methuen, London, 1931.

DUNNETT, ROSALIND, *The Trinovantes*, Gerald Duckworth & Co., London, 1975.

DYER, JAMES, *Hill-forts of England and Wales*, Shire Publications, Princes Risborough, 1981.

EKWALL, EILBERT, *The Concise Oxford Dictionary of English Place-names*, 4th ed., Oxford University Press, Oxford.

FEACHEM, RICHARD, *Guide to Prehistoric Scotland*, B. T. Batsford, London, 1963.

FORDE-JOHNSTON, J., *Hill-forts of the Iron Age in England and Wales*, Liverpool University Press, Liverpool, 1976.

GUILBERT, G. ed., *Hill-fort Studies*, Leicester University Press, 1981.

HANLEY, ROBIN, *Villages in Roman Britain*, Shire Publications, Princes Risborough, 1987.

HARDING, D. W., *The Iron Age in the Upper Thames Basin*, Clarendon Press, Oxford, 1972.

HARDING, D. W., ed., *Hill-forts: later prehistoric earthworks in Britain and Ireland*, Academic Press, London, 1976.

HARDING, D. W., *Celts in Conflict: hill-fort studies 1927–77*, 1979.

HARDING, D. W., *The Iron Age in Lowland Britain*, Routledge & Kegan Paul, London, 1974.

HARTLEY, BRIAN, AND FITTS, LEON, *The Brigantes*, Alan Sutton, Gloucester, 1988.

HERDMAN, MARGARET, *Life in the Iron Age*, Harrap, London, 1981.

HIGHAM, NICHOLAS, AND JONES, BARRY, *The Carvetii*, Alan Sutton, Gloucester, 1986.

HOGG, A. H. A., *Hill-forts of Britain*, Hart-Davies MacGibbon, London, 1975.

HOGG, A. H. A., *British Hill-forts: an index, 1979*.

HOULDER, C., *Wales: an archaeological guide*, Faber, London, 1975.

JACKSON, K., *Language and History in Early Britain*, Edinburgh University Press, 1953.

JESSON, M., AND HILL, D., *The Iron Age and its Hill-forts*, Southampton University Archaeological Society, 1971.

MACKIE, E. W., *Dun Mor Vaul: an Iron Age broch on Tiree*, Glasgow, 1974.

MACKIE, E. W., *Scotland: an archaeological guide*, Faber, London, 1975.

MANNING, W. H., *Usk Fortress Excavations*, University of Wales Press, Cardiff, 1981.

National Museum of Antiquities (Scotland): *Catalogue of Antiquities*, Edinburgh, 1982.

Ordnance Survey: *Southern Britain in the Iron Age*, 1962.

RAMM, HERMAN, *The Parisi*, Gerald Duckworth & Co., London, 1978.

RICHMOND, I. A., ed., *Roman and Native in North Britain*, Edinburgh University Press, 1958.

RITCHIE, ANNA, *Scotland BC*, Historic Buildings and Monuments, HMSO, Edinburgh, 1988.

RITCHIE, ANNA, *Picts*, Historic Buildings and Monuments, HMSO, Edinburgh, 1989.

RIVET, A. L. F., ed., *The Iron Age in Northern Britain*, Trustees of the Edinburgh University Press, Edinburgh, 1966.

SAVORY, H. N., *Guide Catalogue of the Early Iron Age Collections*, National Museum of Wales, Cardiff, 1976.

STANDFORD, S.C., *The Malvern Hill forts*, Archaeological Committee of the Malvern Hills Conservators, 1973.

STEAD, I. M., *The Arras Culture*, Yorkshire Philosophical Society, York, 1979.

TODD, MALCOLM, *The Coritani*, Gerald Duckworth & Co., London, 1973.

TRUEMAN, DON, *Hill-forts and the Iron Age in Gwent*, Newport Museum & Art Gallery, 1988.

WADMORE, B., *Earthworks of Bedfordshire*, Bedford, 1920.

WATSON, W. J., *The History of the Celtic Place-names of Scotland*, Edinburgh, 1926.

WEBSTER, GRAHAM, *The Cornovii*, Gerald Duckworth & Co., London, 1975.

WEBSTER, GRAHAM, AND DUDLEY, DONALD R., *The Roman Conquest of Britain*, B. T. Batsford, London, 1965.

WHEELER, R. E. M., *Maiden Castle, Dorset*, Oxford University Press, Oxford, 1943.

WHEELER, R. E. M. AND T. E., *Verulamium: a Belgic and two Roman cities*, Oxford University Press, London, 1936.

WILSON, DAVID M., *The Collections of the British Museum*, British Museum Publications, 1989.

Index of Sites